Debugging ASP

Troubleshooting for Programmers

About the Author

Derek Ferguson is head of development for InterAccess, one of the largest Data Local Exchange Carriers (DLEC) in the United States and the first company in the world to sell DSL Internet access commercially. He is a Microsoft Certified Solutions Developer (MCSD), a Sun Certified Java Programmer (SCJP), and a Certified Lotus Notes Principal Programmer (CLPP).

Derek received his B.S. in computer science from DePaul University and has authored, co-authored, and tech-edited books on a wide variety of technical subjects, ranging from iMacs to MCSD certification.

You may visit his page on the World Wide Web at www.EvilOscar.com, or contact him via e-mail at dferguson@interaccess.com.

Debugging ASP

Troubleshooting for Programmers

Derek Ferguson

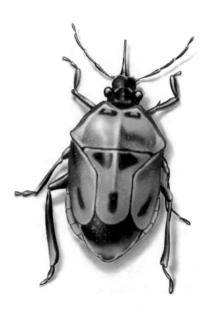

Osborne/McGraw-Hill

Berkeley / New York / St. Louis / San Francisco / Auckland / Bogotá
Hamburg / London / Madrid / Mexico City / Milan / Montreal / New Delhi
Panama City / Paris / São Paulo / Singapore / Sydney / Tokyo / Toronto

Osborne/**McGraw-Hill**
2600 Tenth Street
Berkeley, California 94710
U.S.A.

For information on translations or book distributors outside the U.S.A., or to arrange bulk purchase discounts for sales promotions, premiums, or fund-raisers, please contact Osborne/**McGraw-Hill** at the above address.

Debugging ASP: Troubleshooting for Programmers

1234567890 VFM VFM 019876543210

ISBN 0-07-212539-4

Publisher	Brandon A. Nordin
Vice President and Associate Publisher	Scott Rogers
Editorial Director	Wendy Rinaldi
Project Editor	Pamela Woolf
Acquisitions Coordinator	Monika Faltiss
Technical Editor	Greg Buczek
Copy Editor	Barbara Brodnitz
Proofreader	Rachel Lopez Bell
Indexer	Karin Arrigoni
Computer Designers	Jean Butterfield, Gary Corrigan
Graphic Artists	Robert Hansen, Michael Mueller, Beth E. Young
Series Design	Peter F. Hanick
Cover Design	Dodie Shoemaker, Dian-Aziza Ooka

This book was composed with Corel VENTURA ™ Publisher.

For my daughter, Elizabeth, who was born during
the writing of this book. You can grow up
to be any kind of programmer you like. :)

And to my wife, Erin, for tolerating all the missed family
time that goes along with any book project.

Contents at a Glance

Table of Contents

Acknowledgments

Over the years I've spent at InterAccess, I've had the privilege to work with some of the most wonderful people. I'd like to acknowledge the contributions made by some of them:

- Hoyt Hudson, chief technology officer, for always giving his people the chance to become whatever they could make of themselves. (I've decided I want to be your boss—that's not going to be a problem is it?)
- Bryan Evans, director of technology, for constantly trying to bring order to the chaos that sometime is InterAccess R&D. (Thankless task, isn't it?)
- Lorrie Sparrow, systems analyst, for restoring the chaos! (See Bryan, I *told* you it was a thankless task.)
- Cheryl Wilson, Unix systems administrator, for friendship and advice ever since my very first day at InterAccess. (Just remember: whatever is broken—I didn't do it!)
- John Humanski, senior Unix developer and occupant of the other half of my office, for picking up the pieces whenever I try to use pointers in C. Now, will you please turn down the Stravinsky? (Preferably until the volume knob goes "click!")
- Lewei Shang, Oracle DBA, for keeping 100% of our systems 100% operational 100% of the time. (At least that's what he tells us!)

I'd also like to thank Mr. David Carter of Cambridge University for his assistance with the IMAP email protocol. This has nothing whatsoever to do with Active Server Pages, but you have to admit it sounds really cool to reference Cambridge and "the IMAP email protocol" in the same sentence.

Big thanks to my agent Chris VanBuren at Waterside Productions. Also, thanks to Wendy Rinaldi and Monika Faltiss at Osborne/McGraw-Hill, and my technical reviewer Greg Buczek. I've never enjoyed working on a book as much as I have with all of you!

Finally, I'd like to acknowledge (or is it confess?) that this book was written entirely to the music of Jason Falkner, Spock's Beard, the Who, and Marillion—lots and lots of Marillion!

Introduction

When Osborne/McGraw-Hill first approached me with the idea for this book, I was a little skeptical. After all, I reasoned, Active Server Pages represented one of the simplest means available for quickly creating powerful Web applications. How much could possibly be said about debugging in such an easy development environment?

I returned to my daily work, programming ASP scripts for InterAccess, a large regional Internet service provider (ISP). But, from this point forward, I was on the lookout. Every time a bug was encountered, it went on "the list." At the end of a few weeks of regular development, I was completely convinced—a book on ASP debugging wasn't just needed, it was desperately required!

As experienced developers, we all too often become so accustomed to the eccentricities and short-comings of our chosen tools that we forget how completely arbitrary and illogical they can seem to unfamiliar audiences. In this book, it has been my goal and desire to pinpoint as many of these potential stumbling blocks as possible. In this way, a developer new to Active Server Pages, regardless of his or her level of experience with other development tools, can use this book to spare themselves the hours and days of agony spent by those of us who have gone before.

This book begins by explaining some of the basic tips and tricks associated with successful debugging and configuring a machine specifically for ASP development, as opposed to a production Web server. The bulk of the rest of the book is then spent examining each facet of ASP development in turn, laying bare the nuances and peculiarities that typically cause developers frustration when working with these technologies.

The appendixes provide additional data that you might find useful in crafting your Active Server Pages. Of particular interest is Appendix C, in which I give as concise and complete an overview of Microsoft's forthcoming ASP+ technology as was possible at the time of this writing. ASP+ represents an enormous advance over current Active Server Pages, and I would highly recommend that you embrace and utilize this new technology sooner rather than later.

CHAPTER 1

Fundamental Debugging

To successfully debug Active Server Pages, you need a thorough understanding of the many tools that are available. This chapter helps you comprehend the appropriate ways to set up and configure these tools in order to get the most out of them. Once these tools are correctly established and functioning in a way appropriate for debugging, it is also important that you be able to adequately monitor their feedback for the diagnosis of problems within your scripts.

The single most important tool offered by Microsoft to assist in the debugging of your scripts is the Microsoft Script Debugger. This chapter concludes with a complete discussion of the correct usage of this tool.

Configuring Your Server for Development

It is generally accepted in software engineering circles that systems can be broadly classified into at least two groups: development or production. Development systems are constructed to facilitate access to system internals. For example, the code in a development system may be left to operate in an interpreted state rather than being compiled into directly executable machine language. While representing an obvious loss in the performance of such a system, it is considered an acceptable trade-off on a development system.

A production system operates under an entirely different set of assumptions. In this case, facilitating access to the internals of a system is not only considered unimportant but may very well be actively discouraged for security reasons. To continue the preceding example, code on a production system will almost always be compiled as close to "machine language" as the platform allows, for reasons of performance and security.

In this section we will explain the appropriate establishment and configuration of a system solely for the development of Active Server Pages. While much of the information given here could easily by used in the creation of a production-oriented Active Server Pages system, such a setup would be far from ideal. Many of the ideas expressed here are guaranteed to have negative effects on the overall performance of any system on which they are instituted. *Always make sure you have the consent of your system administrator before making these changes on any computer that may be used for purposes other than Active Server Page development.*

Setting Up Internet Information Server

Internet Information Server provides the ultimate foundation for all Active Server Page activity. It is, after all, Internet Information Server (or IIS) that must first either accept or reject attempted connections by client tools such as the Internet Explorer or Netscape browser. IIS also interprets the code in your Active Server Pages through one of its default extensions (asp.dll) and returns their output across the network. For these reasons, the utmost importance should be given to ensuring that the settings for IIS are optimal from a development standpoint.

Changes in the configuration of IIS are made through the Microsoft Management Console (MMC) interface. The MMC uses a format now standard throughout Windows applications: a tree on the left for navigation and a list on the right for "drill-down." You might see a screen like the following soon after opening MMC for the purpose of administering IIS.

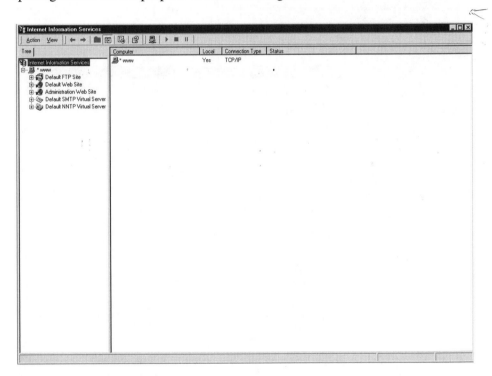

To open MMC for yourself, follow these steps:

1. Select Programs from the Windows Start menu.

2. Open the Administrative Tools group.

3. Select Internet Services Manager.

Web Site Properties

The properties that are set in the Web Site portion of the MMC interface affect everything that runs as part of a given site. It is possible for a single Web server to host multiple sites, so you should always make sure that the site you are changing properties on is the site you are currently developing. The "Default Web Site" listed at the top of the tree contains settings that will be used as the initial values for every new site that is created on this server.

The Web Site tab of the Default Web Site Properties dialog is shown in Figure 1-1.

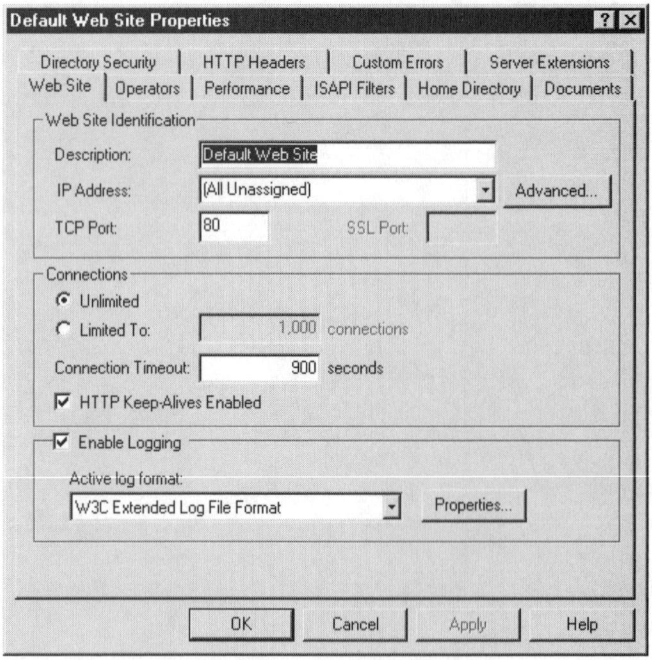

Figure 1.1   The Web Site tab

From a debugging standpoint, the first thing that you should notice on this dialog is the ability to limit the number of concurrent connections. *Concurrent connections* refer to the total number of tools (most typically Web browsers) that you would like to allow to interact simultaneously with your Web application.

Production servers that require guaranteed uptime might use this setting to prevent any sudden spikes in usage that might overload and break their systems. For example, a Web site maintained by a large television network might experience a sudden increase in traffic during the broadcast of large sporting events on that network. By setting this parameter, a system administrator could guarantee that his server would be available to continue servicing client requests throughout even the most dramatic surges in usage. The only ill effects would be that some client requests would inevitably be *temporarily* turned away if they exceeded the maximum number of concurrent connections allowed.

So, where does this leave you in terms of the ideal setting for a development box? Ideally, your development boxes should not be required to fulfill production needs at the same time you are trying to create and debug your Active Server Pages on them. One argument in favor of this proposition is the fact that you might have to reboot any such computer many times during the creation of your applications. Another argument would be that the "exposed" configuration that this section advocates (low security, easily accessible scripts, and so on) is in direct conflict with one of the most basic goals of system administration in a production environment: air-tight security.

Based on the previous statements, the only appropriate setting for this parameter is Unlimited. A development box should not require the kind of traffic control that this setting offers because the usage levels on it will be low at all times. The one exception to this is during performance stress testing.

During stress testing, automated tools are often used to verify that Web applications can handle enormous numbers of client requests in relatively short periods of time. Even under these circumstances, you will want to make sure that IIS is continuing to allow an unlimited number of concurrent connections. This is important to ensure that your tests measure only the performance of your scripts and not the effectiveness of IIS's traffic-control mechanisms. This would be a highly undesirable variable in any stress testing experiments.

The other relevant parameter on this dialog is Enable Logging. *Logging* generally refers to the keeping of records by an application regarding the activity that it conducts over a given span of time. In the case of Internet Information

Server, these logs can give you a great deal of information about the kinds of things that people (and automated tools such as "Web spiders") are doing with your Active Server Page applications.

For a development system, logging is absolutely essential. For this reason, you should make sure that the Enable Logging box is checked on this screen in IIS. Once you have done this, you will be able to select the precise style of logging that you would like from the drop-down list located beneath the checkbox. The options are summarized in Table 1-1.

On a development box, the W3C Extended Log File Format offers the ultimate in flexibility and thoroughness. Unlike the other log file formats, which dictate exactly which pieces of data will be tracked, the W3C standard allows for end-user selection of the fields to be monitored.

Design Tip   *For the sake of code optimization, you may elect to go with the NCSA Common Logging format when you move your applications onto production servers. The reason is that it is the only format currently supported by the vast majority of third-party log analysis tools. These tools allow system administrators and other nondevelopers to pinpoint bottlenecks in production Web sites. Such analysis might prove extremely valuable to you if it uncovered performance issues with your code early enough for you to solve them before they become problematic.*

Once you have selected W3C Extended Log File Format from the drop-down list, you should be able to click the Properties button to specify exactly which pieces of data you want to track. The Extended Properties tab of the Extended Logging Properties dialog is shown in Figure 1-2.

Option	Standardization	Log Format	Configurable Field Choices?
Microsoft IIS Logging	IIS only	Text file	No
NCSA Common Logging	Industry-wide	Text file	No
ODBC Logging	IIS only	Database	No
W3C Extended Log File Format	Industry-wide	Text file	Yes

Table 1.1   Logging Formats

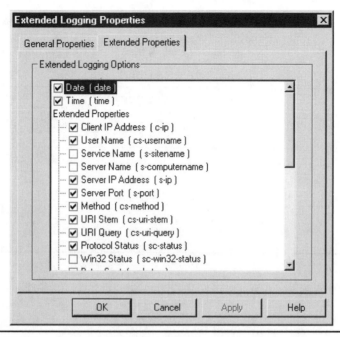

Figure 1.2   The Extended Logging Properties tab

For a development box, you should make sure that every option in this dialog has a check mark next to it. The exact meaning of each of these terms is explained later in this chapter in the section on logging your errors.

HTTP Headers

The second tab on the Web Site Properties dialog that you should be interested in on a development machine is the HTTP Headers tab. This is shown in Figure 1-3.

On this tab, the most salient feature is the Enable Content Expiration checkbox. This should be selected for development servers.

Most modern browsers have the ability to store Web pages locally in order to reduce the number of times that they must request those pages directly from the server. The place where a browser stores a copy of a Web page for local access is called that browser's *cache*.

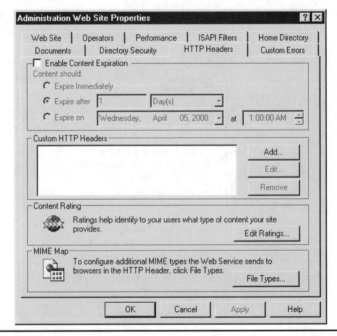

Figure 1.3   The HTTP Headers tab

The idea behind content expiration is that your servers should be able to suggest to browsers how long they should keep your pages stored in their caches. You are given three options to choose from, which are summarized in Table 1-2.

Option	Suitable Content Example	Good for Development Server?
Expire On (a given date)	Planning or promoting a specific event, such as a wedding, movie release, or business meeting	No
Expire After (a certain amount of time)	Material that changes slowly, such as a personal home page	No
Expire Immediately	Up-to-the-minute data, such as stock market quotes, as well as applications under continual development	Yes

Table 1.2   Content Expiration

Error Watch   *Always set your content to expire immediately on development boxes. It is usually a source of intense puzzlement for developers when they make alterations to their scripts and yet their output remains unchanged. This is discussed at length in the next chapter. For now, suffice it to say that the reason for this is the client-side caching that browsers may perform if the Expire Immediately setting is not chosen.*

Server Extensions

The final tab on the Default Web Site Properties dialog that helps us set up a proper ASP development environment is the Server Extensions tab (see Figure 1-4).

You must select Enable Authoring on this tab in order to access the three drop-down lists beneath it. Of these three lists, two are important from a development standpoint: Version Control and Client Scripting.

Version control refers to software that automates the tracking, archiving, and (when needed) roll-back of changes to documents such as Active Server Pages.

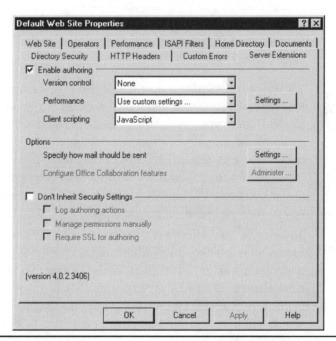

Figure 1.4   The Server Extensions tab

We will discuss the use of version control in greater detail in Chapter 13. For now, you are presented with three choices:

- **None**   This is the default for ASP applications, but it is a bad choice for any serious development effort.

- **Internal**   This is an acceptable choice if you don't have access to more sophisticated source control tools, such as Microsoft Visual Source Safe. The source control provided by IIS is adequate and its use is (unlike Source Safe) thoroughly explained in Chapter 13.

- **External**   This is the best choice you can make for any serious ASP development and/or debugging effort. You must, however, have a third-party source control package currently installed on the same computer as the Internet Information Server that will be running your scripts. You should also understand how to use this software. Explaining the working of a tool such as Visual SourceSafe is beyond the scope of this book. If you don't already know how to use such a tool, then you should probably choose Internal and read the section on source control in Chapter 13 very carefully.

The other drop-down list that must be considered when configuring Internet Information Server for development and debugging purposes is Client Scripting. You are given two options to choose from:

- **VBScript**   VBScript is a subset of the Visual Basic programming language, which is the single most popular programming language in the world. Coding your applications in VBScript has the notable advantage of making vast amounts of support available to you. Numerous Web sites, magazines, user groups, and books (including this one) focus on Visual Basic and the myriad issues with which its users must contend. VBScript is also considered to be relatively simpler and easier to learn than the other option for your client scripts, JavaScript.

- **JavaScript**   JavaScript is not the subset of Java that one might expect; instead, it is a browser scripting language originally developed by Netscape under the moniker "LiveScript" and only recently standardized by the European-based ECMA organization. The primary advantage to JavaScript is that it is available on both Netscape and Internet Explorer browsers, which will be relevant if you wish to maintain platform independence in your browser-based code.

Neither of these two options is a clear-cut winner over the other, but you should make a decision about which language you plan on using for client-side scripting right at the start of your project. In this book, the primary focus will be on server-side scripting in VBScript.

There are additional tabs visible on the Default Web Site Properties dialog. These tabs technically belong to the directory (or virtual directory) under which they are opened. For example, you could see all of these same tabs by right-clicking any of the directories listed in the tree nodes beneath Default Web Site and selecting Properties. An example of this dialog is shown in Figure 1-5.

Directory

The Directory tab (which also may be labeled Home or Virtual Directory) is the first of this group of tabs that you should examine in preparing a system for development and debugging operations.

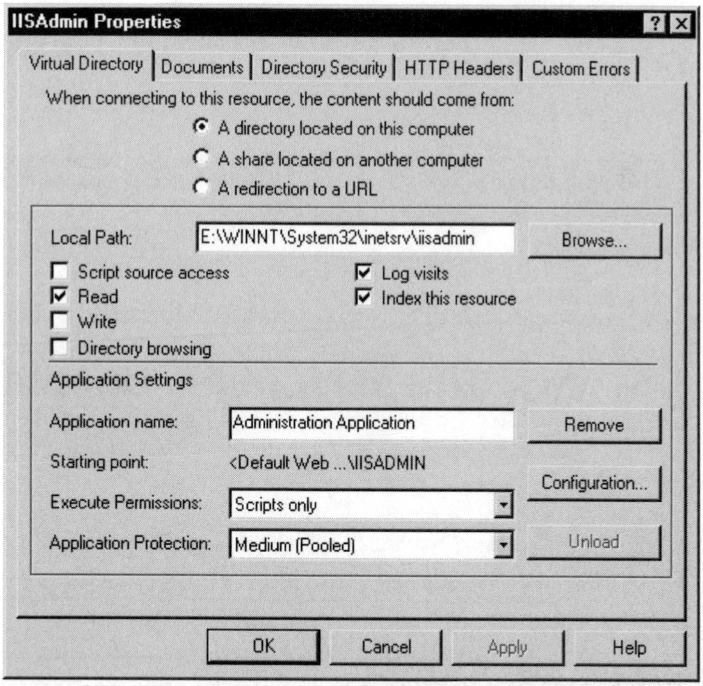

Figure 1.5   A directory's Properties dialog

You should choose Log Visits for your application. This is related to the previous conversation about making sure that logging is enabled for your site. The idea here is that an administrator may choose to have logging turned on in general for their site but may wish to exclude certain directories that they might see as unimportant.

There are no directories on a development box so unimportant as to not need logging! The reason for this is that your scripts may be written in such a way as to cause brief accesses to pages in other directories without you even realizing it. If these pages cause things to happen that break your scripts, you will be unable to hunt down these errors without logging turned on for those directories.

You will probably also find it helpful to enable Directory Browsing for all of the directories in your ASP applications. This is a convenience option: If you create an application of even 20 to 30 scripts with reasonably complicated names, it may become quite difficult for you to remember them all. With Directory Browsing enabled, you can pick the scripts that you would like to run from an automatically generated HTML menu of the files in your directory. Such a listing is shown in Figure 1-6.

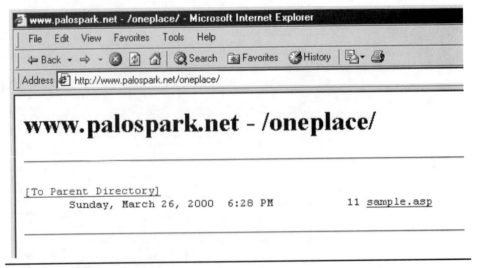

Figure 1.6   Directory browsing

24x7 Directory Browsing and Production Servers

It is important to note here that *directory browsing should almost never be enabled on a production server.* The security hole represented by such a move would be sizable. To begin with, directory browsing would allow a user to run the scripts in your application in any order simply by clicking on their entries in the directory listing. This may create unanticipated and harmful effects upon the files, databases, and other resources used by your system.

Also, any other files contained in the same directory structure as your application would be easily seen and accessed. This might include the "shopping cart" files of other people who have used your e-commerce Web site. Or, it might include the secret player standing information for that online game you run. The possibility for the loss of confidential information is great if you enable directory browsing on a production server.

Application Settings

The next section on this tab with which you should concern yourself is labeled Application Settings.

The application protection drop-down list is the first thing that you will want to make sure is properly set for a development system. Your options are the following:

- **Low (IIS Process)**   Under this setting, your ASP application will run as a part of the general IIS process. Other ASP applications using the same application settings will be running in the same portion of memory. This includes any COM components that any of these scripts might call. The danger in this is that a fatal error in one application could easily bring down all of the other applications in the shared area of memory. Worse yet, since this shared area of memory exists within IIS, the very real potential exists for errors that would result in the complete shutdown of the server! This is the wrong choice for a development machine.

- **Medium (Pooled)**   As with the Low option, applications set to run this way execute in a shared region of memory. For this reason, a fatal error in one application can easily cause failures in any other applications that are sharing the same memory space. Unlike the Low option, however, the area where these applications run is separate from that of the main IIS process.

For this reason, it should not be possible for an ASP application executing under this setting to crash the IIS server itself. This is still a bad choice for development machines.

- **High (Isolated)** System administrators tend to hate this setting on production machines because it is a real drag on performance. Under the High option, every ASP application is given its own area in memory to execute and its own set of resources (such as database connections) with which to work. This represents an enormous increase in both memory and CPU requirements for any hardware that you use under this option in a production environment.

High is absolutely the only option that should ever be used on development machines. Given the reduced load on such boxes, there is really no reason to be overly concerned with memory and CPU requirements at this stage. It is much more important to isolate the problems in your various applications from one another.

One reason for this is that debugging will be much easier if you can narrow the scope of your investigations to just the application with which you are experiencing problems. Without this setting, you will have to constantly suspect the influence of improper coding in the other applications on your system.

Another reason for this is that you want to avoid spending any more time restarting IIS (or, even worse, the machine on which it runs) than you absolutely must. If you were to select the Low option, bad code in any of the COM components called by your application could easily lead to a crash of IIS.

Beneath the Application Protection drop-down list, you will see a setting for Execute Permissions. In order to run—much less debug—Active Server Pages under IIS, you must change this to either Scripts Only or Scripts and Executables. If you choose Scripts Only, you will be able to use standard ASP pages and instantiate whatever COM components on them you wish. You will not, however, be able to directly execute so-called "cgi-bin"–style programs such as standalone executables ending in .EXE.

Dealing with the CGI interface is beyond the scope of this book. So, for our purposes, choose Scripts Only.

Now that you have chosen all of the immediately visible settings on this tab, it is time to move on to the controls that lay beyond the Configuration button. It is located in the Application Settings portion of the dialog, as shown in Figure 1-5. Pressing this button will cause the Application Configuration dialog to open, shown in Figure 1-7.

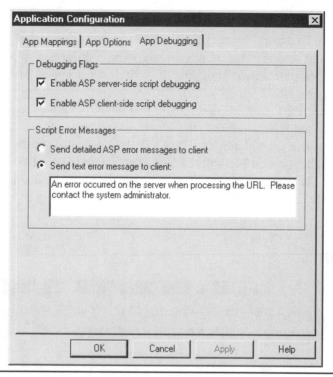

Figure 1.7   The Application Configuration dialog

The tab shown, App Debugging, is the one that you need to be most concerned with in getting your server properly configured for ASP development and debugging. In the Debugging Flags frame, you should make sure that both boxes are checked. Enabling server-side script debugging will allow you to use the script debugger, which you will learn all about at the end of this chapter.

Underneath this frame is one labeled Script Error Messages. It is important that you select Send Detailed ASP Error Messages to Client here. The reason for this is probably fairly obvious to you: It will be a lot easier to debug your script if you are given informative error message whenever they break. Conversely, if IIS were only to report, "I'm sorry, something broke" whenever a problem arose, you would have to do a lot of guesswork and digging even to find out on which line of code your script broke.

Directory Security

The Directory Security tab contains the last options that you will need to worry about setting in order to configure Internet Information Server for the development and debugging of Active Server Pages. The dialog is shown in Figure 1-8.

At the top of this dialog, you will see a frame for the authentication methods. Authentication refers to the way in which users of your applications will be able to prove their identity to IIS. Click the Edit button in this frame to bring up the Authentication Methods dialog, as shown in Figure 1-9.

There are three ways in which you can allow your users to identify themselves to IIS.

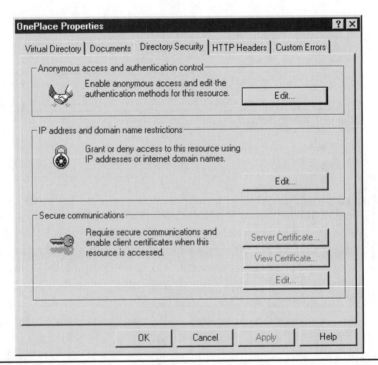

Figure 1.8   The Directory Security tab

Figure 1.9 The Authentication Methods dialog

Anonymous   If you choose to allow anonymous access to your ASP applications, IIS will not always require your users to identify themselves. New connections to your system will first attempt to operate under the IUSR_machinename account. For example, on a computer named MELVIN, an Active Server Page designed to display a certain text file backwards in a user's browser would first attempt accessing that file as IUSR_MELVIN under Anonymous authentication.

If IUSR_MELVIN, or any of the Windows groups to which IUSR_MELVIN belongs (including "Everyone"), has permission to access this file, then everything goes smoothly, and the script runs to completion without incident. If the permissions on the file are stricter than this, IIS will attempt one of the kinds of authentication described next. If neither of these has been enabled on this dialog, neither will be available for IIS to authenticate this user. In this situation, the script will fail with a security error.

Anonymous Access should always be enabled for a development box.

Basic   Basic authentication is the platform-independent standard for Web sites that require their users to identify themselves. To continue the example began above, if Basic authentication were enabled, then a dialog like the one shown in Figure 1-10 would present itself to the user as soon as your script discovered that the IUSR_MELVIN account lacked sufficient permissions for access to the text file.

At this point, your user could enter their username and password as it appears in the Windows security database for the computer on which you are currently running IIS. System administrators often discourage the use of Basic authentication because it send passwords in clear-text mode, which is easy for third parties to intercept as they travel across the network. A development box should not require this kind of air-tight security, however, so *Basic authentication should always be enabled for a development box.*

Design Tip   *Besides the encryption of passwords offered by Challenge/Response authentication, there is a much tighter integration between this kind of authentication and the Windows operating system. If you would like to restrict access to your applications by granting and removing permissions from specific Windows accounts, Challenge/Response authentication may be your best choice. On a Windows computer, Internet Explorer is able to transparently pass information about the account and domain under which a user is currently logged in. You will learn much more about this in the "Permissioning" section of Chapter 3.*

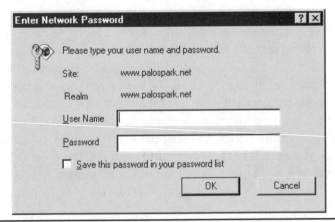

Figure 1.10   A basic authentication dialog

Integrated Windows Authentication   This style of authentication appears to work the same as Basic, but it is slightly different "under the hood." Under Integrated authentication, passwords are not sent in clear text. Unfortunately, the tight integration of this option with the Windows security system restricts its use to the Internet Explorer browser. Nevertheless, some tools (notably some kinds of access to SQL Server) require the use of Integrated authentication. *Unless the nature of your scripts absolutely requires it, you should not enable Integrated authentication on a development box.*

The final setting that you may consider changing on an IIS installation in preparation for serious Active Server Page development involves the restriction of access to certain IPs. If you click the button next to this option, you will get a dialog that looks like Figure 1-11.

Typically, on a development box, it is best to leave this completely blank, so you can be sure that any inability to access your scripts is due to their coding or permissioning—not the IP of whatever client you happen to be using at that moment. If your system administrators insist on having some kind of security on your development systems, however, then this is probably the least invasive place in which to do so.

To use this dialog, type the IPs of all the machines you think you might be using as test clients into the boxes as shown in Figure 1-11. When you have finished, close this dialog to save your changes.

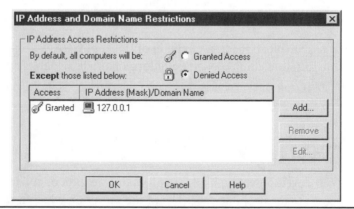

Figure 1.11   A dialog that restricts access by IP

Setting Up for Component Debugging

Active Server Pages often make use of COM components to extend the functionality offered by VBScript and JavaScript. On one hand, the intrinsic ASP objects (Request, Response, Server, and so on) are COM components that almost every server page uses for even the most basic of operations. At the opposite extreme, sophisticated algorithms and procedures may be implemented in advanced languages, such as Visual C++, by you or third-party developers and integrated into your applications in the form of such components.

Along with the power offered by this approach comes a price in terms of potential risk. Unlike such simple languages as VBScript, languages like C++ commonly offer developers the ability to directly manipulate memory and devices. This added flexibility brings with it serious dangers whenever bugs in your components cause them to fail.

Because components are used in compiled (rather than interpreted) form, it can often be difficult to locate the exact spot at which a given component is failing. In the case of third-party components, where source code is typically not even made available, ASP developers are typically at the mercy of their vendors to resolve whatever issues may exist with the bugs in their code.

When source code is available for the components that you intend to use in your Active Server Page applications, it should be installed on your development machine. Whatever tool is required to work with this source code (for example, Visual Basic or Visual C++) should also be installed. Finally, you should obtain and install the Microsoft tool called WinDbg.

WinDbg can help you to pinpoint the precise line in components where failures are occurring. Follow these steps to obtain and install this software:

1. Download the latest version of this tool from http://msdn.microsoft.com/developer/sdk/windbg.asp.

2. Install the software, following the directions included with the download.

3. Start WinDbg.

What's In the Logs?

Web development typically involves the creation of code that has little or no access to the user interface (UI) of the server on which it runs. Active Server Pages are no exception to this rule. Message boxes, dialogs, and all other varieties of windows used for reporting errors under standalone applications are all unavailable means of communication for the ASP developer. The use of logging is one way to overcome this loss of communication.

Web Server Logging

In the previous section on IIS configuration, it was suggested that you select the W3C Extended Logging Format for all of your Active Server Page applications while they are in development. It was further suggested that you elect to record every piece of data that this format allows. The following table is a brief explanation of the meaning of each of these fields.

Date	The date (at your server's location) on which a request is made of your application by a client application.
Time	The time (at your server's location) at which a request is made of your application by a client application.
Client IP Address	An IP is a 32-bit number that uniquely identifies a computer on the Internet at a given point in time. A single IP can be shared by several computers though the use of a firewall or similar proxy. Also, IPs tend to get rotated and reused by multiple computers within the same organization over time. Nevertheless, this field in your Web logs tells you which computer was most directly accessing your server when the request occurred.
User Name	Some applications require that their users log in (or authenticate themselves) before they are allowed access. If your applications are using Basic or Windows Challenge/Response authentication, you will have data here. We will learn more about these authentication options in Chapter 10.
Service Name	The Windows name for the server under IIS that responds to a given request.
Server Name	The name of the computer running your Internet Information Server.
Server IP	The IP of the computer running your Internet Information Server. For more information on IPs, see the previous paragraph on Client IP.
Server Port	The port upon which the given request was made of IIS, and upon which your application made its response via IIS.
Method	This corresponds to (but is not necessarily derived from) the ACTION parameter on HTML FORM tags. GET means that information was delivered to your script primarily via the URL. POST means that information was delivered primarily via HTTP's back-end channel for FORM submissions.
URI Stem	The virtual location on your computer of the requested resource. This is typically everything in your page's URL without the server name on the left or the query on the right.

URI Query	The data passed to your page using the GET method. This is everything to the right of the question mark in your page's URL. If nothing of this sort is passed in the URL, a single hyphen is used to hold this field's place in the logs.
HTTP Status	This field records the industry-standard HTTP status generated by IIS in response to the client's request for this page. "400" is considered success; anything else denotes a problem. Appendix B lists all possible status codes and their meanings.
Win32 Status	This field records the Microsoft-defined status generated by Windows in response to IIS's attempts to respond to the client's request for this page. In the case of standard HTML and many simpler ASPs, IIS can respond to requests with minimal involvement from the OS. In these cases, a 0 will be used by IIS to hold this field's place in the logs. A failure while attempting to instantiate an external COM component would be one example of a situation under which you would expect to see a different value in this column.
Bytes Sent	The total number of bytes sent in response to a given request. This could be useful for diagnosing certain kinds of problems encountered when attempting to send non-HTML content from the server to a client. This is discussed in great detail in Chapter 6.
Bytes Received	The total number of bytes received from a client during a request. This could be useful for diagnosing certain kinds of problems encountered when attempting to receive non-HTML content from clients (file uploads, for example). This is discussed in great detail in Chapter 5.
Time Taken	The total amount of time elapsed between first receipt of a client's request and the completion of the server's response.
Protocol Version	Tells you both the Internet-standard language used to communicate the request from the client to your server (usually HTTP or FTP) and the version of that standard that was used. This can be useful for diagnosing problems arising from differences between protocols and versions.
User Agent	The client tool used to make a given request of your application. This is entirely dependent upon the client tool's ability to identify itself during the making of a request. Both major browsers, Internet Explorer and Netscape, identify themselves and will appear in your logs, though Netscape still refers to itself as "Mozilla." A blank entry in this field typically indicates access by an automated search tool, commonly referred to as a *spider*.
Cookie	All of the data stored by your application within the client tools using it should show up in this field. This can be a vital resource for resolving problems with the maintenance of state across multiple pages. Chapter 4 discusses this at some length.
Referrer	The site containing the link that brought the client to this page is shown in this field. You can use this field to make sure that server redirects are working the way that you think they should be. This is discussed at the start of Chapter 6 in the section on redirection.

NT Event Logging

The Windows 2000 operating system comes with many built-in capabilities for creating, viewing, and archiving logs. The logs dealt with by the operating system may be for applications, services, or even parts of the OS itself. To view the events that are currently being tracked on your system, follow these steps:

1. Select Programs from the Windows Start menu.

2. Open the Administrative Tools menu.

3. Choose Event Viewer from the list of options.

At this point, you should a screen closely resembling the following:

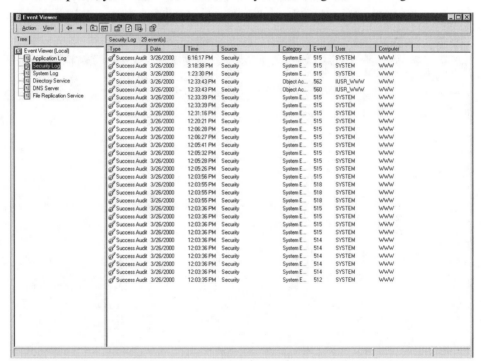

On the left, notice the tree control that allows you to choose from several broad categories of sources for your events. The options here that are most directly related to debugging Active Server Pages are as follows:

Directory Service   If you work with the ADSI components at all in your scripts, errors from these operations will show up in this part of the Event Viewer.

Security Log Problems with user authentication, file permissions, and other such issues will appear under Event Viewer's Security Log heading.

Application Log In Chapter 8, there is a section detailing the inability of COM components running under Active Server Pages to interact directly with your server's user interface. As an alternative way for your components to produce output that can be monitored by your system administrators and yourself, Chapter 8 details how to write information directly to the Windows event logs. When you do so, the events you write will show up in this area.

Because this is the portion of the Windows event logs that is used by most custom applications, it is worth spending a little more time investigating. If you select this from the tree control on the left of the window, you will see a list of columns appear on the right that look much like Figure 1-12.

Type	Date	Time	Source	Category	Event	User	Computer
Information	3/26/2000	12:33:42 PM	Active Server Pages	None	3	N/A	WWW
Information	3/26/2000	12:06:20 PM	Oakley	None	542	N/A	WWW
Information	3/26/2000	12:05:51 PM	ESENT	General	100	N/A	WWW
Information	3/26/2000	12:05:47 PM	NSUnicast	None	300	N/A	WWW
Information	3/26/2000	12:05:46 PM	MSMQ	Kernel	2028	N/A	WWW
Information	3/26/2000	12:05:45 PM	LoadPerf	None	1000	N/A	WWW
Information	3/26/2000	12:05:44 PM	LoadPerf	None	1001	N/A	WWW
Information	3/26/2000	12:05:42 PM	LoadPerf	None	1000	N/A	WWW
Error	3/26/2000	12:05:41 PM	MSMQ	Kernel	2124	N/A	WWW
Error	3/26/2000	12:05:41 PM	MSMQ	Kernel	2121	N/A	WWW
Information	3/26/2000	12:05:40 PM	LoadPerf	None	1001	N/A	WWW
Information	3/26/2000	12:05:36 PM	EvntAgnt	None	2018	N/A	WWW
Information	3/26/2000	12:05:35 PM	ESENT	General	100	N/A	WWW
Information	3/26/2000	12:05:28 PM	MacPrint	Administra...	2010	N/A	WWW
Information	3/26/2000	12:05:20 PM	NSSTATION	None	300	N/A	WWW
Information	3/26/2000	12:05:17 PM	NSMONITOR	None	400	N/A	WWW
Information	3/26/2000	12:05:16 PM	ESENT	General	100	N/A	WWW
Information	3/26/2000	12:05:11 PM	MSDTC	SVC	4097	N/A	WWW
Information	3/26/2000	12:00:50 PM	SceCli	None	1704	N/A	WWW
Information	3/26/2000	12:00:43 PM	SceCli	None	1704	N/A	WWW
Information	3/26/2000	10:41:32 AM	Active Server Pages	None	3	N/A	WWW
Information	3/26/2000	10:32:25 AM	Oakley	None	542	N/A	WWW
Information	3/26/2000	10:32:02 AM	ESENT	General	100	N/A	WWW
Information	3/26/2000	10:31:48 AM	LoadPerf	None	1000	N/A	WWW
Information	3/26/2000	10:31:47 AM	LoadPerf	None	1001	N/A	WWW
Information	3/26/2000	10:31:45 AM	LoadPerf	None	1000	N/A	WWW
Information	3/26/2000	10:31:42 AM	LoadPerf	None	1001	N/A	WWW
Information	3/26/2000	10:31:42 AM	MSMQ	Kernel	2028	N/A	WWW
Information	3/26/2000	10:31:42 AM	NSUnicast	None	300	N/A	WWW
Information	3/26/2000	10:31:37 AM	EvntAgnt	None	2018	N/A	WWW
Error	3/26/2000	10:31:36 AM	MSMQ	Kernel	2124	N/A	WWW
Error	3/26/2000	10:31:36 AM	MSMQ	Kernel	2121	N/A	WWW
Information	3/26/2000	10:31:34 AM	ESENT	General	100	N/A	WWW
Information	3/26/2000	10:31:28 AM	ESENT	General	100	N/A	WWW
Information	3/26/2000	10:31:28 AM	MacPrint	Administra...	2010	N/A	WWW
Information	3/26/2000	10:31:18 AM	NSSTATION	None	300	N/A	WWW
Information	3/26/2000	10:31:16 AM	NSMONITOR	None	400	N/A	WWW

Figure 1.12 An application log event list

The columns in this list each reference a different piece of data given by applications to NT's event logging mechanism. The Application Log portion of the screen typically contains the following:

Type   Error is the most common entry to see here and denotes, as you might expect, an unexpected problem that arose during the execution of a given application. Strictly informational messages may also be stored in the log and will be marked as such in this column.

Date   The date on the server when a given event was logged.

Time   The time on the server when a given event was logged.

Source   The name of the application that requested the logging of the given event. This is usually the application's filename, minus the extension. For example, an executable named "mailer.exe" would usually be shown as a source of "mailer" in the log.

Category   The category assigned to a given event by the application requesting the logging. Most applications will not use this feature, so None is the most common entry to see in this column.

Event   A numeric code assigned to the particular kind of event by the application that requested its logging. The documentation for the application in question must provide a definition for this number in order for you to gain any information from it, because there are no other standards for these codes.

User   The Windows login of the user under which the component was running when the event was logged. In the case of in-process components instantiated by Active Server Pages, this will typically be SYSTEM. Components under Microsoft Component Services, however, are able to emulate any user on the system for whom they have a valid password. Chapter 9 discusses the capabilities and possibilities of this tool quite extensively.

Computer   You can use the Event Viewer to connect to other computers for which you have Administrator privileges and review their logs as well. This column gives you the Windows networking name of the computer on which a given error was logged.

Using the Script Debugger

The Microsoft Script Debugger is one of the most valuable tools you have available to you in your quest to debug Active Server Page applications. Using this tool, you can follow the progress of your application from one line of code to the next. Also, you can observe the values of your variables, as well as change those values on the fly. Finally, you can use the process-monitoring capabilities of the script debugger to identify and move between all of the Active Server Page applications currently executing on your server.

Turning on Debugging

At the start of this chapter, the discussion focused on getting your server properly configured for development and debugging. One of the things that you did in that section was enable debugging of your applications at both the server and client. To get started now, invoke the Microsoft Script Debugger. Follow these steps:

1. Select Programs from the Windows Start menu.

2. Open the Accessories menu.

3. Select the Microsoft Script Debugger group.

4. Choose the Microsoft Script Debugger application.

At this point, the debugger should start, and you should see a window that looks very similar to this one:

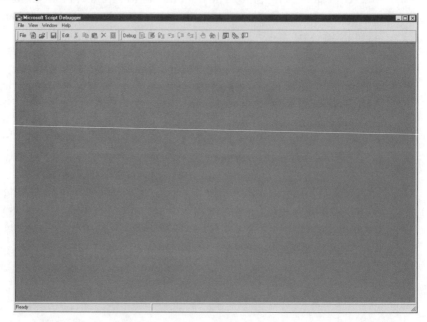

You've probably noticed by now that things look rather blank. To delve a little further into this, choose Open from the File menu and select any of your ASP scripts that you would like to debug. The file should now open in the editing window of the debugger, and you should be able to freely change any of the text in it.

Add a line to the middle of your script that just contains garbage, as shown here:

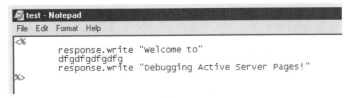

Starting the Microsoft Script Debugger from the Windows Start menu is only one of three ways in which this tool can be started. A second way that the Debugger can be started is automatically in response to errors in your code. Save your script now by choosing Save from the File menu. Next, try accessing your page via IIS from Internet Explorer. When your script reaches a line containing an error, in this case the garbage shown in the previous screenshot, the Debugger will be automatically invoked with the line in question highlighted, as in Figure 1-13.

The third way in which the Script Debugger can be started is whenever a script encounters the keyword "stop" on a line by itself. In order to observe this final way of invoking the Script Debugger, you can repeat the exercise above, only replacing the error in our example with the keyword "stop."

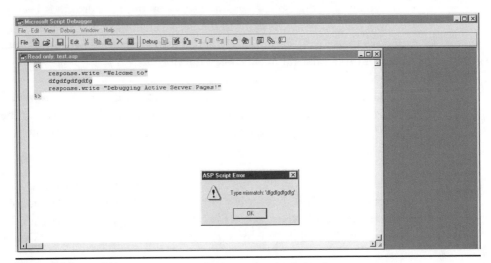

Figure 1.13   The Script Debugger finds an error in the code

Tracing Logic Flows

When the Debugger has been invoked due to a "stop" line or error, you have a number of options available for tracing the flow of your application's logic. Many of these are on the Debug menu of the Script Debugger's main menu bar. Another way to investigate the execution paths followed by your application is via the Call Stack window.

The Debug Menu

The Debug menu is shown next. Its options are as follows:

Debug	
Run	F5
Break at Next Statement	
Stop Debugging	Shift+F5
Step Into	F8
Step Over	Shift+F8
Step Out	Ctrl+Shift+F8
Toggle Breakpoint	F9
Clear All Breakpoints	Ctrl+Shift+F9

Run   This command will immediately resume execution of your script. If the Debugger was invoked in response to a "stop" line, execution will resume with the very next line in the script. If the Debugger was invoked in response to an error, you will not be able to resume execution until the error has been fixed. Because your view at this point in the Script Debugger will be read-only, you will have to use a different tool (Notepad or Visual Interdev, for example) to fix whatever problems you may be encountering.

Break at Next Statement   If you issue this command, the execution of your script will stop, and the Script Debugger will be invoked again on the very next line of code in your script. This is very closely related to the Step Into option discussed next.

Stop Debugging   Issuing this command will cause the rest of your script to attempt executing without further intrusion by the Debugger. Any more "stop" lines encountered in your code will be ignored. Any more errors encountered in your code will simply cause the script to fail without invoking the Debugger.

Step Into   Issuing this command will cause the Debugger to proceed to the very next line in your script. The Debugger will then pause, as in Figure 1-13, and await further instructions. This is closely related to Break at Next Statement.

Step Over   This command will cause the Debugger to proceed to the very next line of code *within the current procedure*. If the current line of code is a call to another procedure, IIS will attempt to execute all of the code in this procedure before returning control to the debugger. If a "stop" line or error is encountered within the procedure that is being stepped over, IIS will immediately return control to the Debugger, and the situation will once again resemble the one shown in Figure 1-13.

Step Out   If you issue this command, IIS will attempt to execute all remaining lines of code within the current procedure before returning to control to the Debugger. If the current procedure was called by another procedure, the Debugger will pause execution immediately following the original call. If the current procedure was the top-level or main procedure in a given script, then IIS will attempt to run the script to completion.

Toggle Breakpoint   A breakpoint is a "mental note" that the Debugger makes to itself that tells it to pause execution and invoke itself whenever a given line of code is reached. The effect is very similar to adding a "stop" line to your code, except that breakpoints can't be saved between debugging sessions the same way that "stop" lines can. If you issue this command on a line that is already a breakpoint, the breakpoint will be removed, and the red dot next to the line will be removed to signify that execution will no longer pause at this point.

Clear All Breakpoints   This is probably the quickest way to remove all breakpoints from whichever script is currently open in the Debugger. You would typically issue this command once you are satisfied that you have resolved (or at least understood) whatever problems are affecting a given script and now would like to proceed to the end of that script's execution as quickly as possible.

Call Stack

The Call Stack window, shown next, allows you to see the name of the currently executing procedure. More importantly, it allows you to see all of the procedure calls leading up to the currently executing procedure. You can view this window by choosing Call Stack from the View menu on the Script Debugger's main menu bar.

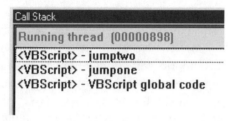

Clicking any of the procedures named in this window will immediately take you to the line of code that issued the call to the procedure located beneath it on the stack. This can be an excellent tool for figuring out how your scripts wind up at the points in their code where they do.

The Command Window

Sometimes, you'd like to be able to change certain things about your scripts while they're running. One problem with this, which the previous section pointed out, is that the copy of your scripts that is opened by the Script Debugger is strictly read-only. Another problem is that sometimes you wouldn't want whatever changes you have in mind to become permanent parts of your scripts, anyhow.

Consider the following example. You might be debugging a set of scripts intended to dynamically create recipes catering to the specific tastes of their users. Now suppose you wanted to see what kinds of recipes might be suggested by your application if you doubled the default amounts of salt and vinegar. The first obstacle that you would face in making this change in the middle of execution is that the Script Debugger would be open in read-only mode. You could circumvent this difficulty by using a different editing tool, but then your changes would become permanent parts of your scripts until you chose to remove them.

The Command Window gives you the ability to change the values of variables in your scripts for the duration of a single script execution. You can also use this window to view variable values that have already been set. Finally, you can call the methods on ASP's intrinsic objects in order to simulate just about any application activity you desire.

To open the Command Window, choose it from the View menu at the top of the Debugger window. Figure 1-14 shows what it should look like.

Most valid VBScript syntax can be used within the Command Window. For this reason, the assignment of new values to your variables here is governed by

```
Command Window
x = 32
Set y = Server.CreateObject("ADODB.Connection")
? x
32


? Request("Preference")
Cheese

Response.Write "Hello World"
```

Figure 1.14   The Command Window

the rules of this language. To assign simple data types to your variables, simply type the name of the variable, followed by an equal sign, followed by the new value that you wish to assign. For object data, use the word "Set" followed by the name of the variable, followed by an equal sign, followed by whatever is the source of the object data (a call to Server.CreateObject, for example). The first line of Figure 1-14 illustrates the assignment of simple data; the second line illustrates the assignment of object data.

Beneath the two assignment examples in Figure 1-14 is an example of how you can display the current values of your variables in the Command Window. Simply type a question mark on a line, followed by the name of the variable in which you are interested. This will only work for data types that it makes sense to display in the text format of the Command Window. Trying to display object data, for instance, would certainly fail (though you can definitely display the property values of objects).

The last interesting thing that you can do from the Command Window is call on the methods and properties of ASP's built-in objects, such as Response, Request, and Server. The last two lines in Figure 1-14 show examples of using these capabilities. The second-from-last line displays the value stored in the Preference field of the Request object. The final line uses the Response object to send "Hello World" (did you really think we could get through Chapter 1 of a computer book without referencing this?) to whatever browser has connected to this application.

The Running Documents Window

If you select Running Documents from the View menu at the top of the Debugger window, you should get a window that closely resembles this:

Underneath the node labeled Microsoft Internet Explorer, you should see a list of all the Active Server Pages currently loaded into memory for execution as part of your applications. If you click on any of these documents, they should open in their own child document window under the Script Debugger. If these scripts are currently in the process of executing, they will be in a read-only mode. Otherwise, you should be able to freely make changes and save these documents.

Here is a shortcut that is worth noting: If you right-click on any of the documents in the Running Documents window, the context menu should give you the ability to request that the script break on the next statement. This can be a very quick way to move from one document directly into debugging mode on another. After you have made this selection from the context menu, you can simply open the document in your browser and be ready to start debugging.

CHAPTER 2

Fundamental Mistakes

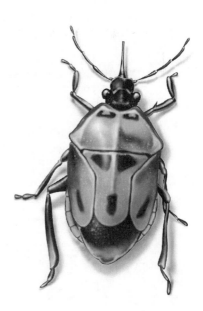

In programming, it is typically the case that 80 percent of all errors are caused by the same 10 percent of all possible mistakes. It is, therefore, most beneficial to pay special attention to those 10 percent of troublesome issues outlined in this chapter. Some of these issues have to do with the way that the Internet Information Server itself has been configured. Others have to do with the ways in which programmers attempt to invoke the procedures in their applications. Finally, the unusual way in which VBScript deals with some data types is a source of frustration for many developers.

Internet Information Server

In the previous chapter, we discussed the best settings for making your Internet Information Server an appropriate tool for development. Apart from the settings covered in that chapter, however, there are many more settings that can seriously impair the ability of IIS to serve Active Server Pages.

Pages That Display Rather than Execute

One of the most mystifying problems experienced by developers working with Active Server Pages is when the pages on which they are working fail to execute. Instead, the code contained within the script itself is sometimes sent directly to the browser. Consider the case of the following code example:

```
<%
      Response.Write "This is the only thing"
      Response.Write "that should show up"
      Response.Write "in the browser"
%>
```

The results produced in the browser by the execution of this script should simply be the words, "This is the only thing that should show up in the browser." If you see something more like the results here, you are definitely experiencing a problem where code is displaying rather than executing.

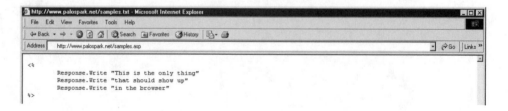

Setting Your Script Mapping Properties

Script mapping properties are used to determine which executables IIS uses to interpret each of the supported kinds of scripting. For example, before there were Active Server Pages, Microsoft offered a technology through IIS called the Internet Database Connector. This tool allowed the formatting of text files in certain special ways so that live data from databases could be "merged" in real time onto HTML pages before they were transmitted to browsers. These files were identified to IIS via their extensions, IDC and HTX. To this day, if you examine the script mappings of your Internet Information Server, you will almost certainly find a listing for these extensions that assigns them to the Internet Database Connector software (httpodbc.dll).

You can verify this for yourself by following these steps to get to your own script mappings:

1. Choose Programs from the Windows Start menu.
2. Open the Administrative Tools program grouping.
3. Start the Internet Services Manager software.
4. Open whichever computer is running your instance of IIS from the tree control on the left.
5. Right-click your development Web site on the tree control and choose Properties from the context menu that pops up.
6. On the Home Directory tab, press the Configuration button to open the Application Configuration dialog.
7. Choose the App Mappings tab, if it is not already in the foreground. It should resemble Figure 2-1.
8. Scroll down to the line showing ".idc" in the Extension column. Note the file pointed to by the Executable Path column: It is the httpodbc.dll file discussed earlier.

For every kind of scripting supported by IIS, there should be at least one line in the App Mappings tab. If your VBScript or JavaScript ASPs are displaying in client browsers rather than executing, you should verify the existence of a line in this dialog for whichever extension you have chosen to give to your Active Server Pages. Typically, this extension is .asp, but you may elect to use any extension not already in use by other scripting languages—provided that you add the appropriate entry to App Mappings.

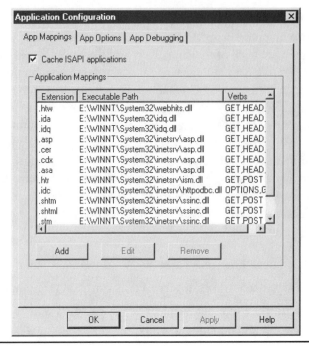

Figure 2.1 The App Mappings tab

To add an entry to the App Mappings tab, follow this procedure:

1. Click the Add button on the App Mappings tab of the Application Configuration dialog under IIS. The Add/Edit Application Extension Mapping dialog appears, as shown in Figure 2-2.

2. Choose the appropriate executable for the kind of scripting that you plan on using. Some of the more common executables are WEBHITS.DLL, HTTPODBC.DLL, SSINC.DLL, and ASP.DLL. ASP.DLL is the library that you will be most interested in within the context of this book, because it contains the code responsible for running all Active Server Pages. You can find the exact paths to these DLLs on your server by using the Find tool available from the Windows Start menu.

3. Enter the extension (beginning with a period) that you plan to associate with this executable. For example, most Active Server Page applications

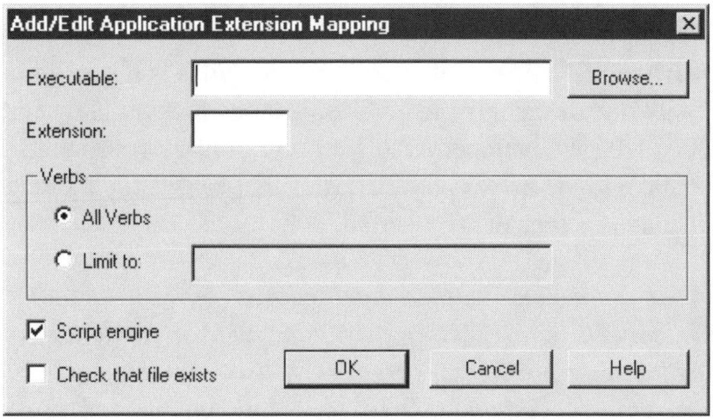

Figure 2.2   The Add/Edit Application Extension Mapping dialog

have at least one entry under App Mappings that has .asp here and another entry with .asa.

4. Select whether you want all kinds of requests passed to the scripting engine in question or only requests using certain kinds of verbs. Active Server Page applications are typically limited to the GET, HEAD, POST, and TRACE verbs. You can achieve this by clicking the Limit To radio button and entering these verbs into the text box, separated with commas. This is shown in Figure 2-2.

5. Enable Script Engine so that IIS will recognize files ending with this extension as scripts, rather than as genuine executable files. This is useful when you want your ASPs to run in directories where you have enabled only script execution, not scripts and executables. For more information, see the section in Chapter 1 on configuring your server.

6. When working with engines other than asp.dll, you may find it useful to enable the Check That File Exists option. This is because, unlike Active Server Pages, many other scripting engines do not fail gracefully if requested files are not available on the server. Refer to your scripting engine's documentation for additional information, as further discussion is beyond the scope of this book.

7. Choose OK to close this dialog.

8. Choose Apply or OK from the Application Configuration dialog to enable your changes.

Including Files

In Chapter 3, the use of server-side includes is discussed at great length. This is easily one of the most troublesome areas for both new and experienced Active Server Page developers. At this point, it is appropriate to discuss one common mistake in the use of included files that causes the included content to be displayed rather than executed.

Design Tip   *If you haven't worked much with server-side includes yet, don't let the caveats in this section dissuade you. A great deal of code reuse can be achieved by storing your frequently used routines and procedures in separate files that you can then ask IIS to include in your scripts at runtime.*

In short, you must understand that content in included files is included by IIS before any execution begins. It is placed exactly where you place inclusion requests within your scripts, and these requests must not occur within script definition tags. This point can be made much clearer through the use of a simple example. Consider the following code:

```
<%
      Response.Write "Include some code..."
      <!--#INCLUDE FILE="two.inc" -->
%>
```

Now, if you place the following code in a file named two.inc, you might expect to see the words, "Include some code...HERE!" in your browser.

```
Response.Write "HERE!"
```

Unfortunately, you will only get the first part, "Include some code..." If you examine the source code for this page, you will see that the "HERE!" is nowhere to be found. The reason for this is that the #INCLUDE directive is invalid and ignored anywhere within the marker tags for server-side code. With this knowledge, you might be tempted to attempt the following code modification to your original source file:

```
<%
      Response.Write "Include some code..."
%>
<!--#INCLUDE FILE="two.inc" -->
```

But at this point you will encounter the problem this entire section has been discussing—code that displays rather than executing! Your output will look like the following:

Fortunately, in this case, the solution is relatively straightforward. Simply include code markers around the text in your two.inc file so that it becomes

```
<%
      Response.Write "HERE!"
%>
```

At this point, you should finally achieve your desired results. This is, of course, assuming that you have placed the two.inc file in the same directory as the script that is trying to include it. In Chapter 3 you will learn about many more difficult problems that arise with the use of include files in Active Server Pages.

Pages That Won't Change

The standard procedure for debugging Active Server Pages is almost no different from the procedure that has been followed by developers for several decades on every machine and platform ever designed. You begin with some code that you think will solve a certain problem for you and achieve a certain result. You try to run this code and are surprised (but probably not much) to discover that the computer hasn't done exactly what you were anticipating.

At this point, you change your code and try running it again. The results are different. Perhaps they are more in line with your desires, or perhaps you have just made matters worse. In any event, it is certainly understood that changes in a program will typically produce changes in the operation of that program. This is not always the case under Active Server Pages.

There are several reasons why changing your ASP code may not always produce a corresponding change in the actions of your scripts. To begin with, IIS can be configured in a way that will cause it to save the output from your scripts for later reuse. Besides IIS, many browsers can be instructed to perform a similar kind of output saving (known as *caching*). A couple of developer errors, such as not accessing the right page or not saving your changes properly, can also exacerbate a bad situation.

Server-side Caching

The server-side caching feature of Internet Information Server can be advantageous under most circumstances. Consider, for example, this code snippet:

```
<%
    a = 2
    b = 2
    Response.Write a + b
%>
```

You could run this over and over again for the rest of eternity, and the results would always be the same. Namely, the printing of the numeral "4" will always be sent to the client.

Now, without IIS's server-side caching, the arithmetic would be performed to add variables a and b every single time that this script was run. With caching, however, Internet Information Server is able to store the results of the very first run of such a script and will continue reusing those results until something in the script changes. Changing the value of *a* to equal 3 would be an example of such a change.

Under some circumstances, however, IIS can become confused about whether changes have been made to a script. Tools such as Visual Interdev can sometimes alter code without altering the date of modification on a given script. In this situation, you can make as many changes as you like but still not see any changes in your results.

If you should start experiencing these problems, follow this procedure to turn caching off for your Active Server Page applications:

1. Select Programs from the Windows Start menu.

2. Open the Administrative Tools program grouping.

3. Start the Internet Services Manager.

4. Right-click the computer running the instance of IIS that you are interested in working with, and select Properties from the pop-up context menu. You should get a dialog like the one in Figure 2-3.

5. Choose WWW Service from the drop-down list as shown in the figure and click the Edit button.

6. Select the Home Directory tab.

7. Click the Configuration button inside the Application Settings frame.

8. Go to the Process Options tab, as shown in Figure 2-4.

9. In the Script File Cache frame, click the radio button labeled Do Not Cache ASP Files.

10. Click OK or Apply to confirm your changes.

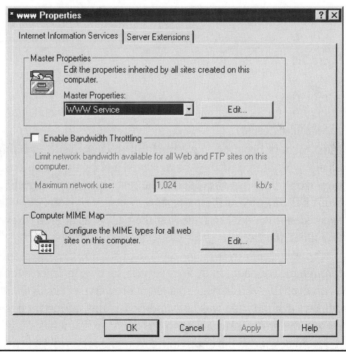

Figure 2.3   A computer Properties dialog

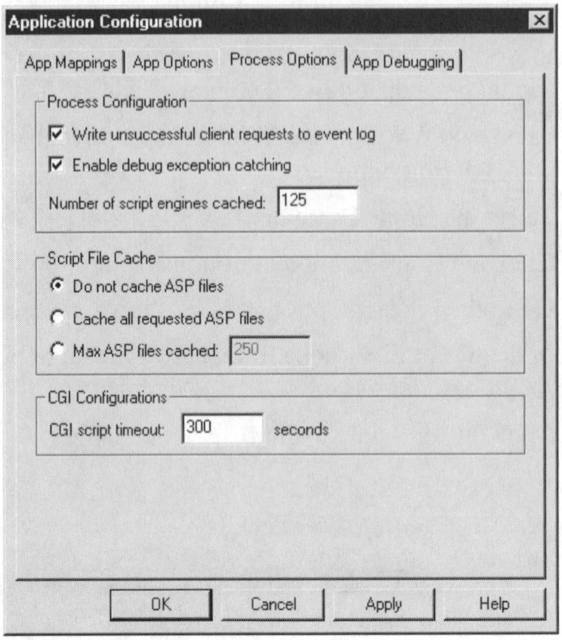

Figure 2.4   The Process Options tab

Last-Modified Headers

Most modern browsers have the built-in capacity for sensing the last time that a page was altered. If they have stored a copy that is at least as recent as this, they won't bother downloading the rest of the page. On the other hand, if they don't have a copy of the page stored locally or if the copy that they have is less recent than the last time that the page was altered, they will go ahead and download the file.

The way that browsers are capable of sensing the alteration times of Web pages is through the cooperation of Web servers such as Internet Information Server. Whenever IIS sends a page to a client browser, it checks the time and date that the OS says that the page was last modified. If this information is incorrect for some reason, the browser may elect to use the page that it has stored locally when, in fact, it should download the entire thing from the server from scratch.

This is typically more of a problem with flat HTML than with Active Server Pages. Except in the case of server-side caching discussed in the previous section, IIS will interpret ASP files every time they are requested and produce output for clients on an up-to-the-minute basis. Standard HTML is often used in Active Server Page applications for taking user input in the way of forms, however. Consider the following:

```
<FORM ACTION="calendar.asp" METHOD="POST">
<INPUT NAME="month">
</FORM>
```

If you were to visit this page once with a browser, a copy of it might be stored on your computer for future reference. Whether this happens depends primarily on whether you have enabled caching on your browser, a topic that is covered at great length in Appendix A. Even if you have enabled caching on your browser, the page should not be stored if you have followed the suggestion in Chapter 1 that you should configure IIS to expire content immediately. Assume for the sake of example that you have enabled caching in your browser and have not followed the advice in Chapter 1 (perhaps because you are working with a production, rather than development, server).

Suppose you decide that the calendar.asp script referenced by the above form should also take a year as input for whatever useful work it is performing. You might change the form to the following:

```
<FORM ACTION="calendar.asp" METHOD="POST">
<INPUT NAME="month">
<INPUT NAME="year">
</FORM>
```

If you revisited this page under normal circumstances, IIS would inform your browser that the last time the page changed was more recently than the copy that it had stored locally, and your browser would request a completely new copy of the page. As the previous section mentioned, however, a number of tools (most notably Visual Interdev) can be used to alter scripts without changing their dates of modification. In this case, your browser would be unaware of the change in your form and would continue to show the now-outdated form in its cache. This would almost certainly cause your Active Server Page not to work.

There are a few ways that you can solve this problem under Active Server Pages.

Content Expiration   Internet Information Server can be configured to instruct all browsers connecting to it that they should not cache any of the information that they receive from it. This can be hard on production servers and so is only recommended for development servers. For more information on this topic, see the section in Chapter 1 on configuring IIS.

Last-Modified Header   The built-in Response object from Active Server Pages can be used to add an HTTP header to your pages that states the last time that they were modified. The best date to use is one far in the future, so it will not have to be manually updated at any point in the near future. This setting overrides any modification date stored by your operating system for the file in which your scripts are stored. The form from our previous example would look as follows using this approach:

```
<%
      Response.AddHeader "Last-Modified", "03-04-2000"
%>
<FORM ACTION="calendar.asp" METHOD="POST">
<INPUT NAME="month">
<INPUT NAME="year">
</FORM>
```

Response Expiration   An approach similar to the one outlined in the previous paragraph is to manually set a given page to expire immediately. This will require the inclusion of server-side script in whichever file you need to make expire. You can only use this approach to prevent a given file from ever being cached by browsers. It is not useful once a file has already been cached. The example form would look as follows:

```
<%
      Response.Expires = 0
%>
<FORM ACTION="calendar.asp" METHOD="POST">
<INPUT NAME="month">
<INPUT NAME="year">
</FORM>
```

Are You on the Right Page?

A fairly obvious reason that changes made to a script may not show up in your browser is if your browser were pointed to an entirely different script. Although this is an obvious problem, it is one to which Internet Information Server makes it particularly easy to fall victim. The reason for this has to do with IIS's whole concept of Web sites and virtual directories.

When you first install Internet Information Server, you typically will have Web sites already installed called Default Web Site and Administration Web Site. These sites can be accessed on the same Web server. More important from the standpoint of this debugging issue is that both sites can contain scripts with exactly the same names.

Open the Administration Web Site Properties dialog by right-clicking its icon in the left-hand navigation tree on the Internet Information Services management console and choosing Properties from the context menu that pops up. On the very first tab, Web Site, you should see the number 7479 in the TCP Port field. This is the port upon which this site will listen for connections—the key to IIS being able to distinguish which requests are for this site, as opposed to other sites on the same computer.

If you change to the Home Directory tab now, you will see a path listed next to the label Local Path. This is the location on your computer's local hard disk where you should store scripts that you intend to make part of this application. Whenever you encounter scripts that aren't changing as you modify their code, you should ensure that you are working at some point beneath the directory listed here.

If you leave this dialog and expand the nodes listed under Default Web Site in the IIS management console, you should (assuming that you installed sample code along with the rest of IIS) see an entry for IISSamples. Right-click on this and choose Properties from the context menu that pops up. The very first tab will be called Virtual Directory and will look like Figure 2-5.

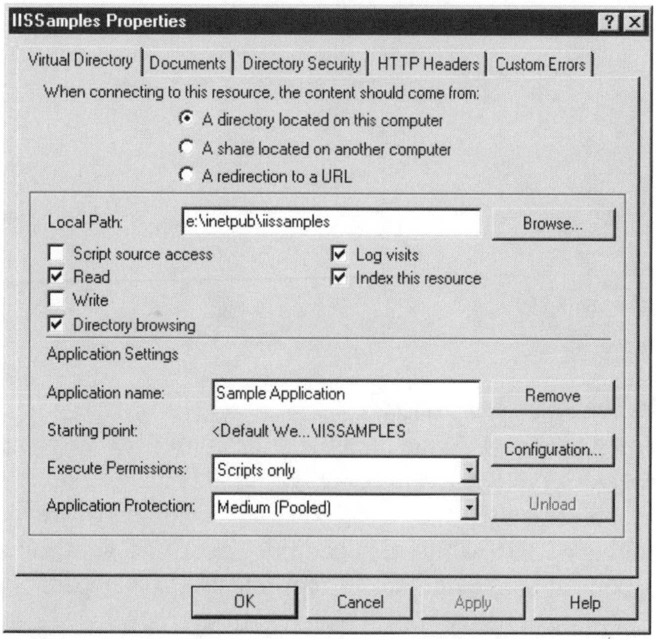

Figure 2.5   The Virtual Directory tab

Notice that this tab contains the same field for a Local Path as the Home Directory tab discussed above. The use and importance of this entry is the same as above, except that all access to this location by browsers will be determined by the TCP Port setting on the Web site of which this virtual directory is a part. In this case, the IISSamples run as part of the default Web site, which listens for requests on port 80 of your computer. This is the standard port for traffic on the World Wide Web.

The other important thing to notice on this tab is the text labeled "Starting Point". This is determined when a virtual directory is first installed on a server. It is assigned by IIS based upon the location chosen for the storage of your files on the local hard disk. Whenever you encounter scripts that aren't changing as you modify their code, make sure that you are prefacing your requests for those scripts with the starting point described here. Here is an example of a request for a script called Learn.asp that is stored in the default directory under the IISSamples virtual directory:

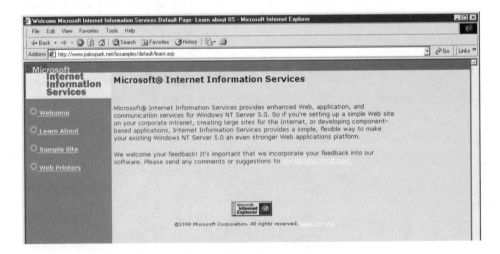

Are You Saving Your Changes?

When you are working directly at the console of the computer from which your Active Server Pages are being served, it is much simpler to ensure that your scripts are truly being saved. The most common way to affect this is via direct editing of the text files that comprise your ASP applications using a text editor. A popular and traditional tool for this task is Notepad.

The main problem with Notepad from a developer's standpoint is that it defaults to the extension .txt for all new files. This is hardly ideal, considering that the most common extensions that IIS expects to see for Active Server Pages are .asp and .asa. If you attempt to access a file under IIS with a .txt extension, the most likely result will be the display of your code rather than its execution. For more information about this, see the previous section in this chapter on pages that display rather than execute.

FrontPage and Visual Interdev are other tools that are commonly used for working with Active Server Pages. Both of these tools allow you to download your scripts to your local box for editing, then transmit them back to your server for execution. The danger here is that both tools offer Save commands under their File menus that could easily be thought to affect the copies of your scripts on the server but which only actually work with your local copies.

Under FrontPage, it is essential that you choose Publish Web from the File menu in order to transmit your changes back to the server. Figure 2-6 shows the dialog that you should see under FrontPage whenever you decide to save your changes using this method.

Under Visual Interdev, you may elect to create new projects in either Local or Master mode. In Local mode, you will have to specifically choose to update the remote copies of your scripts every time that you save them. Under Master mode, two copies of all your scripts will be maintained and updated automatically: one on your own computer and another on the server. For work on development boxes, which is the focus of this book, you should always choose Master mode.

You make this decision in Visual Interdev when you first elect to create a new project. Figure 2-7 shows the dialog under Visual Interdev that comes up during the creation of a new project to allow you to choose between Local and Master.

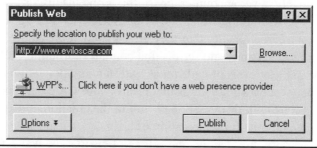

Figure 2.6   The Publish Web dialog

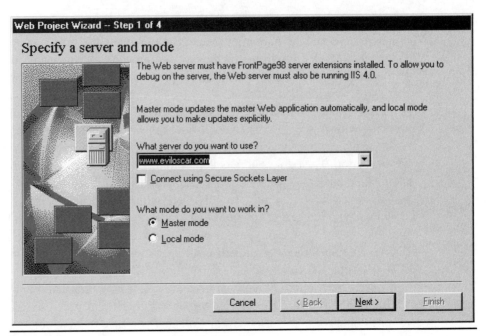

Figure 2.7   The Web Project Wizard dialog

Procedures

The simplest Active Server Pages consist of a single flow of logic from beginning to end. All of this code is contained in the single, unnamed procedure. This procedure begins with the first request of the page and continues until the end of the Web server's response. If all your ASPs use this architecture, you will probably never encounter any of the problems discussed in this section.

You will not, however, be using Active Server Pages at anywhere near the level of functionality that they are capable of providing. Under Active Server Pages, you can create scripts that contain subroutines, allowing you to achieve the highest levels of code reuse within your applications. Furthermore, you can create your own functions that return values as determined by your code.

Along with this great flexibility in the creation of procedures comes an equally great potential for the creation of error-laden code. The ways in which you name your procedures can be one source of errors. The ways in which you attempt to invoke these procedures is another issue that can cause you some grief. Finally, not understanding the differences between functions and subroutines will confuse your code to no end.

Naming Issues

The names that you give to your procedures can result in Active Server Page errors. One way that this can occur is if you choose names for your procedures that are already reserved as keywords by the scripting language that you have chosen to work with (such as VBScript or JavaScript). Another source of trouble is when you attempt to define the same procedure more than one time. This is particularly likely to happen when you are storing your procedures in code libraries and using server-side includes to bring their functionality into your scripts as needed.

Keywords Already Reserved by VBScript

VBScript is a subset of the Visual Basic programming language. For this reason, the predefined functions and routines available to the VBScript programmer are considerable. Chances are, if you have learned VBScript or Visual Basic primarily through on-the-job experience, there are vast portions of the language with which you are currently unfamiliar. This greatly increases the chances that you will try to define a subroutine or function that shares a name with a keyword that has already been reserved by VBScript.

Consider the following code sample:

```
<%
    sentence = "Have a really nice day"
    words = sub(sentence)
    Response.Write "The first word is..." & words(0)

    Function sub(psentence)
       A = 0
       J = 0
       Dim pwords(999)
       For I = 1 to len(psentence)
          C = mid(psentence, I, 1)
          If c = " " then
             pwords(j) = mid(psentence, _
             a + 1, I - (a + 1))
             A = I
          End If
       Next

       sub = pwords
    End Function
%>
```

Here, a programmer is attempting to define a function that facilitates the parsing of words in a string into separate cells in an array. In order to use this, you would simply invoke the function with the string that you would like to have parsed and provide a variable (in this case "words") in which to store the results. There is just one problem with this example: VBScript has already reserved the use of the keyword "sub"! Figure 2-8 shows the error in the Script Debugger that arises when you attempt to execute this script.

The VBScript split function could be considered an improvement on the above insofar as it allows the programmer to pass in an additional parameter that specifies upon which character(s) the given string should be parsed. So, unlike the user-defined function earlier, if the programmer wished to split the string "Have*a*really*nice*day" wherever there are asterisks, then they could simply call the built-in function this way:

```
words = split("Have*a*really*nice*day", "*")
```

In this particular case, it seems fairly obvious that the user-defined split function should simply be dropped in favor of the built-in function. In this case, the code example would become

```
<%
    words = split(sentence, " ")
    Response.Write "The first word is..." & words(0)
%>
```

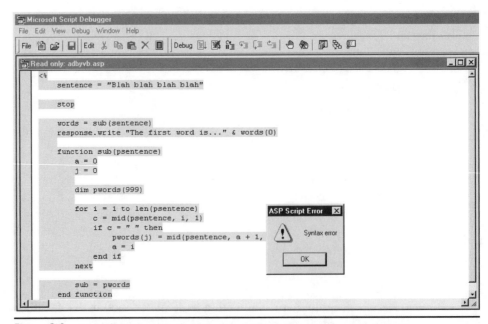

Figure 2.8   Using a keyword already reserved by VBScript causes an error

In some cases, however, you may define a function that works in a way that you prefer to the built-in function. Even in the preceding case, you might find it more convenient for your purposes to never have to specify in an invocation that you want to parse a string on spaces. Perhaps this is because you will always be parsing on spaces and don't want the added complexity that the built-in function's added flexibility brings with it.

If you find yourself in this situation, you will simply have to rename your user-defined function in order to keep it. It is a good idea to decide upon a certain prefix with which you will consistently preface all your user-defined procedures. If you choose something that has meaning to you and your organization, but which would be fairly unusual to anyone else, you stand a good chance of being able to avoid ever having to face naming conflicts with VBScript procedures.

In this case, the example code would become

```
<%
      sentence = "Have a really nice day"
      words = dmf_sub(sentence)
      Response.Write "The first word is..." & words(0)

      Function dmf_sub(psentence)
         A = 0
         J = 0
         Dim pwords(999)
         For I = 1 to len(psentence)
            C = mid(psentence, I, 1)
            If c = " " then
               pwords(j) = mid(psentence, _
               a + 1, I - (a + 1))
               A = I
            End If
         Next

         sub = pwords
      End Function
%>
```

Here, I have prefaced my function with the string dmf (my initials), which has the added benefit of uniquely identifying the procedures that I have created from those created by other developers within my organization. Your company's stock symbol might be a good choice for uniquely identifying the procedures created by your own organization's developers, as opposed to outside contractors, for example.

Procedures Your Application Already Has

The section above discussed situations in which the procedure that you are attempting to define is already a part of the VBScript programming language.

An even more common occurrence is attempting to define a procedure that has already been previously defined by your code!

The most common context in which this kind of error is likely to present itself is when you are storing frequently used routines and procedures in separate files and using server-side includes to use them like script libraries. For example, you might write the routine below to automate the addition of two numerals and store it in a file called maths.asp:

```
<%
    function add(x, y)
        add = x + y
    end function
%>
```

Now suppose that you also wanted to automate the concatenation of two strings. You might write the following routine and store it in a file called strings.asp:

```
<%
    function add(x, y)
        add = x & y
    end function
%>
```

Both of these files could exist quite nicely together in the same application, provided that they were never included as a part of the same script. If some occasion ever arose where you needed to call upon both routines from the same Active Server Page, you would be in serious trouble. *VBScript will always use the last definition given for a subroutine or function and will* not *raise an error to let you know!* In the above case, this means that calling

```
Add(2, 2)
```

would produce a response of "22," because the final definition of add was string concatenation. This is certainly not what was intended.

The easiest way to avoid these kinds of errors is to give all of the procedures in your script libraries unique prefixes that immediately distinguish them as members of specific script libraries. This way, you can be sure that a routine in one script library will never share the exact same name as a routine in another library.

If you like, you can combine the preceding prefixes with prefixes that identify the programmer and/or organization responsible for the creation of the code. In the examples that follow, both code samples are rewritten to immediately indicate the organization (InterAccess), programmer (Derek Ferguson), and libraries to which these routines belong.

```
<%
    function IA_DMF_MATHS_add(x, y)
       add = x + y
    end function
%>
<%
    function IA_DMF_STRINGS_add(x, y)
       add = x & y
    end function
%>
```

Although this can seem like an awful lot to type at first, you will reap considerable rewards if you ever get seriously into the use of code libraries in your Active Server Page applications.

Invocation Issues

The way that programmers call the functionality packaged within their procedures is a common cause of Active Server Page bugs. The proper use of the keyword "Call" is one source of confusion for developers working with VBScript. The appropriate format for scriptlets is another place where errors seem unusually common.

Whether to Use "Call"

The proper use of the Call keyword is dictated by the nature of the procedure and its arguments. In general, *VBScript never requires the use of the keyword Call.* It can, however, be a useful stylistic device within your scripts for distinguishing those procedures with relevant return values from those with irrelevant (or nonexistent) return values. The specifics of this approach are outlined here.

Subroutines Without Arguments   A subroutine without arguments can be called in either of two ways. The first way is to simply place the name of the routine on a line by itself at the point in your code where you want to call the procedure.

```
<%
    Response.Write "One,"
    MiddleProcedure
    Response.Write "Three"

    Sub MiddleProcedure
       Response.Write "Two,"
    End Sub
%>
```

This example prints the words "One, Two, Three" to a client browser. The invocation of the MiddleProcedure subroutine occurs at the line containing just the text MiddleProcedure.

The other way to call a subroutine without arguments is to preface its name with the keyword Call and to place both on a line by themselves at the point in your code where you wish to call the procedure. In this case, the above example would be changed so that the line currently reading MiddleProcedure would now read Call MiddleProcedure.

Subroutines with Arguments   A subroutine with arguments can be called in either of two ways. The first way is to simply place the name of the routine on a line. This should be followed by a space, and then all the required arguments to the function, separated by commas.

```
<%
      Response.Write "One,"
      MiddleProcedure "Two,", "Three,"
      Response.Write "Four"


      Sub MiddleProcedure(first, second)
         Response.Write first
         Response.Write second
      End Sub
%>
```

This example prints the words "One, Two, Three, Four" to a client browser. The invocation of the MiddleProcedure subroutine occurs at the line containing the text MiddleProcedure "Two,", "Three,".

The other way to call a subroutine with arguments is to preface its name with the keyword Call and to surround all arguments required by the subroutine with a single pair of parentheses. In this case, the preceding example would be changed so that the line currently reading

```
MiddleProcedure "Two,", "Three,"
```

would now read

```
Call MiddleProcedure ("Two,", "Three")
```

Functions Without Arguments   A function without arguments can be called in a few ways. One way is to simply place the name of the function on a line by itself at the point in your code where you want to call the procedure.

```
<%
    Response.Write "One,"
    MiddleProcedure
    Response.Write "Three"

    Function MiddleProcedure
        MiddleProcedure = "Two,"
    End Sub
%>
```

This example prints the words "One, Three" to a client browser. Although this is not technically an error in your code, it is probably not the wisest use for a function. The return value is being completely ignored by the calling code and would, therefore, be a much more appropriate place for the use of a subroutine. The section on functions and subroutines later in this chapter discusses this at greater length.

Prefixing this call to MiddleProcedure with the keyword Call would not technically be an error under VBScript either. Unfortunately, it would also ignore the value returned by the function and would, therefore, be an equally poor way of invoking this code.

The approach that is most likely to produce the desired results in this case would be to invoke the function directly from a line that made use of its results. This is demonstrated by the code sample here, which would produce the output "One, Two, Three."

```
<%
    Response.Write "One,"
    Response.Write MiddleProcedure
    Response.Write "Three"

    Function MiddleProcedure
        MiddleProcedure = "Two,"
    End Sub
%>
```

Functions with Arguments   There are two good ways to call functions that require arguments. The first is to place the function's name directly into a statement that will make use of the function's return value. For example

```
<%
    Response.Write "2 + 2 = " & add(2, 2)

    Function add(a, b)
        Add = a + b
    End Function
%>
```

Note the use of parentheses around the parameters for the function. This is required whenever anything is to the left of the function call within a given VBScript statement.

The other good way to invoke a function that requires an argument is by assigning its return value to a variable. The value of this variable can then be used wherever you like. Using this methodology, the preceding example would become

```
<%
   nmb = add(2,2)

   Response.Write "2 + 2 = " & nmb

   Function add(a, b)
      add = a + b
   End Function
%>
```

Once again, the parameters for the add function are surrounded by parentheses during the invocation because there is something "to the left" of the function call within the same VBScript statement. You could choose to invoke the "add" procedure like this:

```
add 2, 2
```

The problem with this, however, is that there is nothing catching the value returned from the add function.

The use of Call would be similarly problematic in this case. The proper way to use the keyword Call with this function would be

```
Call add(2,2)
```

The parentheses around the parameters have returned because the Call keyword is to the left of the function call within the same VBScript statement. As above, however, the problem is that the return value (4) is simply being allowed to vanish into the void. Although this is syntactically correct under VBScript, it is almost certainly not the results that were intended.

Scriptlets

Scriptlets provide a unique shortcut for doing work in Active Server Pages with which you should try to gain some familiarity. A scriptlet allows you to embed a single VBScript expression at any point within an ASP page. When Internet

Information Server interprets the page, the current value of this expression is swapped in and the page continues executing.

Here is an example of a script to show the current time and date as it might be written without the use of scriptlets:

```
<HTML><BODY>
<%
    Response.Write "The time and date are currently..."
    Response.Write Now
%>
</BODY></HTML>
```

Now, here is an example of how you might accomplish the same results using a scriptlet:

```
<HTML><BODY>
The time and date are currently...
<%= Now %>
</HTML></BODY>
```

Notice that most of your page now consists of regular HTML. This can be an advantage when using editing tools such as FrontPage. It can also be advantageous when the text that you would like to place on a page contains a lot of special characters, such as quotes. A typical hyperlink, for example, would look as follows in plain HTML:

```
<a href="http://www.eviloscar.com">My "Site"</a>
```

But in order to send this using Active Server Pages, you would have to code it as follows:

```
<%
    Response.Write "<a href="""
    Response.Write "http://www.eviloscar.com"""'
    Response.Write ">My ""Site""</a>"
%>
```

The main strength of scriptlets, then, is that they allow you to do more of your pages in plain HTML.

The most common mistake that developers make when working with scriptlets, however, is forgetting to begin them with an equal sign. Without the equal sign, IIS will interpret the scriptlet as being a regular segment of Active

Server Pages code. Since the only thing that most scriptlets will contain is a single expression, this will typically generate the error shown here.

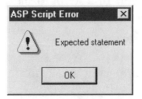

A related, but less common, mistake when working with scriptlets is to attempt actions within the scriptlet. Remember that a scriptlet exists only to return data from a given expression that will be rendered as a part of your HTML. Anything other than a single expression that evaluates to some kind of nonobject data is completely illegal in a scriptlet.

Here is an example of the most common context in which you will see this mistake. Study it carefully and take pains not to repeat it.

```
<HTML><BODY>
The current time and date is...
<%= Response.Write Now %>
</BODY></HTML>
```

You can correct this error either by removing the Response.Write:

```
<%= Now %>
```

or by removing the equal sign:

```
<% Response.Write Now %>
```

Functions Versus Subroutines

Earlier in this chapter, you were cautioned against the inappropriate use of the keyword Call. You should have taken away from this conversation the basic notion that Call should be used only with procedures that will not be returning values. The reason for this is that if you are using the keyword Call; you are filling the spot in your code to which values are typically returned. This begs the question: Which procedures return values and which do not?

Confusing functions with subroutines is a source of some trouble amongst developers. In short, functions are procedures that return values. Subroutines are procedures that do not return values.

One of the hardest-to-track-down mistakes that VBScript developers make is using subroutines for procedures that need to return values. Examine the following code:

```
<%
    Response.Write "The doctor is... "
    Response.Write isDoctorIn

    Sub isDoctorIn()
        If weekday(now) > 0 and weekday(now) < 6 then
            IsDoctorIn = "IN"
        Else
            IsDoctorIn = "OUT"
        End If
    End Sub
%>
```

The result produced by this script is shown here.

Note the complete absence of any indication as to whether the doctor is in or out. Developers making this kind of mistake typically spend hours scratching their heads and wondering how the isDoctorIn procedure could possibly produce a completely blank result when the If condition is so obviously correctly coded.

In order to solve this problem, you must change to a function rather than a subroutine. *Subroutines never accept return values!*

When using functions, developers coming from other languages are often confused by the syntax VBScript uses for assigning return values. In most other languages, the correct format is to use the keyword Return followed by whatever value the function is to return. Using this syntax, the procedure in the above example would become

```
Function isDoctorIn()
    If weekday(now) > 0 and weekday(now) < 6 then
        Return "IN"
    Else
        Return "OUT"
    End If
End Function
```

This shows the error displayed by the script debugger when this syntax is attempted.

It is important to remember that the correct way to return values from VBScript functions is to assign the value to be returned to the name of the function. This is a fairly easy problem to recognize and troubleshoot, but it bears mentioning as it is extremely common with developers from C/C++ and Java backgrounds.

Finally, it should be mentioned at this point that it is a mistake to use a subroutine for any procedure that might fail without producing a visible script error. Consider the following procedure:

```
<%
    sub divide(byref number, divisor)
        if divisor <> 0 then
            number = number / divisor
        end if
    end sub
%>
```

24x7 By Reference Versus by Value

I should take a moment to explain two parameters. The first is defined to be called "by reference"; the second uses the default under VBScript, "by value." Parameters that are passed to procedures "by reference" can be changed by the code within those procedures. Parameters passed "by value" (which all parameters are assumed to be under VBScript unless they are proceeded by the keyword ByRef) cannot be changed by the procedures to which they are passed. Their values may be altered for the duration of the procedure, but they revert back to their original values at the end of the procedure.

In general, you should only pass parameters "by reference" when you have a specific need for changing their values within your procedures. You should do this as little as possible because limiting the number of procedures that can change a variable's values limits the amount of code that you need to check for errors when that variable is being set improperly, and you aren't sure where or why.

An Active Server Page that used this procedure could very easily receive bogus results by passing in 0 as the value for "divisor." Now, as you may already know, division by zero is an undefined mathematical operation and will cause an error if attempted under VBScript. It is good that the programmer accounted for this possible misuse of his or her procedure. However, consider the following call to this procedure:

```
<%
   n = 138
   d = 0
   Response.Write "Did you know that 138 / 0 = "
   Call divide(n, d)
   Response.Write n
%>
```

You will see that this produces output which declares (quite incorrectly) that 138 / 0 = 138! This is because the divide procedure, as coded, skips any division at all when an operation is requested that would result in a division-by-zero error. It is unfortunate that they didn't write this procedure in a way that can signal the calling code to let it know that a problem has occurred.

One approach that some developers take to this situation is to choose a highly unlikely value, such as 999999, and use it to signal calling code that the operation requested was inappropriate and was not attempted. In this case, the complete code would be altered to read

```
<%
   n = 138
   d = 0
   Response.Write "Did you know that 138 / 0 = "
   Call divide(n, d)
   If n <> 999999 then
      Response.Write n
   Else
      Response.Write "An Undefined Value"
   End If

   sub divide(byref number, divisor)
      if divisor <> 0 then
         number = number / divisor
      else
         number = 999999
      end if
   end sub
%>
```

This is one possible approach to signaling your calling code when an operation has failed. It is certainly a step in the right direction. It is not, however, all that it could be. One problem is that however unlikely the value that you choose for your signal (999999 included), it is unlikely that you will be able to find any value that is truly *impossible* for all legitimate operations.

The other problem is that, philosophically speaking, you make purpose and function much less clear for whatever parameter you choose to use as a possible signal. In this case, "number" is the answer *except* when it equals 999999, and then it is a sign of impending doom. This kind of ambiguity in meaning is poor coding.

The best solution, as stated previously, is to use functions for any procedures that might fail to perform their requested operations without producing any kind of error that would be otherwise visible to the calling code. This means that the value returned by your function always indicates whether the function operated as expected. Your calling code checks this value separately from any parameters that it passed to the function to determine whether the requested job has been accomplished.

Here is the preceding code rewritten to use this approach:

```
<%
   n = 138
   d = 0
   Response.Write "Did you know that 138 / 0 = "
   Status = divide(n, d)
   If status = "OK" then
      Response.Write n
   Else
      Response.Write "An Undefined Value"
   End If

   Function divide(byref number, divisor)
      if divisor = 0 then
         exit function
      end if

      number = number / divisor
      divide = "OK"
   end sub
%>
```

Special Data Types

The original BASIC computer language supported only two kinds of data: strings and numbers. Visual Basic supports a bewildering assortment of data types, including one special type that can hold (and be used as) almost any of the other available data types. This special type, known as Variant, is the *only data type supported by VBScript!* It is, therefore, of the utmost importance that you thoroughly understand the problems that working with this kind of data can produce.

The problems associated with working with Variant data are so numerous that they are discussed throughout the rest of this book. At this point in the book, I would like to discuss the errors associated with the complete absence of data.

The Use of NULL

NULL is a data value used by VBScript to denote the absence of data itself. In comparison to colors, you might consider NULL to be like black—which is considered to be the absence of color rather than a color in and of itself. There are four things that ASP developers tend to confuse NULL with:

- **Empty**   An empty value is what is contained by a Variant variable that has been declared but not yet assigned to any value. Once a value is assigned to a variant, the only way that it can be returned to an empty state is by redeclaring it. This can be accomplished using the keyword Redim.

- **Nothing**   A variable is set to Nothing in order to remove any object data that might be stored in it. An object may be set to Nothing both before and after an object has been stored in it. This is an excellent way to signal some objects that they are no longer being used and can reclaim their resources.

Error Watch   *It is important to remember whenever attempting to assign the value Nothing to a variable that you must also use the keyword Set. This is because Nothing is considered a special case of object data, specifically the absence of any currently instantiated object. The proper way to assign any kind of object data is with the keyword Set.*

- **Zero**   Zero is a numeric value. It is most definitely data because all sorts of mathematical operations can be performed on it. You can assign a value of 0 to any variable at any point in time.

- **Zero-length Strings**   A zero-length string is represented by a pair of quotes with nothing between them (""). Because it is a string and can be a part of string operations (such as concatenation), it is definitely a kind of data. You can assign a zero-length string to any variable at any point in time.

Here is a piece of code that should convince you of NULL's separate and distinct nature. When you run it, you will be given a completely blank screen. No output is generated because none of the above data types are the same as NULL.

```
<%
   dim a ' Empty
   b = 0 ' Zero
   c = "" ' Zero-length string
   Set d = Nothing ' Nothing

   if isnull(a) then
      response.write "Empties are NULL"
   end if

   if isnull(b) then
      response.write "Zeros are NULL"
   end if

   if isnull(c) then
      response.write "Zero-length strings are NULL"
   end if

   if isnull(d) then
      response.write "Nothings are NULL"
   end if
%>
```

CHAPTER 3
File System Issues

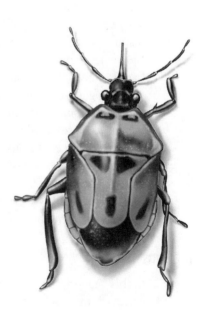

File systems represent the basic structures that applications use to store data. Almost all development platforms allow some degree of access to the file systems of the machines upon which they operate. In some cases, such as Java applets running in a browser, the execution environment may purposely restrict file system access to prevent unscrupulous developers from wreaking havoc on unwitting end-users. At the other extreme, developers working in languages such as C/C++ are often given such low-level access to their file systems that they can perform virtually any operation supported by their operating systems.

The file system model supported by Active Server Pages is a direct result of this platform's grounding in the VBScript programming language and NTFS file structures. VBScript, the subset of Visual Basic supported by Active Server Pages, encapsulates all access to the server's file system in the methods and properties of the FileSystemObject component. NTFS, the file system natively provided by Windows 2000 and NT, allows for very fine-grained control over access to individual files and resources. This control is maintained through a sophisticated system of "permissioning" that may be manipulated using several GUI tools within the operating system.

Permissioning

Permissioning is a concept that has been around the operating systems world at least since the advent of Unix. In short, it refers to placing certain restrictions on resources based upon the identity of the person or tool trying to access them. In a file system context, this might mean restricting the list of people who are allowed to edit a given file to only the administrators of a given system. Figure 3-1 shows the dialog under Windows 2000 that is typically used to place such restrictions.

Permissioning becomes a problem from Active Server Pages primarily when the entity represented by a given script lacks sufficient privileges to access needed system resources. In this section, you will learn how to spot the symptoms that indicate the existence of such a conflict. This section also discusses many tools that Windows 2000 provides for diagnosing the specific causes of any permissioning issues. Finally, this section will explain the many causes of permissioning issues and how they might be resolved.

Symptoms

In this section, you will learn how to spot the symptoms that indicate a permissioning problem with your Active Server Pages. The first of these is

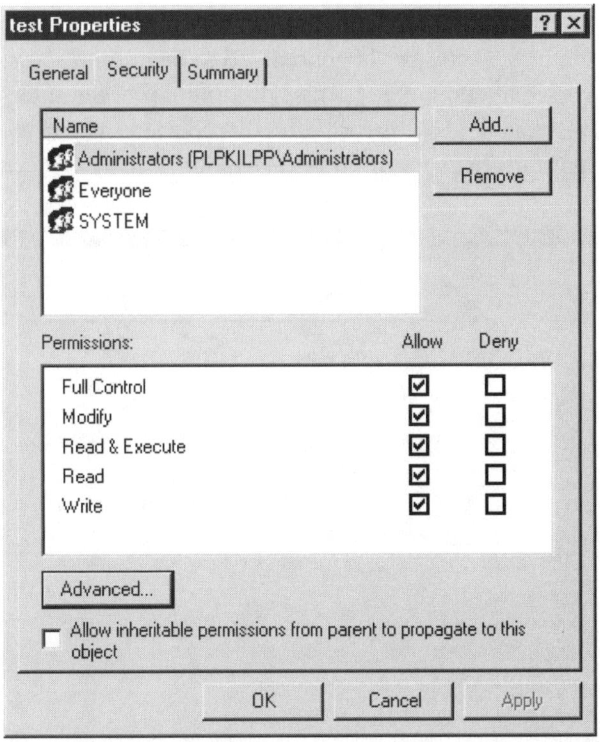

Figure 3.1   Assigning permissions to a file

pages that return messages indicating that you don't have permission to access them. The second would be scripts that fail trying to access network resources, such as shared drives. The third, and final, symptom of a permissioning problem with your Active Server Pages is when your GLOBAL.ASA file fails to execute.

Pages Produce a " No Permissions " Message

The first indication you may have that you are experiencing a permissioning problem with your Active Server Pages is likely to be an error message appearing in your browser window. There are a couple of different errors that you may be given. One is a general warning about IP restrictions; the other is a warning about resource ACLs.

IP restrictions were discussed at length in Chapter 1, under the section " Setting Up Internet Information Server. " To review, you can elect to configure an IIS application in such a way that only certain computers are allowed access. An administrator uniquely identifies computers using numbers called IPs. A computer's IP number is guaranteed to be unique across whatever TCP/IP network that computer is a part of—including the Internet!

Take a look at the error typically reported by a browser when an access attempt fails because of an IP restriction:

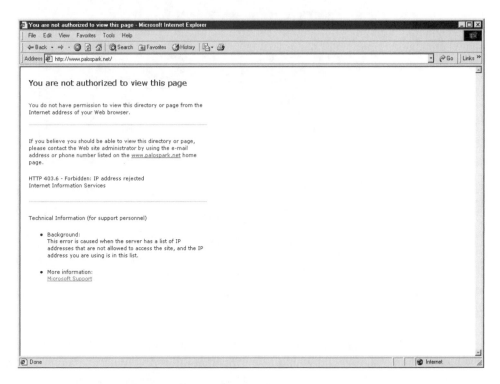

An even more common kind of error involving permissioning concerns the so-called ACL on whatever resource you are attempting to access. ACL stands for Access Control List and refers, logically enough, to the list (maintained by Windows) stating which users are allowed access to a given resource. If a user attempts to access a resource, but they are not on that resource's ACL, then an error is typically generated.

You might first be alerted to the presence of an ACL permissioning issue when a login dialog pops up in your browser as you attempt to run a given script. In Chapter 1 you learned that IIS supports three kinds of authentication: Anonymous, Basic, and Challenge/Response. If you have enabled basic and/or challenge/response authentication, you will see a login dialog whenever IIS needs to verify your identity before giving you access to a given resource. If neither of these kinds of authentication are enabled, the first sign you will have of an ACL permissioning issue will be this error:

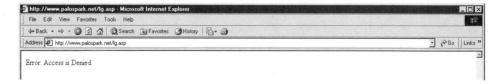

This error will also appear after the entry of an incorrect username/password combination.

It is useful to note that neither of the above errors will cause the Script Debugger to be invoked. In order for the Script Debugger to run, the user must have permission to execute whatever script is being accessed. If this were the case, then neither of the above errors would have been generated. In the next section, you will see an example of a permissioning error that will cause the Script Debugger to be invoked.

Scripts That Try to Access Network Resources Fail

Windows 2000 allows for the use of many different kinds of network resources. The most basic of these has been around since the early days of Windows NT: shared drives. Shared drives allow administrators to make portions of file systems running on one machine appear to be a part of file systems running on other machine. Figure 3-2 shows how this works.

One example of a more recent addition to the list of available network resources would be DCOM components. Using DCOM, developers can partition different pieces of their applications across multiple computers. These pieces can

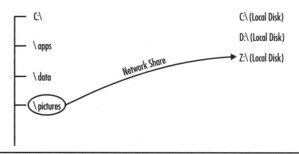

Figure 3.2   Sharing file systems across machines

then communicate and be combined freely to create entirely new applications. Figure 3-3 shows how that works.

All network resources have an associated list of people that are allowed to use them. In the previous section, you learned that such a list is called an Access Control List. The Access Control List, or ACL, used for permissioning shared drives is similar to that used for permissioning most other drives, directories, and files under Windows. The ACLs that govern access to DCOM components, however, are quite different.

Unlike the errors described in the previous section, attempting to access a network resource for which you are not listed in the ACL will never result in the display of a network login dialog. Instead, the script may generate a "File not found" error at the point in the script where such an access is first attempted. Figure 3-4 shows such an error as it might appear under the Microsoft Script Debugger.

GLOBAL.ASA Fails to Execute

Both of the previous errors would be obvious to even a casual user of your Active Server Page applications. But there are other permissioning errors that can cause even more subtle failures in your applications. The most common of these errors prevent the GLOBAL.ASA script from properly executing.

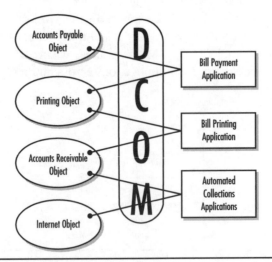

Figure 3.3   Partitioning applications with DCOM

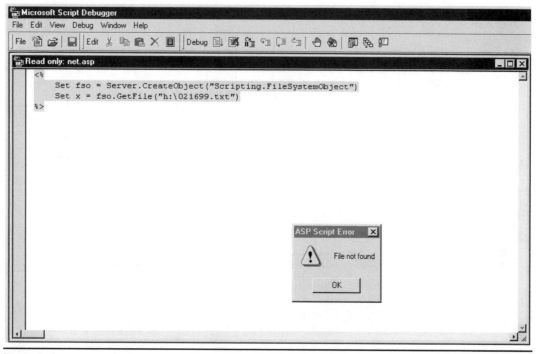

Figure 3.4   Failure to access a network resource

To demonstrate this problem, enter the following code into the GLOBAL.ASA file located in the root directory for any of your applications:

```
<SCRIPT Language="VBScript" RunAt="Server">
Sub Session_OnStart
   Response.Redirect "http://www.eviloscar.com"
End Sub
</SCRIPT>
```

Now, enter the following code for the default script in the same directory. The specific names permissible for this script are configured in the properties for this application. Common names for default scripts include DEFAULT.ASP and INDEX.ASP.

```
<%
   Response.Write "If you are seeing this, "
   Response.Write "then your GLOBAL.ASA file "
   Response.Write "didn't run!"
%>
```

Finally, adjust the permissions on the GLOBAL.ASA file so that the Anonymous IIS user is no longer allowed any kind of access. Make sure that the special Everyone group is off the list as well. If you aren't sure how to do this, simply right-click the file's icon under the Windows Explorer and select Properties. You will see a dialog like the one in Figure 3-5.

If you choose the Security tab you will be presented with the options in Figure 3-6.

Choose Advanced and use the controls on the next dialog to remove the requested entries from the list. When you are done, click Apply or OK to confirm your changes.

Use this same procedure to verify that the Anonymous IIS user (and/or the Everyone group) is included in the permissioning for your application's default

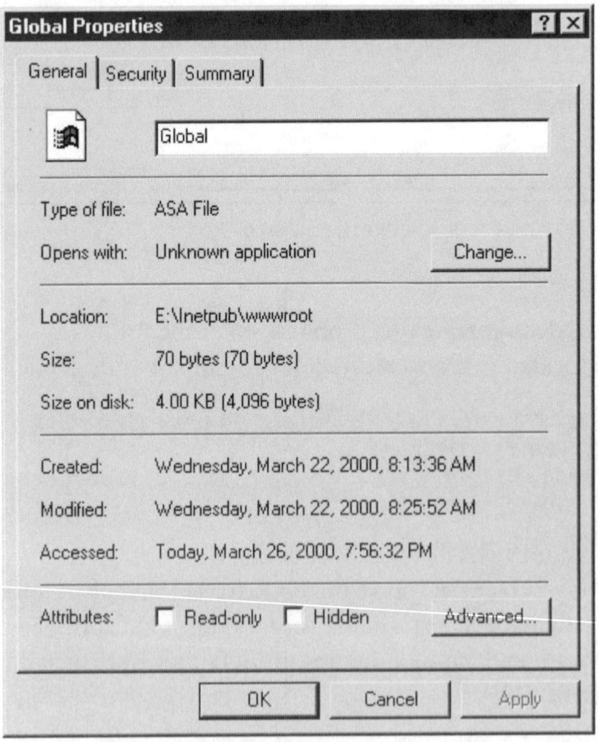

Figure 3.5   A file's Global Properties dialog

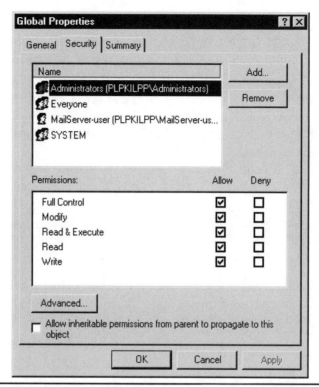

Figure 3.6   The Security tab

script. If you now open a browser from scratch to the DEFAULT.ASP page
(*do not attempt to access the page with a browser that is already open)*, you will
be presented with a login dialog. This might surprise you, considering that the
permissions on the page you are attempting to execute specify that you should be
able to gain access without restriction.

The reason, of course, is that the GLOBAL.ASA script is attempting to
execute before the start of your new session. It is this script that has been
completely restricted by the permissioning above. If you attempt to begin a new
session on any other page in the same application, you will experience the same
login/password request, regardless of the permissioning on the file at which you
point your browser. This can be extremely confusing for the novice Active
Server Page developer.

> ### ▐24x7▌ Always Have a GLOBAL.ASA File
>
> Whenever you begin making a new Active Server Pages application, you should remember to create and test a GLOBAL.ASA file for it. This holds true even if you have no particular plans in mind for such a script. In this case, you can simply "stub out" the Application_OnStart, Application_OnEnd, Session_OnStart, and Session_OnEnd procedures. Visual Interdev performs such an operation for you if you use it to create your ASP applications.
>
> The value to this approach is that it gets you thinking right from the start about where your GLOBAL.ASA file is going to be located. You can also begin thinking right from the start about the kind of permissions your application will need in order to ensure that a GLOBAL.ASA file will work appropriately for you. The section on "Causes and Resolutions" later in this chapter discusses this topic in more depth.

In the section "Causes and Resolutions" later on in this chapter, we will show you that entering a correct login and password is not always a guarantee that your GLOBAL.ASA script will run.

Diagnosis

In the previous section, you learned to spot permissioning problems. This section will introduce you to the techniques you need to pinpoint the sources of such problems. The first of these techniques involves the echoing of a server variable to the user's browser in order to help you identify who they are currently logged in as. The second technique leverages Windows 2000's capabilities to audit all attempted accesses to a given resource. The final two techniques suggest "opening up" access to your resources as much as possible in order to pinpoint the source of your problems by gradually "closing them off" again.

Once you understand these techniques, you will be much closer to mastering the use of permissioning with your Active Server Page applications.

Verifying Your Identity

The permissioning of Windows resources can best be thought of as the assignment of specific rights and privileges for specific users and groups to use certain system resources. For example, you can permission a file (a system resource) in such a way that Joe Shmoe (a user) can read it (a right or privilege) but cannot delete it (a different right or privilege). This gives us three distinct aspects to permissioning: resources, users/groups, and privileges.

The technique discussed here is for diagnosing problems with the users/groups portion of permissioning. In particular, problems can arise if you or your users are attempting to access resources under a different identity than you believe that you are. You may, for example, only be logged in as yourself when you think that you are actually logged in as the system administrator. This difference would have a vast impact on most permissioning situations.

There are a couple of different ways you can determine which user account is being used to attempt access to a given resource. The first method is to echo the server variable LOGON_USER back to the browser window whenever the script that must perform the access is executed . The other way would be to review the IIS logs containing the access attempt in question.

Design Tip   *The LOGON_USER server variable can be echoed to a browser or written to a file or even passed as a parameter to a component for recording directly into the Windows event logs. It is an extremely valuable piece of information that should not be neglected as you design your applications, as it can make future debugging quicker and less painful.*

Here is an example of code that makes use of the echoing method:

```
<%
    Response.Buffer = False ' So we can see output

    Dim fs ' Holder for the FileSystemObject instance
    Dim fl ' Holder for the file pointer
    Set fs = Server.CreateObject("Scripting.FileSystemObject")
    Set fl = fs.OpenTextFile("e:\inetpub\wwwroot\example.txt")
%>
```

If you place the preceding code in an application that only supported anonymous access, all the code would be guaranteed to run under the IUSR_<machine> account. This account name is what you would expect to see echoed by the first line of the script. If the file EXAMPLE.TXT is permissioned in a way that allows for access by this account, the script would then run to completion without incident. Otherwise, an error will be generated.

Figure 3-7 shows a situation where the anonymous account has been denied access to the EXAMPLE.TXT file. In the next section, you will learn what steps a system administrator or developer can take to resolve this permissioning failure.

The previous technique works whenever a script attempts to access a resource for which the user lacks sufficient permissions. But what about cases where the user lacks sufficient permissions to access the script itself? To continue the

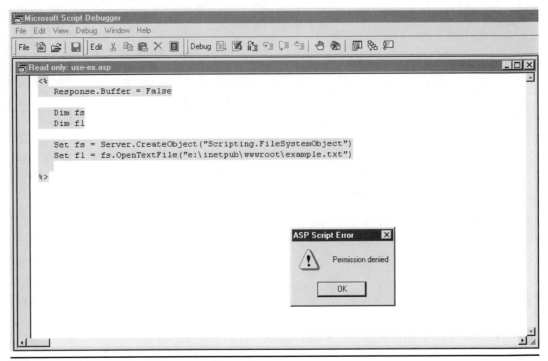

Figure 3.7   Access failure shown by script debugger

previous example, try removing all permissions for the anonymous user to the Active Server Page script that you entered from the listing. Now, assuming that you have placed the script (as requested) in an application that denies anonymous login, you should get a login dialog when you attempt to execute this script. Click the Cancel button; you will get the ACL error screen.

Echoing the LOGON_USER server variable didn't enter into this discussion because the script was aborted before execution even began. So how do we know which account was being used to attempt access to this resource? The IIS log files contain this information. An example is shown in Figure 3-8.

Note in Figure 3-8 that a single dash indicates an attempt to access a resource as the anonymous user. Accesses under other accounts are shown either (in the case of basic authentication) with the login or (in the case of challenge/response) with the Windows domain followed by a slash and then the login.

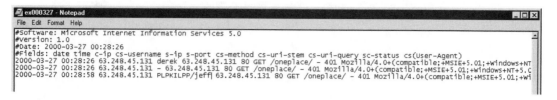

Figure 3.8   Log files showing user authentication attempts

Windows 2000 Auditing

The Windows 2000 auditing mechanism can be of invaluable assistance when it comes to sorting out permissioning problems with your Active Server Page applications. Using auditing, you can ask the operating system to log most attempts at operations on the files and directories that comprise your applications. These logs can provide extremely useful information when you need to figure out which accounts and operations are involved in whatever problems you are experiencing.

To turn on Windows 2000 auditing for a script or directory that you suspect may be involved in a permissioning problem, follow this procedure:

1. Locate the script or directory within the Windows Explorer.

2. Right-click the icon representing the script or directory in question.

3. Choose Properties from the pop-up context menu.

4. Select the Security tab on the Properties dialog (shown previously in Figure 3-6).

5. Click the Advanced button at the bottom of the dialog.

6. Select the Auditing tab on the Access Control Settings dialog shown in Figure 3-9.

7. Click Add at the bottom of the dialog.

8. Choose the user, computer, or group that you wish to audit from the list, as shown in Figure 3-10. If you aren't sure, choose the group called Everyone.

9. For every operation listed in the Auditing Entry dialog, click Successful if you wish to audit attempts that succeed, or click Failed if you wish to audit attempts that fail.

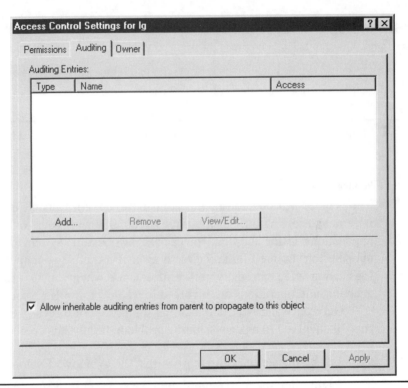

Figure 3.9   The Access Control Settings dialog

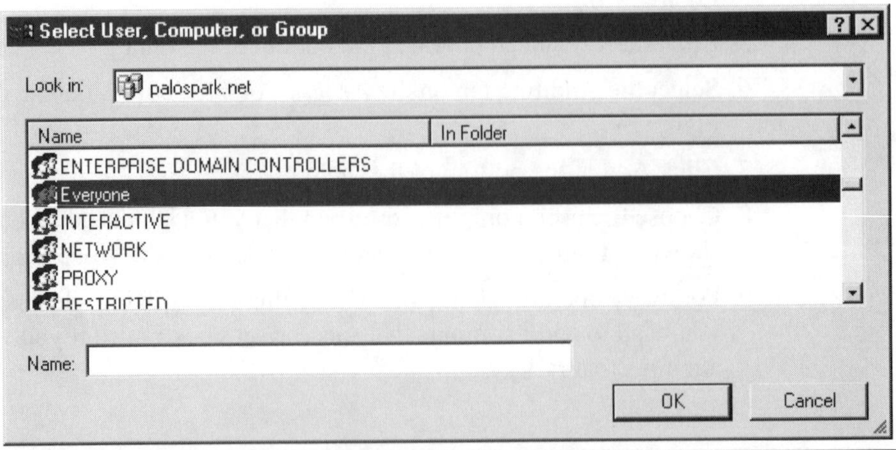

Figure 3.10   Selecting a user, computer, or group for auditing

The operations available to you for auditing include the following:

Traverse Folder/Execute File　A folder is traversed whenever any resource (such as a file) inside of it is accessed in any way, shape, or form. A file being executed will most often mean IIS running an ASP script within the context of this book. It may, however, also refer to the interpretation of a PERL script through CGI or the running of a binary executable from the workstation console or Explorer interface. This is a common operation to audit when debugging Active Server Pages.

List Folder/Read Data　A folder is typically listed under IIS when a browser requests a directory for which no default document exists. IIS can be configured to refuse such requests, but it is typically better to allow them on development machines (as discussed in Chapter 1). On the other hand, a file is read whenever IIS passes the contents of an HTML page to a browser. This is a common operation to audit when debugging Active Server Pages.

Read Attributes　Before IIS can serve any kind of file to a requesting client, it must first examine that file's basic attributes. It must do this to determine the type of the file and to ensure that it is appropriate for serving. For this reason, this is a common operation to audit when debugging Active Server Pages.

Read Extended Attributes　Examining advanced attributes for the file system resource in question (whether a file or directory) will cause this operation to occur. Advanced attributes include such things as the Archiving and Encryption settings. This is not a very common operation to audit when debugging Active Server Pages. The exception to this might be if your scripts make extensive use of an Active Directory API such as ADSI.

Create Files/Write Data　A file may be created or written to if any of the forms in your ASP application support file uploads. Otherwise, these operations are typically only audited when attempting to debug Active Server Page operations that use the Scripting library's FileSystemObject component (discussed later in this chapter).

Create Folders/Append Data　An ASP application can only create folders or append data through the operations of a COM component. Therefore, these operations are typically only audited when attempting to debug Active Server Page operations that use the Scripting library's FileSystemObject component (discussed later in this chapter).

Write Attributes   Changing the attributes of the file system resource in question (whether a file or directory) will cause this operation to occur. This is not a very common operation to audit when debugging Active Server Pages. The exception to this might be if your scripts make extensive use of an Active Directory API, such as ADSI.

Write Extended Attributes   Changing advanced attributes for the file system resource in question (whether a file or directory) will cause this operation to occur. Advanced attributes include such things as the Archiving and Encryption settings. This is not a very common operation to audit when debugging Active Server Pages. The exception to this might be if your scripts make extensive use of an Active Directory API, such as ADSI.

Delete Subfolders and Files   An ASP application can only delete subfolders or files through the operations of a COM component. Therefore, these operations are typically audited only when attempting to debug Active Server Page operations that use the Scripting library's FileSystemObject component (discussed later in this chapter).

Delete   This operation refers to the deletion of the very file system resource that is currently being audited. For this reason, auditing will always cease after the performance of this operation. Since the only way that Active Server Pages can directly delete a file system resource is through the operations of a COM component, these operations are typically only audited when attempting to debug Active Server Page operations that use the Scripting library's FileSystemObject component (discussed later in this chapter).

Read Permissions   Examining the permissions of the file system resource in question (whether a file or directory) will cause this operation to occur. This is not a very common operation to audit when debugging Active Server Pages. The exception to this might be if your scripts make extensive use of an Active Directory API, such as ADSI.

Change Permissions   Changing the attributes of the file system resource in question (whether a file or directory) will cause this operation to occur. This is not a very common operation to audit when debugging Active Server Pages. The exception to this might be if your scripts make extensive use of an Active Directory API, such as ADSI.

Take Ownership   Taking ownership of a resource is almost always accomplished from the Windows Explorer interface. This is not a very common operation to audit when debugging Active Server Pages. The exception to this might be if your scripts make extensive use of an Active Directory API, such as ADSI.

Once you turn on auditing for the file system resource that you want to track, the operations selected will begin generating log entries in your system's Event Viewer. Figure 3-11 shows a punch-down on one such event: a successful visit to the page log.asp.

In the background, you can see that the log summary for this punch-down has been highlighted. In addition to other information available in this summary view, you can see the date and time when the access was attempted. You can also see that the account used for the access attempt was the anonymous account for this machine (which is named WWW), IUSR_WWW.

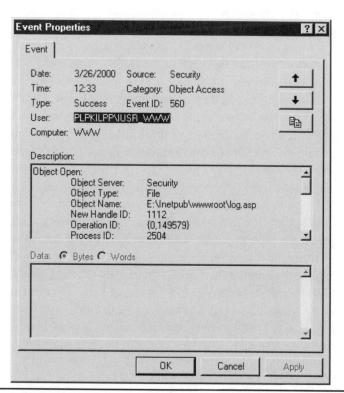

Figure 3.11   Event properties for a successful Web page visit

Opening up IUSR_<Machine>

The anonymous account has been discussed at great length in this chapter. It is probably the single most important user account to the typical Internet Information Server, because it is the account through which all unauthenticated access occurs. Given that the vast majority of sites on the World Wide Web are completely open to the public, the case could be made that the anonymous account is the single most commonly used Windows account on the planet!

This situation changes somewhat in the case of sensitive or internal-use Web sites. In this case, it is fairly common to want to restrict access to a more select choice of users and groups. The first step in achieving this goal is to remove the IUSR_<Machine> account from the ACL of the pages and resources to be used by your application. Theoretically, you would then place only the specific accounts that you would like to have access to these resources in their ACLs, and users would be required to authenticate into your application before they could use them.

What do you do when an authenticated user is getting ACL errors and you have no idea why? Suppose, for example, that you have given the account eviloscar full access to every script in your application, yet they still can't use them. At this point, you can fall back to the IUSR_<machine> account and begin opening things up until you are finally able to gain admission.

For example, you might begin by giving IUSR_<machine> access to the specific script in your application that you are trying to access. Then, you might give the account access to your GLOBAL.ASA file. You could then proceed adding this account to every resource in your application until things started working successfully. The left side of Figure 3-12 shows what this workflow might look like.

Using this approach, you would be able to pinpoint the resource used by your application that required greater permissioning. Once you know this, you can begin experimenting with ways to close off access again so that you can feel comfortable operating your application in a production environment. You would begin by swapping the IUSR_<machine> account with the right account(s) for this application on the specific resource that had been causing a failure. Once you manage to get this working, you can work your way back up the right side of Figure 3-12, restricting access once again. It would be important to test every step of this to make sure that you had not shut yourself out again!

Opening Up Operation Permissions

A point closely related to the above method of opening up the IUSR_<machine> account is the liberalization of the operations that are permitted for the resources

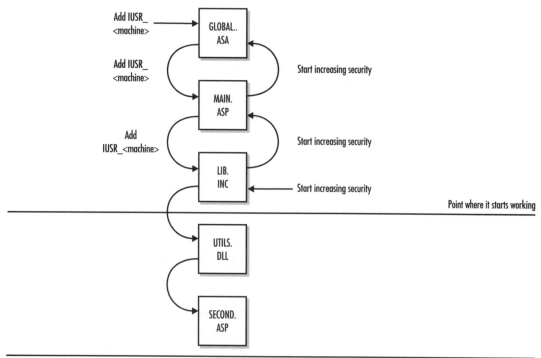

Figure 3.12   Opening up the IUSR_<machine> account

used by your application. To clarify, in the previous method it was suggested that you temporarily add the IUSR_<machine> account to all your application's files and scripts. To follow this method, you would make sure that whatever users and groups are already on your ACLs have the maximum freedom to perform any operations possible.

Examine the following listing:

```
<HTML>
<HEAD>
<TITLE>What is wrong here?</TITLE>
</HEAD>
<BODY>
Can you spot the problem with this code today?
Or is <%= Now %> not a good time to ask?

</BODY>
</HTML>
```

If you were a system administrator and a developer handed you this file, you might give it a quick look and decide that it was just regular HTML. You would then probably put it in an HTML file and assign the read but not execute permission to it. The first time that anyone tried to access it, they would notice that the scriptlet buried inside displayed itself in the browser window rather than executing. This situation was discussed at length in Chapter 2.

At this point, the developer would probably call you and ask for the extension on this file to be changed to .asp. This way, as you learned in Chapter 2, Internet Information Server would know that it needed to try interpreting scripts inside of the file before sending them on to the browser clients. The only problem is, with only read permissions for this file, whichever account attempted access would get the results shown in Figure 3-13.

At this point, you first use the methods outlined previously in this section to assure that you are accessing this file under the account that you think you are. Once you were certain of this, you could implement the method of diagnosis being described here by assigning whatever account you are using permissions for every kind of operation on this file. Figure 3-14 shows a file that has had its operation permissions completely opened for the oscar account.

If this didn't work, you could proceed through the rest of the resources in your application, opening their operation permissions the same way for your test account. This would be useful in case your script made use of another file of which you were unaware. Once your application began working, you could begin trimming back the operations allowed for your account, such as changing execution permissions to script only permissions. This would prepare your application for use in a security-sensitive production environment.

Causes and Resolutions

By now, you should feel quite comfortable recognizing when you are experiencing a problem with Active Server Page permissioning. Furthermore, in the previous section you were given the techniques necessary for narrowing

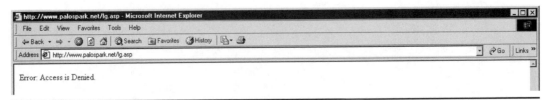

Figure 3.13 Accessing an Active Server Page with only read permission

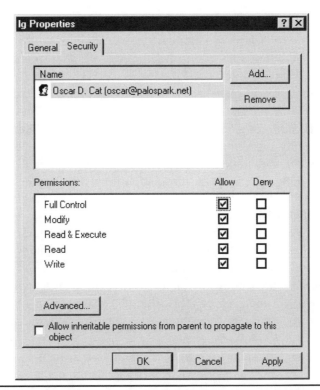

Figure 3.14   File with completely open operation permissions

down the causes of such problems. At this point, you should be quite prepared for a discussion of the specific causes of permissioning problems and their resolutions.

The most obvious and common cause of permissioning problems under Windows 2000 is an unacceptable setting of the permissions on required resources. A potentially less obvious but equally troublesome cause of permissioning errors is Internet Explorer's tendency to pass along the Windows identity of its current user without asking. The use of *automatic password synchronization* can also be a problem when trying to access network resources. Finally, applications that require authentication may cause GLOBAL.ASA scripts to fail to execute.

Resources Lacking Permissions

In the last section, you learned about opening up the permissions on the resources in your applications in order to verify the minimum and maximum settings required in order for your scripts to be both secure and fully functional. It should be clear from that discussion that the most direct way to resolve most permissioning issues is to alter the ACL of the file containing whatever script you are trying to execute. If a file is flat HTML, whatever account(s) you plan to use it to access must have at least read permissions. If a file contains server-side script, the account(s) should have execute permissions.

Besides the ACLs of the files that make up your applications, you should also carefully examine the permissioning options presented by the Internet Information Server configuration screens. These options were discussed at length in the section on configuring Internet Information Server in Chapter 1.

Internet Explorer Passing Identity

More so than any other browser currently on the market, Microsoft's Internet Explorer (IE) is deeply integrated into the Windows operating system. One example of this is IE's capability to directly support the Windows challenge/response authentication for access to secured Web applications. It is important to realize, however, that this strength is based largely upon IE's capability to directly access the security information of whichever user is currently logged into the Windows system.

The downside to this kind of integration is that you may occasionally wish to log into your Active Server Pages application under some account other than the one that you have used to log into Windows. If challenge/response authentication is enabled for your application, Internet Explorer may pass your current Windows identity without even telling you! This can create enormous confusion when permissions for your application are set in expectation of a different account.

In this case, the method discussed previously in which the LOGON_USER server variable is echoed to the client may prove particularly helpful. Once you understand that the wrong account is being used to access your application, you may decide to enable forms of authentication besides challenge/response. Alternately, you may switch to a browser that is less integrated with the Windows operating system (such as Netscape).

Automatic Password Synchronization and Network Resources

You should be aware that version 4 of Internet Information Server contained a bug that prevented some Active Server Pages from accessing Microsoft Access files stored on network drives. This typically occurred when Access databases stored on local drives contained tables linked to files on network drives. Attempts to use ODBC to work with these linked tables typically failed.

This bug has been fixed in IIS 5, which is the version of Internet Information Server assumed by this text.

GLOBAL.ASA Versus Authentication

You should be aware that version 4 of Internet Information Server contained a bug that prevented the successful execution of GLOBAL.ASA scripts in applications that required authenticated access. Typically, applications that allowed anonymous access were unaffected. Applications that only supported basic or challenge/response access, however, experienced problems in this respect.

This bug has been fixed in IIS 5, which is the version of Internet Information Server assumed by this text.

Included Files

The inclusion of files within other files is accomplished through a simple server-side directive. The ability to leverage this functionality prior to the interpretation of any scripting in your Active Server Pages is a great benefit to you as a developer. Among other things, you can use this facility to dramatically increase the clarity of your scripts by reducing the number of common functions that you would otherwise have to hardwire into your scripts. Figure 3-15 graphically demonstrates the clarity of code that can be achieved through the use of server-side includes.

Experience has also shown, however, that included files also represent a tremendous source of potential errors in your Active Server Pages. In some cases, you may find that the files you wish to include cannot be found by Internet Information Server. At other times, the peculiar rules governing what you can and cannot do with included files may lead you into serious code errors. This section thoroughly discusses both of these possibilities.

File Not Found

Internet Information Server most often fails to include files as requested by server-side directives due to differences between the virtual and real paths to those files. The enabling of parent paths on the server can also cause such a failure. Finally, the permissioning problems that were examined in the previous portion of this chapter can cause failures during server-side include attempts.

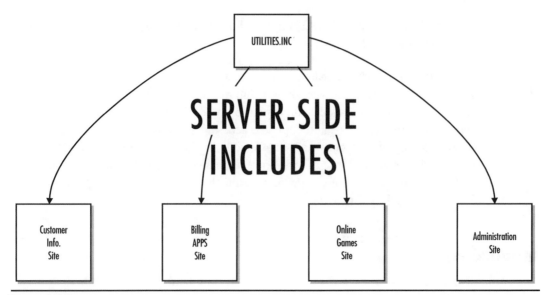

Figure 3.15   Server-side includes

Virtual Versus Real Paths

A virtual path is best thought of as the path to a file that might appear in the URL field of a browser. A real path, on the other hand, is the path that you would use to access a file under the Windows command console (sometimes still referred to as DOS by old-time programmers). Problems can easily arise with your applications if you attempt to use virtual paths where real paths are required, or vice versa.

The paths required by server-side include directives are virtual paths. Attempting to use real paths here will result in an error in your Active Server Page application. Consider the dialog shown in Figure 3-16.

The dialog in Figure 3-16 shows that the Local Path for the directory that serves as the starting point for the Debugging application is e:\book\chapter3\debugging. This is the real path. Further down in the figure, you will also see that the starting point for this application is described as <Default Web...\debugging. This is the virtual path. In order to access a script called EXAMPLE.ASP in this application, you might use your browser as shown here:

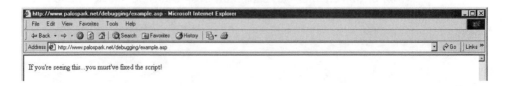

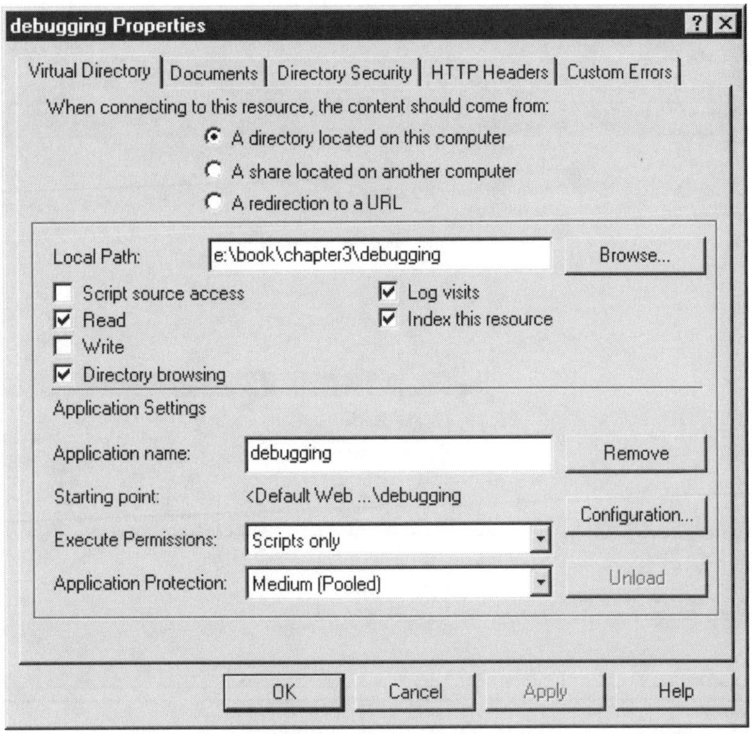

Figure 3.16   Properties for the Debugging application

Note that the path in the browser incorporates the virtual path from Figure 3-16, not the real one. Now, suppose that the source code for this page was modified to include another file in the same directory on the server. Here is one way that such an attempt might be made:

```
<!-- #INCLUDE FILE="e:\book\chapter3\debugging\includeme.txt" -->
<%
   Response.Write "If you're seeing this…"
   Response.Write "you must've fixed the script!"
%>
```

Figure 3-17 shows the error that you will get from the Script Debugger if you attempt to run the preceding script.

This error can be fixed only by changing the real path in the include directive to the virtual path instead:

```
<!-- #INCLUDE FILE="includeme.txt" -->
```

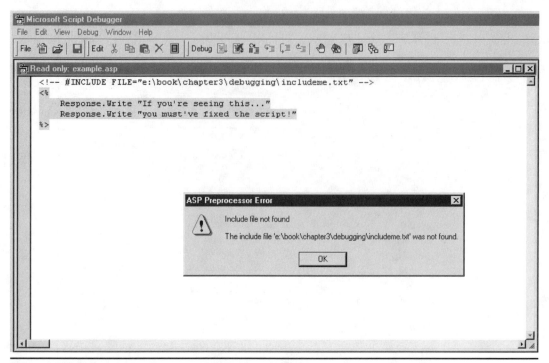

Figure 3.17   Using a real path in a server-side include

In this case, since the file is located in the root directory of the application, no path is required to precede the filename in the include directive.

Enabling Parent Paths

A *relative path* is a path that specifies the location of a resource by giving directions from the current position within the file system structure. The following path requests the inclusion of a file that is two directories above it in the file structure.

```
<!-- #INCLUDE FILE="../../includeme.txt" -->
```

It is capable of making this request via the parent path symbol "..."; whenever you use this symbol in a relative path it means, "Go up one level in the directory structure."

Internet Information Server can be configured to not allow the use of parent paths. This is typically done is to prevent ill-intentioned hackers from abusing this capability to gain access to parts of your system. On a production system, this may be a real concern.

On a development box, however, access should be limited enough that you shouldn't need to worry about this kind of abuse. You may wish to think twice about using relative paths in your applications, however. If you use them on your development server, you will either have to enable parent paths on your production server or radically alter your code before you can put it into production. To enable parent paths, follow this procedure:

1. Choose Programs from the Windows Start menu.
2. Open the Administrative Tools program group.
3. Select Internet Services Manager.
4. Right-click the Site or Virtual Directory for the application you are debugging.
5. Choose Properties from the pop-up context menu.
6. Select the Home Directory tab.
7. Click the Configuration button.
8. Select the App Options tab.
9. Make sure the Enable Parent Paths checkbox is enabled.
10. Click Apply or OK to verify your changes.

Permissioning

In the previous section, permissioning issues were discussed at great length. The peculiar effects of improper permissioning on included files warrants special mention here, however. In short, problems can arise if a user attempts to access a page that *includes* files to which the user doesn't have sufficient access permissions. This is true even if the user has sufficient access to the file containing the server-side include directive.

The error raised by such an attempt is odd. The script debugger is *not* invoked by this kind of script failure. Instead, you will simply get a message in your browser like this one:

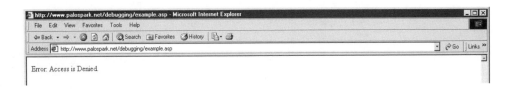

If you see this error in your browser, look for include directives in the script being accessed and verify the permissions on the files being included.

Code Errors

The interaction between your code and the code of files that are included at the server is complex. For this reason, programmers often fall foul of Active Server Pages when they first begin digging deep into the possibilities of server-side includes. This section covers some of the most common pitfalls in the use of included files from the perspective of an Active Server Page developer.

Run-time File Selection

When Internet Information Server reads a file into memory for the first time, it goes through a specific series of steps as it renders it for a browser. This series of steps begins with processing all the server directives within that file. Once all the directives have been processed, the server goes on to interpret any server-side code within the file. Only then does it send the page on to the client.

If you consider the preceding sequence of steps, it should become clear that you cannot use server-side code to specify the name of a file that you would like to have included at the server. Consider the following code:

```
<%
    If Request.Form("UserPreference") = "" then

%>

        <HTML>
        <HEAD><TITLE>Vacation Preference</TITLE></HEAD>
        <BODY>
        What kinds of things do you prefer to experience on vacation?
        <FORM METHOD="POST">
        <INPUT TYPE="RADIO" NAME="UserPreference" VALUE="Sun">
        <INPUT TYPE="RADIO" NAME="UserPreference" VALUE="Fun">
        <INPUT TYPE="RADIO" NAME="UserPreference" VALUE="Culture">
        </BODY>
        </HTML>
<%
    Else
%>
        <!--#INCLUDE FILE = "<%= Request.Form("UserPreference") &
        ".htm" %>" -->
<%
    End If
%>
```

This application asks the user what kind of things they are looking for in a vacation, and then it returns a bunch of information about possible destinations that meet the description. The developer who wrote this was hoping to avoid hardwiring three rather lengthy HTML responses into her script. The only problem with this is that, by the time the scriptlet in the server-side include is actually interpreted by IIS, the include directive itself will already have been executed.

Since the scriptlet will not have been interpreted at the point in time when the include is executed, IIS will try to interpret the code within the scriptlet as the name of the file to be included. This will probably cause your script to fail, as in Figure 3-18.

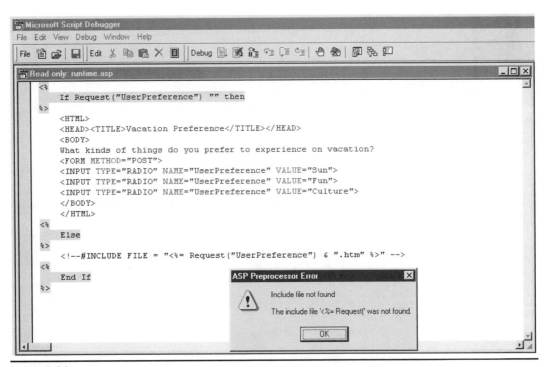

Figure 3.18 Trying to dynamically assign a server-side include

The best way to work around this limitation is through the Response.Redirect functionality of Active Server Pages. Using this approach, the preceding example becomes

```
<%
   If Request.Form("UserPreference") = "" then
%>
      <HTML>
      <HEAD><TITLE>Vacation Preference</TITLE></HEAD>
      <BODY>
      What kinds of things do you prefer to experience on vacation?
      <FORM METHOD="POST">
      <INPUT TYPE="RADIO" NAME="UserPreference" VALUE="Sun">
      <INPUT TYPE="RADIO" NAME="UserPreference" VALUE="Fun">
      <INPUT TYPE="RADIO" NAME="UserPreference" VALUE="Culture">
      </BODY>
      </HTML>
<%
   Else

      Response.Redirect Request.Form("UserPreference") & ".htm"

   End If
%>
```

Breaking Code Across Files

Another common mistake, closely related to the previous mistake, is attempting to partition a single procedure between multiple files. This occurs whenever a procedure begins in one script and is intended to end in an included file. Here is an example of such an attempt:

```
<%
   If Request.Form("EmployeeType") = "" then
%>
      <HTML>
      <HEAD><TITLE>Salary Calculation</TITLE></HEAD>
      <BODY>
      What kind of position do you hold within the company?
      <FORM METHOD="POST">
      <INPUT TYPE="RADIO" NAME="EmployeeType" VALUE="Manager">
      <INPUT TYPE="RADIO" NAME="EmployeeType" VALUE="Peon">
      </BODY>
      </HTML>
<%
   Else
      Salary = Calculate(Request.Form("EmployeeType"))
End If
```

```
function Calculate(et)
    if et = "Manager" then
%>
<!-- #INCLUDE FILE = "manager.asp" -->
<%
    else
%>
<!-- #INCLUDE FILE = "peon.asp" -->
<%
    end if
%>
```

Here, the developer would like to calculate salaries differently for managers and peons. The Calculate procedure that begins in this file has different conclusions in either the MANAGER.ASP or PEON.ASP files. For example, the MANAGER.ASP file might read

```
<%
    Calculate = 100000
End Function
%>
```

Unfortunately, this doesn't work at all. Instead, it produces this error:

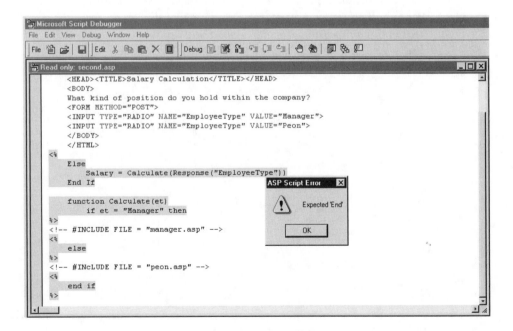

The reason for this failure is that the directives are processed before any of the server-side script is interpreted. This means that both cases are included in the file before any script is given a chance to execute. The proper way to achieve the desired results here would be to either include the entire functions in the MANAGER.ASP and PEON.ASP files or to completely abandon the separate files and incorporate their code directly into the main file. Done this way, the procedure would look like this:

```
function Calculate(et)
     if et = "Manager" then
        Calculate = 100000
     else
        Calculate = 50000
     end if
end function
```

Included File Loops

The final common mistake that is made when working with included files under Active Server Pages is to create a situation in which your directives create circular references to each other. Figure 3-19 depicts the way that this might occur: file A is including file B. File B is including file C. File C tries to include file A, at which point the entire process becomes an infinite loop. Active Server Pages will automatically detect situations like this and refuse to execute any application where they occur.

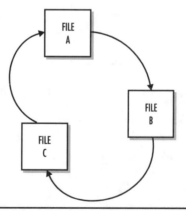

Figure 3.19   Circular file inclusion

FileSystemObject

All access to the server's file system is encapsulated under Active Server Pages via the FileSystemObject scripting component. This component supports many of the same file I/O operations that are typically available to more traditional development environments such as C/C++ or Visual Basic. The ways in which it differs from these environments, however, has proven an enormous potential source of errors for the neophyte Active Server Page developer.

Constants

One source of errors that is commonly observed when using the FileSystemObject component is in the constants used with its methods and properties. If you are not very familiar with discovering, defining, and using constants in a Visual Basic–derived environment, you will want to read this section with special care.

Not Understanding Constants

Not understanding what constants are is understandable for people who have only worked with scripting languages such as VBScript. In short, a constant is like a variable, insofar as it is a user-assigned name that can be associated with a given quantity. For example, this code assigns the value 32 to the variable X:

```
<%
   X = 32
%>
```

Similarly, this code assigns the value 42 to the *constant Y*:

```
<%
   Const Y = 42
%>
```

So what is the difference between these two? A variable can have many different values assigned to it over time, while a constant is guaranteed to always have the value to which it was originally assigned. So, the following code is valid:

```
<%
   DailyTemperature = 68 ' Monday
   DailyTemperature = 72 ' Tuesday
   DailyTemperature = 69 ' Wednesday
%>
```

but the following code is not:

```
<%
   Const RoomTemperature = 68 ' This is set-in-stone
   Const RoomTemperature = 72 ' Since when?!?!
   RoomTemperature = 69 ' This won't work either
```

After you assign a value using the Const keyword, consider that value set in stone and unchangeable from that point forward. The preceding script produces the error under the Script Debugger that is shown in Figure 3-20.

Getting Constants from the Object Browser

Besides the constants that you can define in your own code, some built-in objects have a set of constants all their own. So, for example, you might imagine a component called CreditCard that features a method called Destroy. Rather than taking the strings Fold, Spindle, or Mutilate as a parameter that describes how

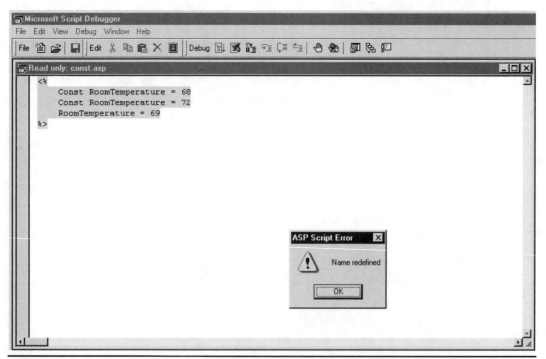

Figure 3.20   Trying to change a constant value

this destruction is to be accomplished, it might internally define them as three integer constants. The code inside the component might look like

```
Public Const destroyFold = 1
Public Const destroySpindle = 2
Public Const destroyMutilate = 3
```

This is great, assuming that the client programmer has some way of finding out which numbers equate with which actions. But how can this be accomplished? In most cases, the objects that you deal with will have documentation available either in printed or electronic form. The constants for the FileSystemObject are available electronically as a part of the Microsoft Developer's Network Library (search for FileSystemObject constants at http://msdn.microsoft.com).

Follow the procedure described below to discover the constant values used by any component for which you can't find documentation.

1. Start Visual Basic.

2. Click Open in the New Project dialog (shown in Figure 3-21) to create a new Standard EXE project.

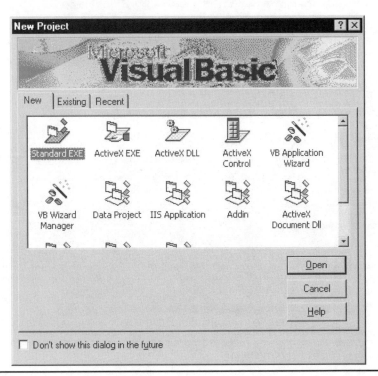

Figure 3.21   The New Project dialog

3. Choose References from the Project menu.

4. Click Browse on the References dialog (shown in Figure 3-22) to locate the file containing your component.

5. Select the DLL, OCX, or TLB file for your component. For the FileSystemObject, this file is SCRRUN.DLL and is located in the Windows System directory.

6. Click OK to close the References dialog.

7. Choose Object Browser from the View menu.

8. Choose your component from the drop-down list in the top-left corner of the object browser. For the FileSystemObject, it is called Scripting.

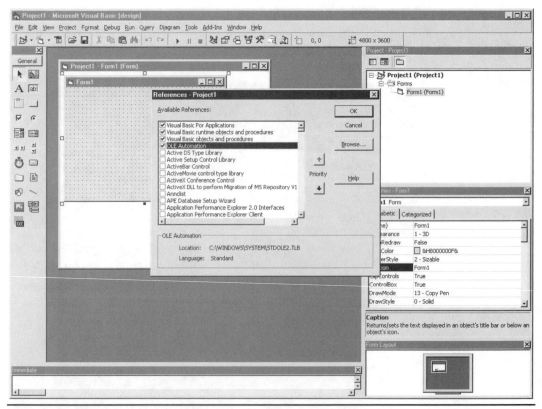

Figure 3.22   The References dialog

9. Choose Globals from the list in the lower-left pane of the object browser. The constants for this component are now indicated by the lines with little "equals" icons in the lower-right pane of the object browser.

10. Click on any of the constants to view their correct value in the bottom pane of the object browser. This is shown in Figure 3-23.

Design Tip *If you are going to be doing any serious work with Active Server Pages and their debugging, you should strongly consider investing in a copy of Microsoft's Visual Studio. Visual InterDev is a part of this collection and is an excellent tool designed primarily for developing in Active Server Pages. Visual Basic provides the object browser discussed in this section; additionally it enables you to instantly leverage a great deal of your VBScript knowledge for building genuine Windows applications.*

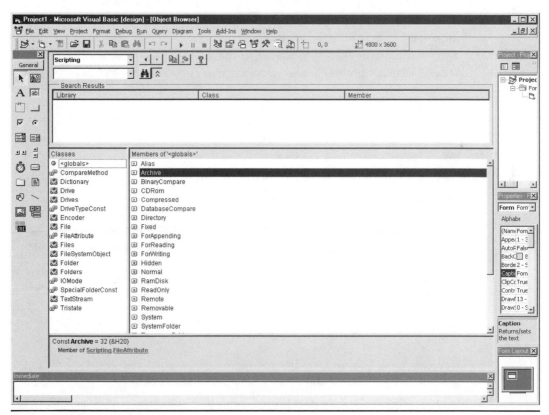

Figure 3.23   Viewing a constant value in the object browser

Defining the Constants

Once you know how to look up the values of constants using the object browser and/or the component documentation, you should have no difficulty using them in your code. Chapter 13 suggests a particular style that you should probably follow when building an application that uses constants to any great extent.

There is just one stylistic matter that warrants discussion here, because it is the source of a great many errors in Active Server Page applications. Examine the following code sample:

```
<%
    Set fs = Server.CreateObject("Scripting.FileSystemObject")
    fs.OpenTextFile "c:\example.txt", 1
%>
```

This code is perfectly correct in terms of VBScript syntax and usage. If you look up the IOMode.ForReading constant in the documentation or object browser, you will see that it is associated with the value 1. This code is, therefore, simply opening a text file strictly for reading.

The problem with this approach is that the value 1 tells the casual reader of your code virtually nothing about its meaning. A better approach might be

```
<%

    Const READ_ONLY = 1
    Set fs = Server.CreateObject("Scripting.FileSystemObject")
    fs.OpenTextFile "c:\example.txt", READ_ONLY
%>
```

This approach goes much further toward the goal of creating truly self-documenting code. It is, in fact, the best approach that you have available to you when working within the confines of server-side script. When you are creating your own components using higher-level languages such as C++ and Visual Basic, however, there is an even better way available to you.

```
Sub main()
    Dim fs as New Scripting.FileSystemObject
    fs.OpenTextFile "c:\example.txt", Scripting.IOMode.ReadOnly
End Sub
```

This Visual Basic procedure is truly the ultimate in self-documenting code. Fully leveraging Visual Basic's ability to "early bind" with component code, it uses a direct reference to the IOMode constants stored within the Scripting library. This enables different developers working with the code in the future to understand its purpose immediately upon first encounter.

Code Issues

Two methods of the FileSystemObject component seem to create much more than their fair share of confusion amongst ASP developers. The first of these is the ReadAll method and its supposed ability to facilitate the run-time inclusion of one script within another. The other of these is the FileCopy method and some peculiarities in the format that it expects its parameters to have.

The ReadAll Method

Some developers mistakenly believe that they can use the ReadAll method of the FileSystemObject to affect a run-time determination of which files to server-side include in their scripts. This chapter has already explained why this is an impossible quest. The following listing might be familiar from that previous discussion:

```
<%
    Const READ_ONLY = 1
    Const FOR_WRITING = 2
    If Request.Form("EmployeeType") = "" then
%>
    <HTML>
    <HEAD><TITLE>Salary Calculation</TITLE></HEAD>
    <BODY>
    What kind of position do you hold within the company?
    <FORM METHOD="POST">
    <INPUT TYPE="RADIO" NAME="EmployeeType" VALUE="Manager">
    <INPUT TYPE="RADIO" NAME="EmployeeType" VALUE="Peon">
    </BODY>
    </HTML>
<%
    Else
        If Request.Form("EmployeeType") = "Manager" Then
            Set x = fs.OpenTextFile ("c:\manager.asp", READ_ONLY)

        Else
            Set x = fs.OpenTextFile ("c:\peon.asp", READ_ONLY)

        End If

        buffer = x.ReadAll
        x.close
        Set x = fs.OpenTextFile ("c:\raises.asp", FOR_WRITING)

        x.WriteLine buffer
        x.close

        Salary = Calculate(Request.Form("EmployeeType"))
    End If
%>
<!-- #INCLUDE FILE = "raises.asp" -->
```

The problem with this approach, just as with all previous attempts at runtime include-file selection in this chapter, is that the #INCLUDE directive is always executed before any of the server-side script! This means that the text included at the location of the directive in the preceding script will be whatever was written into the RAISES.ASP file during the *previous* execution of this script. If this is the first time that this script has been run, execution will fail because the RAISES.ASP file will not even exist yet. Figure 3-24 shows what this looks like in the Script Debugger.

The only way to achieve the desired results would be to follow the same methodology outlined in the previous section on runtime selection of included files. In short, you could define a single procedure that is capable of dealing with both kinds of raises. Alternatively, you could define two different procedures in the same include file and simply call one or the other based on what kind of raise you are attempting.

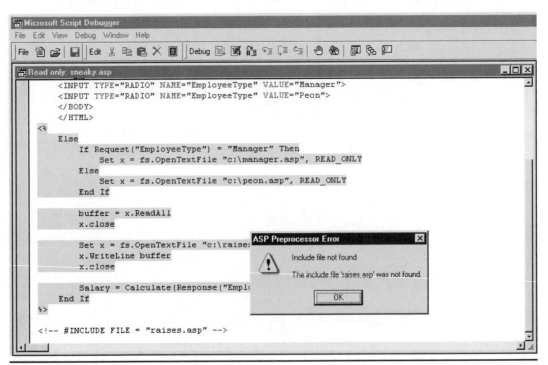

Figure 3.24   The Include file not found error

The Copy Method

Sometimes, you may find yourself wanting to write a script that copies a file from one directory to another. An example of this might be an e-commerce application that accumulates items to be purchased into shopping cart files on the server. Whenever a customer checks out and completes their visit to your site, you might want to copy their finalized file to a different directory for archiving purposes. Here is a snippet of code that might be attempted for this purpose:

```
<%
    Set fso = Server.CreateObject("Scripting.FileSystemObject")
    Set sc = fso.GetFile("e:\inetpub\wwwroot\5318842.txt")
    sc.Copy "e:\inetpub\wwwroot\archives"

%>
```

Error Watch *VBA components often use a method called FileCopy for the same purpose as the Copy method discussed in this section. Be careful not to mistakenly attempt to call FileCopy on the FileSystemObject component, or your script will break with a syntax error.*

The preceding script begins by instantiating an instance of the FileSystemObject. It then obtains a reference to the current customer's shopping cart file, which we have hard-coded as 5318842.TXT. In a real application, this filename would have to be something different for each new visitor to your site. Finally, our application attempts to copy the shopping cart file to the archives subdirectory.

Internet Information Server will not like this syntax at all. It will, in fact, produce an almost inexplicable permissioning error, as shown in Figure 3-25.

If you followed the advice in our previous section on diagnosing permissioning problems, you might go to the archives subdirectory and give everyone full permissions. You would then be quite stunned to find that the error would still occur. The reason for this is that IIS is interpreting the above Copy command as a request to overwrite the archives directory. This is because you have left the trailing slash off of the parameter!

```
sc.Copy "e:\inetpub\wwwroot\archives\"
```

This line works as intended.

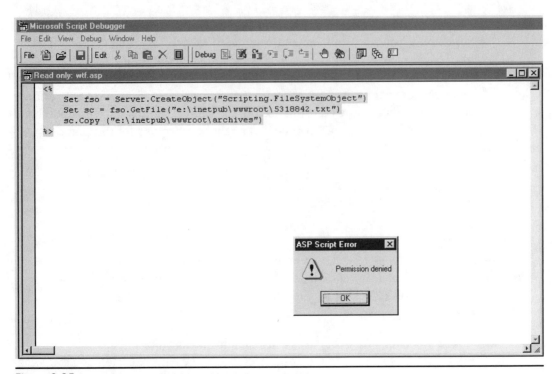

Figure 3.25   A permissioning error when copying a file

CHAPTER 4

Maintaining State

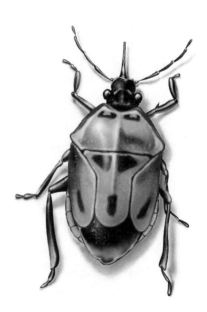

In the early days of the World Wide Web, pages were strictly static affairs that provided, but did not receive, information. A little bit later, with the introduction of the Common Gateway Interface (CGI), simple forms allowed the entry of basic data by end-users. This data was then processed by executables stored on the server and acted upon—all within the context of a single page visit.

Sometimes the data being dealt with needed to exist over several page visits. For example, online stores needed to let customers select products for purchase on multiple catalog-style pages before proceeding to a final checkout page to pay for everything. In these cases, CGI scripts needed to use elaborate schemes for *hidden fields* that passed all of the data to be stored back and forth between the browser and the server for every single page visited.

Fortunately, Active Server Pages offer an infinitely more elegant and advanced solution to this problem. For storing information across page visits on a user-by-user basis, ASP applications are able to leverage the features of the intrinsic Session object. For storing Application-level information that can be shared by different users visiting completely different pages, you can use the Application object.

At the Session Level

A session typically begins the first time that a user's browser accesses any page within your application. At this point, a single session is created for exclusive use with this client. If the client were to be terminated for any reason (for example, if the user turned off his or her browser), then that session would be terminated, and all information stored within it would be lost. If the user returned to your application after such a termination, a completely new session would be created. The process looks like Figure 4-1.

Figure 4-1 shows two users visiting over time various pages in your ASP application. Notice that the first page visited by either of the users results in the creation of a Session object for that user.

It is particularly important for a developer who wants to debug ASP Session objects to understand the exceptions to the workflow described earlier. Numerous things can limit the life span of your sessions besides the termination of the client. Similarly, choosing to manage multipage data (referred to as "state") yourself through the use of cookies can present its own host of difficulties. Finally, the incorporation of HTML frames into your applications can confuse the session-management features that are built in to Internet Information Server.

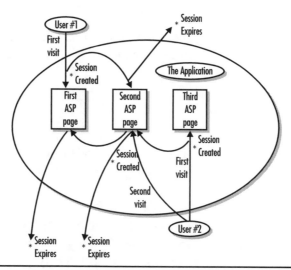

Figure 4.1   Two users visiting one application of three pages

Life Span

Not understanding the typical cycle of life for Active Server Page sessions can lead to a myriad of errors in your code. You might, for example, set Session.TimeOut too high or too low for the specific needs of your application. Or, in a more extreme case, you might elect to disable session state maintenance altogether! In this section, you will learn how to avoid these costly mistakes, as well as a couple of others.

Setting Session.TimeOut Incorrectly

Typically, a new session is created every time a new visitor comes to your Web site. You might think that this session is destroyed as soon as the visitor leaves your site. But what does this really mean in terms of the World Wide Web? A Web server like IIS breaks its connection with client browsers after serving each page, so how can it possibly know when a visitor has left the site for good?

The answer is that it doesn't. Internet Information Server waits for a specific number of seconds to elapse between requests from the same client. If this number of seconds is ever exceeded, the session associated with that client is destroyed ("abandoned" in IIS terminology) and all data lost.

So, when a browser leaves your site and goes on to other places on the Web, the session associated with it may not be abandoned immediately. If the amount of time allowed between client requests is very long, a client could potentially visit many other sites and still return to your site to find all of his/her data still intact. You could create such a situation using code such as

```
<%
    Session.TimeOut = 1400 ' Time in minutes
    Response.Write "I'm going to live FOREVER!! :)"
%>
```

The main problem with the preceding code is that allowing a session to remain open for such a long time is not very secure. It is entirely conceivable that one user could stop using a browser and still leave it running. If another user were to visit the same site using this browser within the 23-hour window of opportunity, they would have access to all the first user's session data.

The other problem with setting session timeouts to be this long is that, on a particularly busy server, it is easy to imagine servers slowly accumulating Session objects. Over time, the number of Session objects could grow to a point that the hardware running IIS would not be able to continue running the operating system acceptably. At this point, IIS, the computer, and your application would all grind to a halt!

Now, let's consider the opposite of the above situation. A developer might set the timeout threshold for sessions to be something abnormally low. Consider the following:

```
<%
   Session.TimeOut = 1 ' Time in minutes
   Response.Write "I'll be dead before you know it!"
%>
```

The problem here is that any information stored in the Session object by this application could easily be gone by the time that the next script is invoked. The reason for this is that there will only be one minute allowed between page requests before any given Session object is abandoned and all of its data lost.

Whenever you are experiencing problems with lost session information, one of the first things that you should check is the amount of time that is being allowed for session expiration. Fortunately, this is easily accomplished by echoing the Session.TimeOut parameter to the browser using the Response object.

```
<%
   Response.Write "I'm going to live for "
   Response.Write Session.TimeOut & " minutes!"
%>
```

The default value for this parameter is 20 minutes and should only be changed if you have some specific reason in mind for doing so.

Disabling Sessions

It is possible to completely disable the use of sessions under Internet Information Server. As strange as it may seem, there are some valid reasons for doing this. Later in this chapter, in the section on frames, you will learn that performance concerns are one such reason.

From a development standpoint, disabling sessions is an obvious showstopper to proper maintenance of session state. So, if you suspect that your administrator may have configured IIS this way, you can use the following procedure to verify this setting:

1. Select Programs from the Windows Start menu.
2. Open the Administrative Tools group.
3. Select the Internet Services Manager.
4. Expand the tree control on the left to reveal the application that you suspect might have its session ability turned off.
5. Right-click this application.
6. Choose Properties from the pop-up context menu.
7. Click Configuration in the Application Settings section of the dialog.
8. Select the App Options tab.
9. Verify that the Enable Session State box has been checked.
10. Click OK or Apply to verify your changes.

Before Sessions Begin

Trying to retrieve information from a session variable before that variable has been initialized is a common error in Active Server Page applications. Consider the following code:

```
<%
   If IsNull(Session("FavoriteIceCream")) Then
      Response.Redirect "PickIceCream.asp"
   Else
      Response.Write "So, you think that "
      Response.Write Session("FavoriteIceCream")
      Response.Write " is the best ice cream?!"
   End If
%>
```

The idea here is that a visitor to your site should go first to the PICKICECREAM.ASP page. There, they should choose their favorite ice cream before proceeding to the page containing the preceding script. This illustrates one key reason why developers often wind up trying to access session variables before they have been set: You can never be sure of the exact order in which users will visit the pages comprising your applications.

The developer who created the preceding piece of code is trying to safeguard against this mistake by checking the session variable to make sure that it isn't NULL. If it is, then she is redirecting the user back to the page on which this value is initially set. The problem with this approach is that unset session variables are not equal to NULL; they are equal to the empty string "". For more information on the difference between these values, see the section on special data types in Chapter 2.

Turning On Buffering

On a development machine, your main focus should be on doing things in a way that facilitates the creation of easily understood, bug-free code. Because the creation of some bugs along the way is unavoidable, you should also strive to design your applications in such a way that errors and their causes are obvious when encountered.

When you move to a production box, however, your emphasis may change noticeably. In this context, it may be useful to squeeze every last drop out of your

---

24x7 Setting Defaults in GLOBAL.ASA

You might think that the best way to rewrite the preceding code would simply be to make sure that the session variable isn't equal to the empty string before proceeding. It is true that this will solve your problems in most cases, but there is a better way. The Session_OnStart event in the global.asa script is guaranteed to execute at the start of every session. Deciding on some unique default value for each of your session variables and setting them in this procedure is the best way to design bug-free applications.

```
Sub Session_OnStart
    Session("FavoriteIceCream") = "None"
End Sub
```

The code in your pages then could check for the value None and be completely certain that, if they saw this value, no assignment of this session variable had occurred beyond the default.

computer's performance that you possibly can. Turning buffering on for the pages in your application is one technique that you should consider in this kind of production environment.

Generally, if sessions are enabled for an Active Server Page application, they are instantiated at the start of a client's very first visit and remain in effect for every page rendered thereafter. By turning on buffering, you allow IIS to first determine whether a given page actually *uses* the Session object before loading it into memory. If a user selects a path through your application that avoids the use of sessions completely, you can save your server the burden of ever instantiating a Session object for that client at all!

This may seem a trivial savings at first, but consider the scale of the problem as a Web application grows in size and popularity. An application consisting of 100 scripts might easily be visited by tens of thousands of users every day on the World Wide Web. This would require a total number of session accesses given by the following formula:

```
100 pages * 10,000 users = 1,000,000 session accesses
```

There are two ways to turn buffering on for your Active Server Page applications. The first is by including the following statement at the top of every file for which you want to use buffering:

```
Response.Buffering = True
```

The second approach turns buffering on for all of the pages in your application. Follow this procedure:

1. Select Programs from the Windows Start menu.
2. Open the Administrative Tools group.
3. Select the Internet Services Manager.
4. Expand the tree control on the left to reveal the application that you suspect may have its session capability turned off.
5. Right-click this application.
6. Choose Properties from the pop-up context menu.
7. Click Configuration in the Application Settings section of the dialog.
8. Select the App Options tab.
9. Verify that the Enable Buffering box has been checked.
10. Click OK or Apply to verify your changes.

Cookies

The Session object is fine for storing simple data between page accesses during a single browser visit. What if your data isn't quite so simple, though? Or, what if you would like to continue storing your data even after a browser has left your application and been terminated? These are just a couple of the situations in which you would need to make use of cookies.

Like Session and Application objects, cookies are stored on the client's machine during a visit to your Web application. Unlike these intrinsic objects, however, cookies allow for the storage of much more complicated data hierarchies, as well as for the persistence of data between multiple sessions.

Design Tip   *Never make the assumption in your Active Server Pages that cookies will always work the way that they should. Given the media hype that has surrounded cookies and their alleged security problems, many users have chosen to disable them on their browsers. For more information on detecting this and working around it, see the section in Appendix A on browsers and security.*

Traveling Off the Path

Most of the time when developers use cookies, they are interested only in talking to their own application. A system designed to assist in the ordering of prefabricated houses might use the following code to set a cookie so that the user's preference in building materials can be remembered from one session to another.

```
<%
   Response.Cookies("Material") = "Brick"
   Response.Cookies("Material").Expires = "April 1, 2030"
%>
```

Now, suppose that another application was designed by the same company to facilitate the ordering of house insurance. Assuming that this application was to be housed on the same server, the following line could be added to ensure that it, too, was able to retrieve this information from client browsers:

```
Response.Cookies("Material").Path = "/"
```

This line tells IIS to record the cookie in client browsers in such a way that any application located within the same domain as the current application can access the information. The problem is, Internet Information Server is capable of hosting multiple domain names on a single server. If your system administrator chose to operate the house-buying application as www.derekshousebuyingapplication.com and the insurance application as www.derekshomeinsuranceapplication.com, then there would be no way of exchanging cookies between the two.

The best way to work around this limitation is simply to store the required information in files on your server. Any application requiring access to this information must then require users to log in before reading the data stored in these files into their associated session variables. The whole workflow looks like Figure 4-2.

Here is some sample code that you could adapt for the start of any Active Server Page application to accomplish the log in and session variable population:

```
<%
   If Session("Username") = "" then
%>
   <HTML>
      <HEAD><TITLE>LOG IN</TITLE></HEAD>
      <BODY>
      <FORM Method="POST">
      Username: <INPUT NAME = "Username"> <br>
      Password: <INPUT NAME = "Password"> <br>
      </FORM>
      </BODY>
   </HTML>
<%
   Else
      Const FOR_READING = 2
      strFileName = "c:\datastores\" & request("username")
      Set fso = Server.CreateObject("Scripting.FileSystemObject")
      If not(fso.FileExists(strFileName)) Then
         Response.Write "Invalid Login!"
      Else
         Set ds = fso.OpenTextFile(strFileName, FOR_READING)
         strBuffer = ds.ReadLine
         If strBuffer <> Request("Password") Then
            Response.Write "Invalid password!"
         Else
            Session("Username") = Request("Username")
            Session("Password") = Request("Password")
            Do Until ds.EOF
               strBuffer = ds.ReadLine
               key = split(strBuffer, chr(9))(0)
               value = split(strBuffer, chr(9))(1)
               Session(key) = value
            Loop
            Response.Redirect "appstart.asp"
         End If
      End If
```

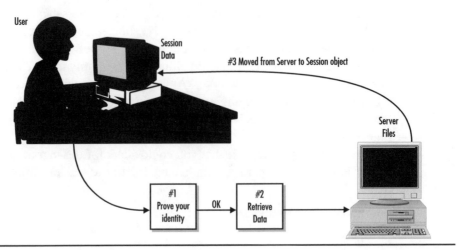

Figure 4.2 Retrieving Session object data

This code begins by checking if a username has already been specified. If it has not, the script asks for it along with a password and terminates. Otherwise, it attempts to find a file in the datastores directory with a filename that matches this username. If none exists, the user is told that they have given an invalid username.

If the file does exist, it is opened and the first line is read. If this line is the same as the password given, the rest of the data in the file is parsed in tab-delimited format. The bit of each line before the tab is used as a key and the bit after the tab is used as a value. The key and value together are used to populate the session object associated with the current user.

The only other bit of code that you should need is something to write this data back into the data files when the current session is finished with it. This code should be located in the Session_OnEnd event of the GLOBAL.ASA file and can be quite simple:

```
Sub Session_OnEnd
    Const FOR_WRITING = 1
    strFileName = "c:\datastores\" & Session("username")
    Set fso = Server.CreateObject("Scripting.FileSystemObject")
    Set ds = fso.OpenTextFile(strFileName, FOR_WRITING)
    ds.WriteLine(Session("Password"))
    ds.WriteLine("Material" & chr(9) & Session("Material"))
    ds.WriteLine("SocNumber" & chr(9) & Session("SocNumber"))
    ' ETC ETC ETC ETC
    ds.Close()
End Sub
```

Traveling Off the Server

In the previous section, you learned that cookies are always restricted to the paths that are set for them when they are created. If you set a path of /homebuyingapp for a cookie, all the scripts located in or under this virtual directory on your server will be able to retrieve it. If you set a path of / for a cookie then all the scripts located in the entire domain in which your application operates will be able to retrieve it.

What if you need to retrieve a cookie that is set by another computer? If this were allowed, it would constitute an incredible security hole in the World Wide Web. Imagine if your bank could set cookies in your browser indicating your account numbers and balances, and these could then be retrieved by whatever other sites you happened to visit. Since this is a patently bad idea, it is completely disallowed by all major Web servers and browsers (including IIS and Internet Explorer).

The problem this presents for you as a developer is that sometimes your application may shift from one machine to another without your knowledge and for reasons beyond your control. This could happen very easily in a system that makes use of so-called Web "clusters." A cluster is a group of machines running special software that allows them to work together and act as a single machine. You might think of them as clones because they typically have identical files and settings at all times. If any one of the machines fails or is too busy to respond to an incoming request for a Web page, any of the others can respond.

In order to overcome the limitations of this situation you must do two things. First, you must ensure that all the links in your application are relative rather than absolute. Second, you must force all page requests made by the same session to go to the same machine.

The concept of relative links should be a fairly simple one to grasp. So long as a given URL doesn't include the name of a machine at the start of it, it is relative. Without a machine at the start of it, a URL is interpreted to mean "on the current machine." This distinction is important because if you give the name of the machine in your URLs, Web browsers following these links will stand a chance of being redirected by the clustering software on your Web servers. Relative addresses always stay on the same machine.

The best way to force a session onto a single machine in a cluster is by putting the following code in your application's GLOBAL.ASA file:

```
Sub Session_OnStart
   RealMachineName = Request.ServerVariables("SERVER_NAME")
   ApplicationPath = "/homebuyingapp"
   strURL = "http://" & RealMachineName & ApplicationPath
   Response.Redirect strURL
End Sub
```

To use the preceding code, just change the ApplicationPath variable to match the starting point of your application as listed in the IIS management console.

Traveling into Other Applications

At this point in the discussion, you should be quite prepared to debug issues involving applications that attempt to retrieve cookies for which they are out of scope. Sometimes, however, you will find that the problem with your cookies is exactly the opposite. It is possible to set cookies in one application that interfere with those being used by others.

To continue the home and home-insurance buying examples from the previous two sections, imagine that these applications both exist on the same server but are not affiliated. This could easily happen if these applications are being hosted by a third-party Web-hosting organization. Now, suppose that at some point a visitor to the home-buying application is asked for the name of their realtor. The application might save this information to a cookie using code like this:

```
<%
    Response.Cookies("Name") = Request("RealtorName")
    Response.Cookies("Name").Path = "/"
    Response.Cookies("Name").Expires = "April 1, 2030"
%>
```

Because this cookie's expiration date is set so far in the future, it will remain stored on the client's computer even if the browser is stopped and restarted. To see how this may lead to confusion and the failure of Active Server Page code, imagine that this user were now to visit the home insurance–buying site.

```
<%
    if Request.Cookies("Name") <> "" then
        strInsuranceAgentName = Request.Cookies("Name")
    else
%>
    <FORM METHOD="POST">
    Please give us your insurance agent's name:
    <INPUT NAME="Name">
<%
    end if
%>
```

This code demonstrates one situation in which trouble could arise. The insurance-buying application tries to determine whether the current user has already been to this site and chosen an insurance agent. It determines this by looking for a value in the cookie named Name. If it finds a value here, it uses that value as the insurance agent's name. If it finds this cookie to be blank or nonexistent, it asks the user to choose.

If a user has already visited the home-buying site, they will have the name of their favorite building material stored in this cookie. The script preceding will interpret it as the name of their insurance agent. Unless this firm happens to have a Mr. Brick or Mrs. Frame working for them, chaos is guaranteed to ensue.

It is important to note that this would only be an issue if both of the sites shared the same domain name. This situation is most common when a low-budget start-up decides to share server space with many other companies via the services of a third-party Web hosting outfit. This can be considered a strong argument in favor of bringing such Web hosting "in house."

There are also many other morals to this story…

Choose Unique Identifiers for Your Cookie Names   You can't control the actions of other developers on your server, but you can make it harder for them to choose cookie names that will fluster your own applications. Choosing a cookie name like Password or Total is a guaranteed recipe for disaster. If you must use terms like this, preface them with something distinct. This way, Password might become HOMEINSURANCE_Password, or Total might become HOMEINSURANCE_Total.

Choose the Most Restrictive Path Possible for Your Cookies   This is partly good citizenship. If you are sharing space on a common Web server, other developers shouldn't need to worry about your cookies encroaching on their applications' space. On the other hand, it is also good security, because you really don't want those other developers being able to retrieve a cookie you set called AccountNumber or DoomsdayPassword.

Try to Avoid Sharing Domain Names with Other Applications   If you really must use cookies and can afford it, spend the extra cash to get a unique domain name for every application.

Multilevel Cookies

Unlike the built-in Session object, cookies allow for the creation of hierarchical structures in which to store your information. For example, a system designed to let people sign up for Internet service might want to track the three telephone numbers on which a customer thinks that they are most likely to dial in. Using normal Session object syntax, these numbers would have to be stored like this:

```
<%
   Session("DialInNumber1") = Request("FirstDialupChoice")
   Session("DialInNumber2") = Request("SecondDialupChoice")
   Session("DialInNumber3") = Request("ThirdDialupChoice")
%>
```

There is nothing wrong with this approach, but it requires you to go through some string-concatenation contortions in order to simply iterate through the list of dial-up numbers.

```
<%
   For I = 1 to 3
      Response.Write Session("DialInNumber" & i)
   Next
%>
```

Besides the decidedly unsophisticated use of string concatenation that this approach requires, it also locks you in to a specific number of data members. The previous example that loaded the data into the Session object supports exactly three dial-in numbers, no more or less. Similarly, the code that retrieved these values expects exactly three to have been stored. If any more than this were stored, they would not be retrieved. If any fewer were stored, empty strings would be returned for any missing members.

The hierarchical scheme supported by cookies allows for the dynamic allocation of storage space under a given key. The code snippet below could be repeated for every field on an incoming form that provides optional space for multiple entries of the same type.

```
<%
   If Request("DialInNumber1") <> "" then
      Response.Cookies("DialInNumber")("One") = _
Request("DialInNumber1")
   End If
%>
```

These values can then be retrieved using an iterative construction that allows for any number of values.

```
<%
   For each x in Request.Cookies("DialInNumber")
      Response.Write Request.Cookies("DialInNumber")(x)
   Next
%>
```

Error Watch   *In the previous example, it is important to note that the variable x is referring to the name of the subkey for DialInNumber and not the subkey itself. If you attempted to write the value of x to the browser without prefacing it with the reference to the DialInNumber cookie, you would just get a list of the names of the subkeys. Since you will most often be interested in the values of subkeys rather than their names, this is a likely source of bugs.*

After you have created a cookie with subkeys, you must be careful never to attempt to set a value at the top level of this hierarchy. If you do this, all subkeys within the cookie will be erased and the cookie will become a single-level data store once again. As an example, the following script stores only Blue. The other values stored in this cookie are erased when this value is stored.

```
<%
        Response.Cookies("Colors")("One") = "Red"
        Response.Cookies("Colors")("Two") = "White"
        Response.Cookies("Colors")("Three") = "Black"
        ' The following line erases all the data stored above
        Response.Cookies("Colors") = "Blue"
%>
```

Setting Cookies to Exist

Application developers that are new to Active Server Pages often try to simply set cookies to exist, without providing specific values for them. They theorize that simply using a cookie must reserve space in the client's browser for them and therefore register their existence in some way. Here is an example of a developer trying to store the information on the client that its user has children:

```
<%
    Response.Cookies("HasChildren")
%>
```

The code that is typically seen trying to determine whether this cookie has been set looks like the following:

```
<%
    If Response.Cookies("HasChildren") Then
        Response.Write "They're a parent!"
    Else
        Response.Write "They're childless (but probably better _
rested :)"

    End If
%>
```

This test will always fail for a cookie that has been set using the method outlined earlier. A cookie that is simply referenced in code (as shown above) has no more existence on the browser than one that hasn't been referenced at all. A better way to achieve the results desired would be simply to set the cookie equal to the value True.

```
<%
    Response.Cookies("HasChildren") = True
%>
```

In this case, the application designed to test for the existence of this cookie can remain unchanged. It will now function properly.

Error Watch   *Cookies are not case-sensitive. If you are used to working with Visual Basic and other Window tools, this may not come as much of a surprise to you. If you come from a Unix or Java background, however, you will be surprised to learn that cookies are not even case-sensitive on these platforms. This can prove problematic if you are expecting case-sensitivity to play a part in distinguishing one cookie (say "employee_hours") from another ("EMPLOYEE_HOURS"). In this case, all statements intended to set or retrieve either cookie will be operating on exactly the same cookie.*

Frames

The use of HTML frames can greatly improve the look and feel of your Active Server Page applications. If you are using ASP's built-in Session-state management, however, it can also lead to problems that can be particularly hard to deal with.

Session.SessionID

To begin understanding the problems that can arise when trying to combine frames with Active Server Page sessions, you must first envision a typical situation in which frames might be used. Imagine a Web site for a large travel agency that allows customers to assemble a complete vacation for themselves over the Internet. A visitor to the site picks out transportation, accommodations, and attractions in separate frames of the application. The frames are arranged like this:

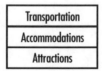

When this visitor is finished shopping, he or she then proceeds to the checkout area. This is also a multiframed page, but the purposes to which the frames are put is different.

| Address Info. |
| Shipping Info. |
| Payment Info. |

At the end of their efforts, the developers working on this checkout page would make a horrifying discovery. *When Active Server Page sessions begin in framesets, every frame in the set is typically given a different session!* The impact of this on the checkout page would be that the top frame could only possibly work with session data about transportation. The middle frame could only work with session data about accommodations. And, the bottom frame could only work with session data about attractions. This would make it very difficult to put together a comprehensive checkout page.

You should suspect that you are a victim of this phenomenon whenever

- You are using frames.

- You are using Session, Application, or Cookies objects.

- You are experiencing a loss of state between pages.

If you meet all the preceding criteria, you should try a simple test to figure out whether this is really the cause of your problems. First, figure out every page loaded by the first frameset in your application. For example, in this frameset

```
<frameset rows="50%,50%">
    <frame src="top.asp">
    <frame src="bottom.asp">
</frameset>
```

the pages being loaded are TOP.ASP and BOTTOM.ASP.

Add the following line of code to each of these files at some point where you can be sure that it will get executed during the first run of your script:

```
<%
    Response.Write Session.SessionID
%>
```

Now, visit your application with a fresh instance of your Web browser. It is important that the instance be fresh to avoid the retention of data from previous sessions. If the output from the preceding line of code is a different number in each frame, you are experiencing a different session in each of these frames! It may look something like Figure 4-3.

Fixing Your Frames

The problem with HTML framesets producing multiple sessions occurs because of the way that browsers and servers cooperate in the rendering of individual frames. In Chapter 2, you learned that one of the first things a Web server examines when serving a page is the extension of that page's filename. If the extension is .HTM or .HTML, the server interprets this to mean that the file

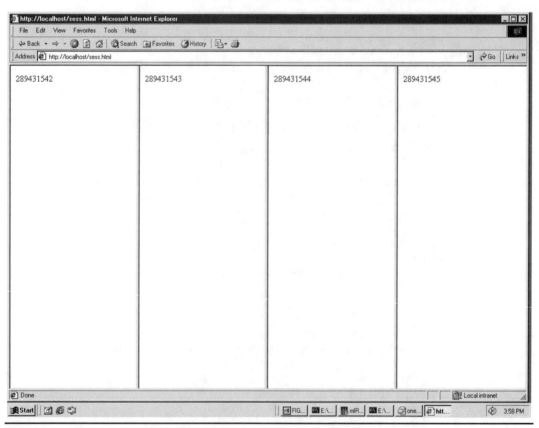

Figure 4.3   Different sessions in every frame

24x7 Embedding the SessionID in a Tag

A little-known fact about the HTML specification is that it requires browsers to skip any tags that they don't understand. This was originally intended to allow older browsers to "fail gracefully" when presented with features added to HTML after their initial creation. For example, a very early browser that complies only with version 1.0 of the HTML specification will have no understanding of frames and framesets. It will respond to the use of these tags simply by skipping over them.

You can use this feature of browser design to embed information such as the SessionID permanently in your pages. This data will not be displayed by browsers, so it won't get in the way of pages for which you no longer need the information. On the other hand, it will be plainly visible from these browsers by displaying the source if you should ever need it for debugging purposes.

To put this technique into practice, simply place the bit of code that echoes the data in which you are interested, in this case the SessionID, inside of an HTML tag.

```
< <%= Session.SessionID %> >
```

The preceding code will produce no visible output on a browser interface. If you view the source for a page using it, however, you will be able to see the data quite clearly:

```
<847081893>
```

contains plain HTML, which should be passed to the client browser without further interpretation or action on the server's part.

If this page contains a frameset, the browser iterates sequentially through each of the frames within this set. For each frame, a separate request is made to the browser. Each request asks for the server to send whatever page is referenced by the frame in question. The server responds to these requests in the order received. If any of these pages are Active Server Pages, the server checks for an existing Session object before creating a new one.

The problem is that if the top-level page containing the frameset is merely HTML, no Session object was created when this page was first loaded. This means that Internet Information Server will never detect an existing Session object when it is first generating pages to fill all the top-level pages' child frames. This results in the creation of a different Session object for every frame.

The way to solve this is usually simply to change the extension on the main frameset page to .ASP. This way, IIS generates a new Session object the first time that a browser visits the main frameset page. When the browser begins making requests for the contents of all this pages' child frames, IIS is able to detect that a Session object already exists and uses it rather than creating an entirely new one.

Design Tip   *If you consider all of the steps just described, you can probably see how managing sessions can be a very performance-intensive task for Internet Information Server. If you are using frames, IIS must, at the very least, check for the existence of previously created Session objects before rendering every single frame of your application. At worst, if you have used plain HTML for the top-level frameset in your application, it will also have to create and manage an entirely new and separate Session object for every frame in your application. This is true whether you plan on using Session objects or not. For this reason, performance should be seriously considered whenever you attempt to combine the use of frames and session-based state management.*

At the Application Level

Applications that make use of the Session object built into Active Server Pages are fairly common. This is probably because almost every application requires more than a single page in order to finish its job, whether that job is registering employees for a corporate 401(k) or selling CDs on the Internet. The need to maintain information at the application level, however, is significantly less common.

Information stored at the application level is typically information that needs to be shared between multiple users. For example, a site that offered arcade games over the Internet in the form of Java applets might use Active Server Pages to maintain a list of high scores. Because this is information that would be of equal interest to all users currently logged into your site, it would make sense to store it in the intrinsic Application object.

In order to use the Application object appropriately, you should be familiar with a few aspects of its design and limitations. To begin with, there are certain boundaries that determine the limits of where Application object data may be set and retrieved. Within these boundaries, the existence of multiple, simultaneous user sessions will inevitably lead to problems with data consistency. Finally, the all-encompassing scope of the Application object requires certain contortions in order to reset its data when needed.

Boundaries

The boundaries that limit the extent of Application-level state maintenance are essentially the same as those limiting Session-level state. The first of these is the directory structure of the application itself as defined by Internet Information Server. The other is the possible use of multiple servers within the architecture of your solutions.

Directory Structures

In the section on included files in Chapter 3, the difference between real and virtual paths was discussed at length. To review, the starting point of an Active Server Pages application is a virtual path under which all of the scripts and other files used by your application must fall. This is related to, but not the same as, a real path on your server's hard disk at which the virtual path is based.

Suppose that you are running an online stock-trading Web site based at the virtual path /stocktrade and the real path e:\inetpub\wwwroot\stocktrade. The amount of cash that each of your users has available for trading would be a matter for their eyes only and would, therefore, be stored in Session-level state (meaning the Session object). Something like an up-to-the-minute Dow Jones or NASDAQ index number, however, would be of general interest to your users. This would be stored in the Application object.

If you chose to store this information in the Application object, it would be accessible to every script stored under the /stocktrade virtual path and the e:\inetpub\wwwroot\stocktrade real path. But what if you needed to share it beyond these boundaries? For example, perhaps you made an agreement with another Web site that would help put current stock market indexes into historical perspective via the use of online graphs and charts. You might like to let your users pass the most recent NASDAQ index from your site to your partnered site.

One way that you might consider working around the path boundaries for the Application object is by putting the data that you want to pass into the query string of a URL. In the case described earlier, you would be making the NASDAQ index a bit of a hyperlink pointing to your partner's Web site. Assuming that the URL for your own Web site was http://www.eviloscar.com/stocktrade, and your partner's Web site was at http://www.eviloscar.com/stockhistory, then you might use code like this:

```
<%
   Response.Write "Click "
   Response.Write "<A HREF = ""/stockhistory?INDEX="
   Response.Write Application("INDEX")
   Response.Write ">here</a> for historical information!"
%>
```

Assuming that your partner's Web site also used Active Server Pages, it could then access this index information as follows:

```
<%
   strIndex = Request.QueryString("INDEX")
%>
```

Other Servers

The same boundaries apply to Application-level data where multiple servers are concerned. This may be a concern for you if you ever need to share information with applications housed on different computers. This might also be a concern for you if your own Web server uses clustering technology to operate a single application on multiple computers simultaneously. The details of clustering technology were discussed in the previous section on Session-level state problems.

You have already seen two ways to work around boundary issues in your state management. One suggestion was to store your data in files on your server. Another was to encode your data as part of your query strings. One final approach that you might try is to encode your data in hidden fields on standard HTML forms.

Imagine that you are still trying to make your stock-trading application described in the previous section work with your partner's Web site for delivering historical stock market information. Your partner may have objected to placing Application-level data in the query string because it is too visible to an end-user there. In order to hide Application-level data in a standard HTML form, you can use code like this:

```
<FORM METHOD="POST" ACTION="http://www.stock-historeeeez.com">
<INPUT TYPE="hidden" VALUE="<%= Application("INDEX") %>" NAME="SECRET">
<INPUT TYPE="submit" VALUE="Click here for historical information!">
</FORM>
```

In this case, your partner's Web site could easily be on a completely different machine. The current stock market index maintained in your application's intrinsic Application object is encoded as part of the hidden field named SECRET. Assuming that your partner's Web site also used Active Server Pages, it could then retrieve this data in this manner:

```
<%
   strIndex = Request("SECRET")
%>
```

Multiuser Problems

Whenever you attempt to have data in your applications that may be accessed by more than one user at a time, you court disaster. The chief form that this disaster may take is that of data inconsistency. The answer to preventing data inconsistency in an Active Server Page application is the use of the Application object's Lock method.

Inconsistencies

An inconsistency in the Application-level data for your application may arise anytime that more than one instance of your application tries to access the same data simultaneously. In some cases, one or more instances of your application may simply wind up with incorrect information as the result of such a conflict. Under more dire circumstances, the Application-level data itself may become corrupted in a way that renders it permanently unfit for use by any of your application's current instances.

If you consider the case that was mentioned earlier of a gaming site's high score server, the nature of a typical inconsistency problem can be easily explained. In order for a given user's current score to be certified as a part of the "top 10" for your entire site, it must be compared against every one of the ten scores currently occupying this space. The list of these scores might be stored as a Variant in the Application object.

```
<%
    topscores = Application("TopScores")
    for I = 0 to 9
        if CurrentPlayersScore > topscores(i) then
            Call InsertScoreAbove(CurrentPlayersScore, topscores(i))
            CurrentPlayersScore = 0
        end if
    next
    Application("TopScores") = topscores
%>
```

This code begins by retrieving the list of top scores from the Application object. It then iterates through all ten of the entries, which are assumed to be stored in order from lowest to highest. If it finds a score that is lower than the score of the current player (previously stored in the CurrentPlayersScore variable), it calls a routine to insert the current player's score into the list at this point. It then sets the current player's score to 0 to ensure that it is only recorded in the "top 10" list once. The routine concludes by placing the variant list of top scores back into the Application object.

The only problem with the approach taken in the preceding string is that more than one person using your application may wind up executing the code above at approximately the same time. Consider the following chain of completely possible events:

1. Player #1 achieves a score of 50,182.

2. Player #2 achieves a score of 50,200.

3. Player #1 retrieves the current "top 10" list from the Application object.

4. Player #2 retrieves the current "top 10" list from the Application object.

5. Player #1 discovers that her score is higher than the fourth entry.

6. Player #2 discovers that his score is higher than the fourth entry.

7. Player #1 inserts her score between the fourth and fifth entries.

8. Player #2 inserts his score between the fourth and fifth entries.

9. Player #1 saves the revised "top 10" list to the Application object.

10. Player #2 saves the revised "top 10" list to the Application object.

As you can see, the upshot of all this is that Player #1's modifications to the Application object in step 9 wind up being completely overwritten by Player #2's modifications in step 10. This is a data consistency issue.

Application.Lock

The preceding error would not have occurred if the two processes could have somehow signaled each other that they were both trying to work with the same data at the same time. Fortunately, Active Server Pages provides such a mechanism in the form of the Application object's Lock and Unlock methods. In order to use these methods, the code from the previous section would need only slight modifications:

```
<%
    Application.Lock
    topscores = Application("TopScores")
    for I = 0 to 9
       if CurrentPlayersScore > topscores(i) then
          Call InsertScoreAbove(CurrentPlayersScore, topscores(i))
          CurrentPlayersScore = 0
       end if
    next
    Application("TopScores") = topscores
    Application.Unlock
%>
```

By calling the Lock method immediately before you begin working with the Application object, you prevent any other processes from working with it at the same time. By calling the Unlock method when you are finished with your task, you make the object available again to other processes. If the same series of events were attempted with the modifications shown earlier, the outcome would be quite different.

1. Player #1 achieves a score of 50,182.
2. Player #2 achieves a score of 50,200.
3. Player #1 retrieves the current "top 10" list from the Application object.
4. Player #2 attempts to access the Application object but finds it locked.
5. Player #1 discovers that her score is higher than the fourth entry.
6. Player #1 inserts her score between the fourth and fifth entries.
7. Player #1 saves the revised "top 10" list to the Application object.
8. Player #2 is notified that the Application object is now available.
9. Player #2 retrieves the current "top 10" list from the Application object.
10. Player #2 discovers that his score is higher than the fourth entry.
11. Player #2 inserts his score between the fourth and fifth entries.
12. Player #2 saves the revised "top 10" list to the Application object.

In this case, Player #1 and Player #2 will both have their scores added to the "top 10" list in the appropriate order.

Restarting an Application

Clearing out the data stored in a given Session object is quite easy: Simply stop and restart the browser associated with the session in question. Clearing out an Application object is significantly more complicated because it holds the data for an entire ASP application.

Restarting Your Computer

One (particularly brutal) approach that you might take to resolving this dilemma might be to restart the computer hosting your Web server. One obvious disadvantage to this approach is the prolonged service outage that it is likely to cause for your users. Completely restarting a Windows computer can take anywhere from one to several minutes. During this time, users will not be able to access your application or any other applications hosted on the same computer.

24x7 If You're Using Locks, You'd Better Be Quick!

You shouldn't use Lock and Unlock just when you are accessing the variables stored in the Application object.

If multiple processes try reading the same information simultaneously, this probably won't cause an error. It is only when multiple processes try reading and writing the same data at the same time that problems can occur.

Under such circumstances, you should call Lock as late as possible in your code—immediately before performing the reading and/or writing that may lead to conflicts. You should also try to call Unlock as soon as possible thereafter. This is to prevent the application slow-downs that can occur for end-users if they are forced to wait for several previous locks on the Application object to be removed before they can continue executing their code.

Restarting IIS

A less severe tactic might be simply to restart the Web server itself. To restart Internet Information Server, follow this procedure:

1. Choose Settings from the Windows Start menu.

2. Select the Control Panel.

3. Double-click the Administrative Tools icon.

4. Double-click the Services icon. You should see a screen like that in Figure 4-4.

5. Right-click on the IIS Admin Service entry.

6. Choose Restart from the pop-up context menu.

7. If you see this dialog, click Yes.

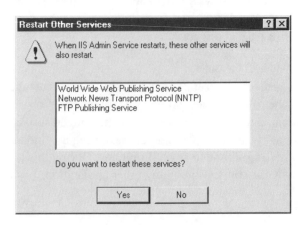

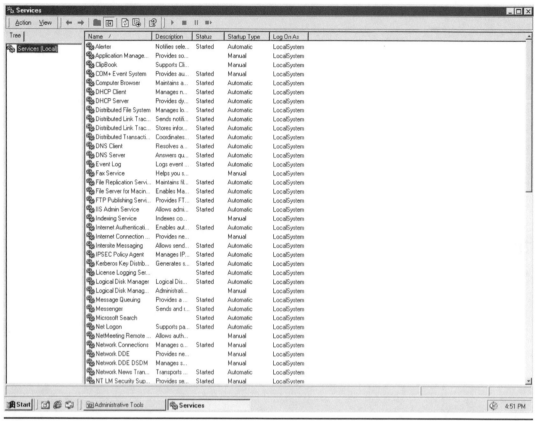

Figure 4.4   The Services screen

Changing the GLOBAL.ASA

The best way to reset the state of your Application object is by making some kind
of trivial modification to your GLOBAL.ASA file. The reason for this is that IIS
checks the modification time and date on an application's GLOBAL.ASA file
every time that it is asked to serve a page from that application. If the
modification date and time is more recent than the date and time that it last
served a request for this application, the entire application is restarted.

One good example of a trivial modification might be the addition of a
comment to the GLOBAL.ASA file. Another way to modify the GLOBAL.ASA
file without changing anything is to insert white space into an otherwise
legitimate statement. You might even consider performing a simple instruction,
such as adding two plus two, just to modify your script in a way that you can be
sure will not lead to changes in your application's behavior.

CHAPTER 5

Taking Requests

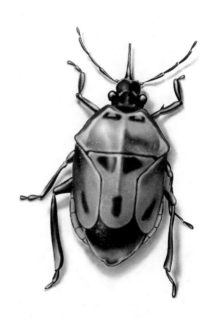

M ost Active Server Page runs begin with a request from a client browser. The server then loads the page into memory (if it has not already done so) and begins interpreting whatever code may be inside of it. After the script has run to completion, the server sends its output across the network back to the client browser. The complete process looks like Figure 5-1.

This chapter's discussion will focus on the first step in the execution of an Active Server Page: the interpretation of the client browser's request. There are several caveats of which you should be aware when attempting to deal with such requests. On the other hand, we will also show you a few not widely known techniques that you can use to your advantage.

Headers

During the initial stages of a page request, a great deal of information is passed to the Web server by your browser. This probably happens without your knowledge because the entire transfer is accomplished using HTTP headers.

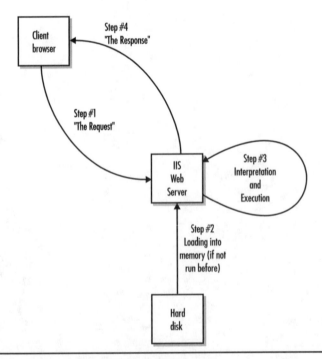

Figure 5.1   Client/server communication sequence

HTTP headers are bits of information about browsers and the systems on which they run that are made generally available whenever a connection to a Web server is made.

You might be concerned that some of this information is personal and not something that you want to share. For the most part, you can relax. The World Wide Web Consortium (W3C) maintains a specific list of which pieces of information clients may send as HTTP headers:

FROM	The e-mail address of the client's current user.
ACCEPT	Every MIME type that the client is willing to accept in your response.
ACCEPT-CHARSET	A list of all of the character sets in which the client can handle a response.
ACCEPT-ENCODING	Every kind of encoding (such as Zip compression) in which your client would be willing to accept your response.
ACCEPT-LANGUAGE	The locale in which the client is being used. See the "Internationalization" section in this chapter on for more information.
USER-AGENT	The name of the client's browser. Netscape is still referred to as Mozilla.
REFERER	The URL of the site (if any) that contained the link followed by this client in order to arrive at your application.
AUTHORIZATION	Username and password for use with basic authentication.
CHARGE-TO	Data to support charge-back systems.
IF-MODIFIED-SINCE	Conditional support for content expiration.
PRAGMA	This header means different things depending on its content. One setting can request a client-side redirect. Another can cause a constant refreshing of a given page.
IF-NOT-MODIFIED-SINCE	Supports the rejection of pages that a client thinks may be out-of-date.
HOST	The IP address of the client computer. For more information on this, see the section "Security" in this chapter.
MAX-FORWARDS	Sets a limit on the total number of redirections that a given client is willing to accept.
PROXY-AUTHORIZATION	Any special information that a proxy server may need to allow a request to complete.

Internationalization

One of the hottest topics in software design right now is that of internationalization. The Internet has opened up global markets to even the smallest of corporations. A modest e-commerce site running on a desktop in Toledo, Ohio, could easily process orders from as far away as Asia and Africa on a daily basis. For this reason, it is important to make sure that your pages convey information in a way that will be readily understood from wherever your applications are accessed.

It is, of course, primarily important to make sure that the output of your scripts is in the language(s) of your target audience. It is clearly beyond the scope of this book, much less this section, to teach you how to speak every potential target language fluently. Assuming that you have (or are in a position to hire) the required expertise in this area, however, there are still some issues in the design of your code that must be addressed.

Imagine that you are building a site to sell raincoats over the Internet. It rains everywhere, and Germany is no exception—so you might decide that the German raincoat market is as worthy of pursuit as any other. You might write a special German version of your order-confirmation script to look something like this:

```
<!-- #INCLUDE FILE = "PRICES.INC"-->
<!-- #INCLUDE FILE = "LEAD_TIMES.INC"-->
<%
    Option Explicit
    Dim nmbr
    Dim shipdate
    ' If they haven't specified a number of coats to purchase yet,
    ' then send them back to the purchasing page specially
    ' created for their language
    If Request("NumberOfRaincoatsToPurchase") = ""Then
        Response.Redirect "GermanRaincoatPurchasingPage.asp"
    Else
        nmbr = Request("NumberOfRaincoatsToPurchase")
        ' This constant is taken from the PRICES.INC file
        total_cost = nmbr * GERMAN_PRICE;
        ' This constant is taken from the LEAD_TIMES.INC file
        shipdate = dateadd("d", now, GERMAN_LEAD_TIME);
        ' Tell the customer their total cost
        Response.Write "Total Cost = " & total_cost
        ' Tell the customer their shipping date
        Response.Write "Shipping Date = " & shipdate
    End If
%>
```

One good thing about this code sample is that it uses include files to encapsulate the prices and lead times for various nationalities. It would be much harder to maintain this script for several languages if each one hard-coded these values.

Unfortunately, this use of include files hasn't gone far enough. The static portions of the response strings could probably also stand to be stored in include files.

```
Response.Write GERMAN_COST_STRING & total_cost
Response.Write GERMAN_SHIPPING_STRING & total_cost
```

This recoding would definitely be a step in the right direction, but there is still major room for improvement. Examine the same output from this script in Figure 5-2.

Now, what's wrong with this picture? To begin with, ask yourself, "What date is being referred to?" If you are in North America, you have probably decided March 11, 2000. But, if you are in Europe, November 3, 2000 is the date communicated to you by this display. This is problematic, because it means that a

Figure 5.2   Poorly internationalized output

server running in one part of the world may use a date format that communicates valid (but completely wrong) dates when accessed from other parts of the world.

There is something else wrong with Figure 5-2. Americans format currency using commas where Germans would typically use periods and using periods where Germans would typically use commas. The currency in this figure is clearly formatted in the American style. This could cause considerable confusion whenever your application was used outside of America.

The solution to both of the issues raised in the preceding paragraphs is to make use of the special HTTP_ACCEPT_LANGUAGE server variable to determine at runtime in which countries your clients are located. With this knowledge, you can customize your output on the fly to match the specific expectations of your users. To see how this works, place the following simple script on your Web server and access it from a browser.

```
<%
    Option Explicit
    Dim code

    code = Request.ServerVariables("HTTP_ACCEPT_LANGUAGE")
    Response.Write "The LCID for your client is..."
    Response.Write code
%>
```

You should see something like this:

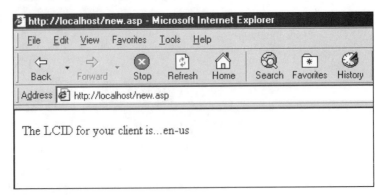

Now, follow this procedure:

1. Choose Settings from the Windows Start menu.

2. Open the Control Panel.

3. Double-click Regional Settings.

4. Choose any entry from the drop-down list other than your current setting.

5. Restart your computer.

If you now access the same page again, you should find that the LCID value has changed. LCID stands for *locale identifier*, which is an appropriate name because it is intended to help applications identify the language expectations for the locale where they are being used. Using this information, you should be able to customize the output of your scripts at runtime, rather than having to create different versions for each target audience.

Here are some of the most common LCIDs:

LCID	Location	Numeric Value
en-us	United States English	1033
de	Standard German	1031
fr	Standard French	1036
el	Greek	1032
it	Standard Italian	1040
ru	Russian	1049
es-mx	Mexican Spanish	2058
es	Traditional Spanish	1034

Some languages are associated with more than one LCID, depending upon the specific dialect to which the LCID is referring. Notice, for example, that Mexican Spanish is given an LCID of "es-mx," while traditional Spanish is simply referred to as "es."

In order to put this information to use in your applications, you must set the LCID property for your Session object to reflect the locality that you are attempting to serve. This is where the numeric values shown in the table come in handy. The Session object expects to see these values rather than the short strings returned in the server variables. You will need to write some code to do the conversions for whichever localities you are interested in. An example of this is shown here

```
<%
    Option Explicit
    Dim code
    Dim nmbr

    code = Request.ServerVariables("HTTP_ACCEPT_LANGUAGE")
    if code = "en-us"then
       nmbr = 1033
    elseif code = "de"then
       nmbr = 1031
    elseif code = "fr"then
       nmbr = 1036
    end if
%>
```

For a complete list of the numbers associated with all LCIDs supported by Windows, refer to Microsoft's page at http://www.microsoft.com/Java/sdk/40/pg/pg_i18n_lcidref.htm. Here, you should find a hexadecimal number for any LCID with which you might want to work. To convert hexadecimal to decimal, you can use code such as this:

```
<%
  if code = "en-us"then
     nmbr = val("&H0409")
  end if
%>
```

Once you have this number, just assign it to Session.LCID, and your formatting should start matching your target locality.

```
' Set to Germany's LCID
Session.LCID = 1031
' Now display properly
Response.Write "Total Cost = " & total_cost
Response.Write "Shipping Date = " & shipdate
```

The output from this script is greatly improved. As you can see in the following, the numbers are grouped using periods, with a comma for decimal delimitation. Also, the day, month, and year of the date are in German ordering and separated with periods instead of slashes.

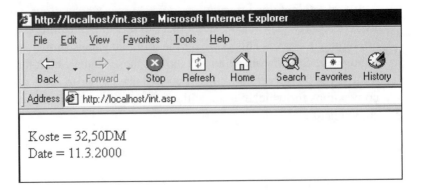

Security

The security of your Web server is primarily a concern for the server's administrator. In Chapter 1, you learned about many of the settings IIS provides for restricting unauthorized access. Some of these settings allow the administrator to stipulate support for different kinds of authentication. Other settings allow administrators to grant or refuse access to other machines based solely upon the IPs of those machines.

You will recall that an IP is a number that is guaranteed to uniquely identify a certain computer on a TCP/IP network. The world's largest TCP/IP network, the Internet, has a central authority that sells blocks of IPs for use by smaller networks, such as Internet service providers (ISPs) and large companies. The exact manner in which these organizations then choose to grant these IPs to their customers and employees differs from one organization to the next.

One methodology for distributing IPs from a block to individual machines is called *static IP*. As you might guess, under this scheme, the same computer will get the same IP every time that it connects to the network. This is popular with DSL companies and other providers of dedicated connections to the Internet because if a computer is constantly connected to a network, then it is easiest just to have it constantly retain the same IP (see Figure 5-3).

Another approach to IP distribution is that of *dynamic IPs*. This is exactly the opposite of the previous approach, insofar as a computer may be given a different IP every single time that it connects to the network (see Figure 5-4). This is by far the most popular choice for ISPs that provide so-called "dial-up" connections to the Internet over standard telephone lines. It is good wherever many computers must share a relatively small block of IPs.

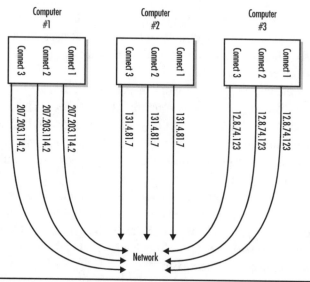

Figure 5.3   Computers with static IP connections

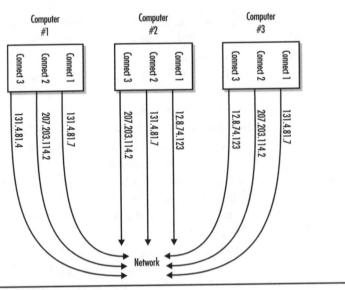

Figure 5.4   Computers with dynamic IP connections

If you are going to use IP-based security, it is important that you understand the previous two approaches for IP assignment. Suppose you notice undesirable activity from a certain IP at a certain point in time—posting harassing messages to your free e-mail application, for example. You might choose to restrict access from this IP in response. This approach will work only if the user that you are trying to ban is connecting to a network that uses static IP assignment. If this person has a dedicated connection, this scenario is likely. If this person has a dial-up connection, it is very unlikely.

If the target user's network uses dynamic IP assignment, they will probably get a different IP the next time that they connect. This means that they will probably be able to connect to your application with little or no problem. Meanwhile, whoever is assigned the IP that you have banned will not be able to access your application in the future. This will undoubtedly cause them much confusion.

Now that you understand the theory behind IPs, it is time to look at the actual practice of granting and restricting access based on them. You have already seen (in Chapter 1) how to use the IIS Management Console to administratively grant and restrict access on this basis. You can also accomplish this goal programmatically, however.

The following code retrieves the IP of whatever client computer is currently attempting to connect. If this IP is on a certain list of "bad boys," the client is redirected to another page that basically says, "Go away, we hate you!"

```
<%
   Option Explicit
   Dim ip
   Dim fso, File, TextStream

   Const FOR_READING = 1

   ip = Request.ServerVariables("REMOTE_ADDR")

   Set fso = Server.CreateObject("Scripting.FileSystemObject")
   Set File = FSO.GetFile("c:\badboys.txt")
   Set TextStream = File.OpenAsTextStream(OpenFileForReading)

   Do While Not TextStream.AtEndOfStream
      if ip = TextStream.ReadLine then
         response.redirect "badboys.html"
      end if
   Loop

   TextStream.Close
%>
```

Notice in the preceding sample that REMOTE_ADDR is the server variable containing the IP of the client computer making the request. This kind of approach is good to remember in cases where you are working on machines for which you have no access to administrative controls. One example of such a situation might be when working on space that is leased from a Web-hosting company.

Performance

Besides the headers sent to your applications by Web browser clients, your Web server is also capable of sending numerous headers back to the clients themselves. Cookies, which you read about in Chapter 4, are an excellent example of information that is conveyed to browsers via headers sent directly from Internet Information Server. Other headers convey additional information about the content of the page being sent, such as MIME type and encoding method.

One piece of information that can prove particularly useful in debugging performance issues in your Active Server Page applications is the time and date at which a script was last modified. By manipulating this value, you can prevent

24x7 Using IPs to Avoid Denial-of-Service Attacks

The approach suggested in this section can be extended to preventing so-called "denial of service" attacks on your ASP applications. Hackers use denial-of-service attacks to crash Web sites by overloading the applications running them with more requests than they can possibly hope to accommodate.

```
<%
   Option Explicit
   Dim old_ip, new_ip
   Dim count

   old_ip = Application("IP")
   new_ip = Request.ServerVariables("REMOTE_ADDR")

   if old_ip = new_ip then
      count = Application("NumberOfVisitsBySameIP")
   else
      count = 0
   end if

   count = count + 1

   if count > 25 then
      response.redirect "http://www.fbi.gov"
   end if

   Application("IP") = new_ip
   Application("NumberOfVisitsBySameIP") = count
%>
```

This code begins by retrieving data from the Application object about the previous visit. If the current visit appears to be from the same IP, the total count of visits from this IP is incremented by 1. If the total count is now in excess of 25, this visit is redirected to the FBI's Web site. The script concludes by saving the revised count back to the Application object for reference by future runs of this script. If another script visits this page, the count will be returned to 1, and the banned IP will once again be capable of accessing your application.

Many denial-of-service attacks generate enormous quantities of requests such that they can crash Internet Information Server itself. This approach is not intended to counter such overwhelming fire power. It will work, however, in cases where the weakest link in the chain is the performance of your own application, rather than IIS. It also assumes that all the requests will be coming from the same IP, an assumption that might not be valid, depending on the sophistication of the hacker in question.

many browsers that already have local copies of your pages from making additional visits. If you are responsible for the maintenance of a particularly busy Web application, the reduction in traffic afforded by this technique can dramatically improve your scripts' performance.

```
<SCRIPT LANGUAGE="JavaScript"RUNAT=SERVER>
    function toUTCStr(vbDate)
    {
        var d;

        d = new Date(vbDate);
        return d.toUTCString();
    }
</SCRIPT>
<%
    Option Explicit

    Dim fso, fl
    Dim vpath, rpath
    Dim fdlm, UTCfdlm

    vpath = Request.ServerVariables("PATH_INFO")
    rpath = Server.MapPath(vpath)

    Set fso = Server.CreateObject("Scripting.FileSystemObject")
    Set fl = fso.GetFile(rpath)

    fdlm = fl.FileDateLastModified
    UTCfdlm = toUTCStr(fdlm)
    Response.AddHeader("LAST-MODIFIED", fdlm)
%>
```

The first bit of the preceding code taps into Internet Information Server's capability to run JavaScript, in addition to VBScript, as server-side code. This capability is used to define a function that accepts a date in typical VBScript format and returns it as a string representing that date in Universal Coordinated Time. It is much easier to perform this operation in JavaScript than in VBScript, thus justifying the added complexity of a mixed-language application script.

Error Watch *Whenever you work with headers that take dates as parameters (LAST-MODIFIED, for example), you should make sure to always convert your dates to Universal Coordinated Time. If you pass dates that are not in this format, client browsers probably will not generate any obvious errors. Instead, they will simply act as if no headers have been passed at all.*

The VBScript portion of the listing encompasses the main flow of the script's logic. It retrieves the virtual path to the file in which it is currently located. Then, it uses functionality available in the Server object to map this virtual path to the real path on your server's hard disk. It is able to retrieve the date on which this file was last modified via the FileSystemObject discussed in Chapter 3. Finally, it calls our JavaScript routine to encode this information as a UTC string and then packages it in the appropriate header.

You can place the preceding code in a file and use server-side include directives to make it a part of any script that you would like to protect from needless browser accesses. This can have a positive impact on the performance of applications with static output.

HTML Forms

The earliest Web sites consisted entirely of flat, unchanging HTML files. This structure provided for a flow of information in only one direction—from the server to the client:

Soon, the Common Gateway Interface (CGI) was introduced, and Web servers became capable of executing files in response to specific requests from browsers. In order to pass information to these executables, schemes were devised to allow for the encoding of data as part of extended URLs. This is the GET method used with the QueryString property of the modern Request object (see Figure 5-5).

Eventually, the need for more sophisticated user interfaces and complicated types of data drove the development of the HTML form. Information entered into an HTML form may be sent to a Web application using either the GET method described previously or the POST method. The POST method allows for all kinds of data to be transmitted to a Web application using a back-end transmission channel that is (unlike an extended URL) invisible to the browser's user (see Figure 5-6).

Uploading to Active Server Pages

Eventually, you may want to create an Active Server Page application that allows users to send complete files to your Web server from their client browsers. Perhaps

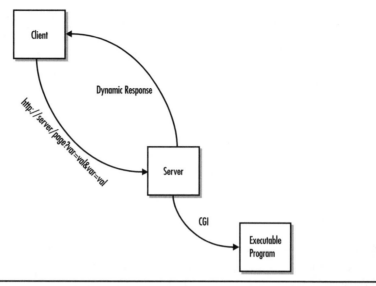

Figure 5.5 Dynamic response in a Web site

you would like to establish a space on the Internet where friends and relatives can exchange pictures of themselves across vast distances. Or maybe you would just like to allow for the exchange of information in formats (such as Microsoft Excel or Word) that would typically not be supported by standard HTML.

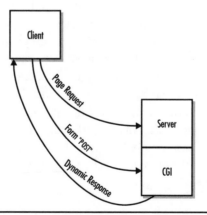

Figure 5.6 Using forms on a Web site

Unfortunately, Active Server Pages provides no direct support for file uploads. A naïve approach such as the one here is guaranteed to produce a cryptic error message in the window of whichever browser attempts it.

```
<%
    If Request("file") = ""Then
%>
    <FORM METHOD="POST"ENCTYPE="multipart/form-data">
    <INPUT NAME="file"type="file">
    </FORM>
<%
    Else
        Response.Write "Thanks for the upload!<br>"
        Response.Write "Total bytes received was " & Request.TotalBytes
    End If
%>
```

 Always remember to specify an ENCTYPE of multipart/form-data when you are trying to upload files to your server.

The reason for this is that uploading files via HTTP requires an entirely new set of functionality that is not an out-of-the-box part of Internet Information Server. As soon as the browser begins uploading a file in the preceding example, IIS realizes that it has no idea what is going on and returns an error message. The code thanking the user for the upload and giving them their byte count never even gets a chance to execute.

Under IIS 4, uploading capabilities could be added to the server via a component called the Microsoft Posting Acceptor. The Posting Acceptor runs as an ISAPI filter, which is basically an application that runs in the same process space as IIS and listens to all requests and responses for items that may be of interest. When it finds such items, it is empowered to act upon them in ways that may alter the content of the request or response in question. (If you think about it for a moment, you may realize that this sounds a lot like Active Server Pages. This is because an Active Server Page is, indeed, an ISAPI filter.)

In the case of the Microsoft Posting Acceptor, the ISAPI filter listens for incoming requests that include file upload attempts. When it finds such items, it is capable of completely handling the intricacies of the file transfer. ASP code can then treat the contents of the upload as binary content passed to the intrinsic Request object.

As of the time of this writing, the exact status of Microsoft Posting Acceptor and IIS 5 (the default Web server for Windows 2000) is unclear. The DLL that used to contain the ISAPI filter code is definitely not a part of the base installation. Furthermore, the software will not function when installed from Visual Studio 6 or Option Pack 4.

The best way to overcome this particular roadblock on your path to creating exciting Active Server Pages applications is to obtain a copy of some free software from a French company called Advantys. Visit their Web site at http://www.advantys.com and look for a product called aspSmartUpload. After following the links and filling out a short questionnaire, you will be able to download the complete package in the form of a compressed archive. Extract the files from this archive into a temporary directory structure and follow the installation instructions in the setup.htm file that is located in the Help subdirectory.

After you have installed this software, uploading files to your Web server is a breeze. Compare the following listing to the previous listing in this section. Notice that we have simply added one line to instantiate the aspSmartUpload component, another line to actually receive the file upload, and a final line to save the file to the c:\uploads physical directory.

```
<%
    Option Explicit

    Dim upComp

    If Request("file") = ""Then
%>
    <FORM METHOD="POST"ENCTYPE="multipart/form-data">
    <INPUT NAME="file"type="file">
    </FORM>
<%
    Else
        Set upComp = _
Server.CreateObject("aspSmartUpload.SmartUpload")
        upComp.Upload
        upComp.Save("c:\uploads")
        Response.Write "Thanks for the upload!<br>"
        Response.Write "Total bytes received was " & _
        Request.TotalBytes
    End If
%>
```

Error Watch   *It is important that the account executing your Active Server Pages application has write permissions on the directory in which you plan on storing your uploaded files. For example, if a nonauthenticated user ran the script above, you would need to make sure that the IUSR_<machine> account had write permissions on the c:\uploads directory.*

Dynamic Sizing

The typical HTML form is really designed for accepting specific answers to specific questions. It provides checkboxes, lists, radio buttons, and even text areas, but the specific quantity of information held by each of these items must be determined at the time of the form's creation, not thereafter.

Sometimes, you might not know in advance exactly how many blanks you will need to provide in order to collect the information in which you are interested. Take, for example, the case of a business with a rapidly expanding sales area. This organization may request a Web application that would allow managers to quickly assign sales people to new sales areas. A first stab at creating a form for such an application might look like this:

```
<FORM METHOD="POST">
    Seattle Salesperson: <INPUT NAME="Seattle">
    Chicago Salesperson: <INPUT NAME="Chicago">
    London Salesperson: <INPUT NAME="London">
    Edinburgh Salesperson: <INPUT NAME="Edinburgh">
</FORM>
```

This is all well and good until the next time the company opens a new sales office. At this point, the developer in charge of maintaining this form will need to go in and add another row to reflect the new branch. If a branch is ever closed or renamed, the form will also need to be modified. If any of the code in the script to which this form feeds its input is expecting a specific number or ordering of these fields, the potential exists for all hell to break loose.

Fortunately, a better method is available. Using the database access capabilities provided by Active Data Object (ADO), a developer could store the fields in which he or she is interested in a table. Forms can then be built on the fly by code that looks at this table. Rows can be freely added and removed from this table without the need to modify any code.

```
<FORM METHOD="POST">
<table border>
```

```
<tr><th>Sales Territory</th><th>Sales Person</th></tr>

<%
   Option Explicit

   Dim cn, rst
   ' Instantiate the ADO objects that give us data access
   Set cn = Server.CreateObject("ADODB.Connection")
   Set rst = Server.CreateObject("ADODB.Recordset")
   ' Use Microsoft's OLEDB Provider for Oracle
   cn.provider = "MSDAORA"
   ' Database=salesdb, User=manager, Password=bigshot
   cn.open "salesdb", "manager", "bigshot"
   ' Now, retrieve the list of territories from the database
   rst.open "select territory, salesperson from sales_areas", cn
   ' Built a pretty HTML table to accept salesperson names
   do until rst.eof
      response.write "<tr>"
       ' First column shows the name of the territory
      response.write "<td>"& rst.fields(0) & "</td>"
       ' Second column accepts the input, using the name of
       ' the territory as the name of the field
      response.write "<td><INPUT NAME="""& rst.fields(0)
      response.write ""VALUE="""& rst.fields(1) & """></td>"
      response.write "</tr>"
   loop

   cn.close
%>
</TABLE>
</FORM>
```

Design Tip *In the preceding listing, it is assumed that the names of the sales territories all make good names for fields in HTML forms. This could easily be a bad assumption. If any of the sales territory names contained a quote, for example, the entire HTML tag that is being built by the code above would become mangled and illegitimate. If you suspect that this situation might arise in your own data, simply add a numeric key value to your table and use this as the name for your input fields.*

The preceding code solves the issue of creating a dynamically resizing HTML form, but what about processing it in your scripts? In order to accomplish this, you must leverage VBScript's capability to iterate through a collection of arbitrary size via the For Each construction.

```
<%
   Option Explicit

   Dim cn, rst
   Dim x
   Dim strCmd

   Set cn = Server.CreateObject("ADODB.Connection")
   Set rst = Server.CreateObject("ADODB.Recordset")
   cn.provider = "MSDAORA"
   cn.open "salesdb", "manager", "bigshot"

   for each x in request.form
      strCmd = "update sales_areas "
      strCmd = strCmd & "set salesperson = '"& request.form(x)&
      _"' "
      strCmd = strCmd & "where territory = '"& x & "'"
      cn.execute strCmd
   next

   rst.close
   cn.close

   Response.Write "All changes made as requested!"
%>
```

This approach accesses the value of the salespeople's desired names through request.form(x) and the name of their territories simply through a reference to x. This is made possible through our previous decision to use the names of the territories as the names of our fields.

The only drawback to this approach is that it produces a number of database updates that is always equal to the number of sales territories possessed by the organization. This will, under most circumstances, be far in excess of the number of territories actually modified during any given execution of your script.

A more sophisticated approach might encode the original values for each of these fields in hidden fields on the same form and compare these before making any database modifications. This fun is left as an exercise for the reader!

Odd Field Types

The final issues that should be touched upon in debugging your ASP applications are those dealing with field types other than text.

Radio Buttons

Developers used to working in other development environments often bring their understanding of radio buttons with them from those platforms. Under Visual Basic, for example, the following code snippet is perfectly legitimate:

```
If RadioButton1 Then Debug.Print "YES"Else Debug.Print "NO"
```

This is because, under Visual Basic (and many other GUI platforms, such as Java), radio buttons are legitimate objects. As objects, they feature full compliments of methods and properties. Typically, they have a default property that reflects whether they are currently set as a Boolean value that can be used in expressions such as the one shown earlier.

Under HTML, however, radio buttons have specific string values with which they are associated. Their fields in the Request object reflect this string value if they are selected. If no string value if specified then Internet Explorer uses "on." If they are not selected, their fields are empty strings.

So, for a radio button defined as

```
<INPUT TYPE="radio"NAME="eyes"VALUE="blue">
```

an appropriate value test under VBScript might be

```
<%
   If Request("eyes") = "blue"Then
      Response.Write "The button is selected!"
   Else
      Response.Write "The button has been left unselected!"
   End If
%>
```

Checkboxes

Checkboxes are similar to radio buttons, insofar as the Boolean tests that you may be familiar with from other programming environments won't get you very far under VBScript. Checkboxes are also associated with specific string values that they either

- will reflect because they are currently selected, or

- won't reflect because they are not selected. (In this case, they will simply return an empty string.)

Things are even more complicated with checkboxes, however, because HTML allows several checkboxes to share the same name. This is so that you can have a list of items associated with a single item on your form. For example, you should be able to order a hot-fudge sundae with a whole host of ingredients.

```
<FORM METHOD="POST">
<INPUT TYPE="checkbox"NAME="ingredients"VALUE="Nuts">Nuts
<INPUT
TYPE="checkbox"NAME="ingredients"VALUE="Strawberries">Strawberries
<INPUT TYPE="checkbox"NAME="ingredients"VALUE="Cream">Cream
</FORM>
```

Using this form, you can create a list of ingredients including nuts, strawberries, and cream—or any combination! The approach shown for dealing with radio buttons in the last section probably won't work very often here, however. If you were to test for the presence of strawberries in your list of ingredients this way

```
If Request("ingredients") = "Strawberries"Then
```

you would only get a positive result when the list of ingredients contained only strawberries! The addition of nuts and/or cream to the list would cause this test to fail.

There are two ways to approach this problem. The simplest way should be used only if you are absolutely certain that the item you are testing for does not constitute a substring for any of the other items on your list.

```
If Instr(Request("ingredients"), "Cream") > 0 Then
```

This test looks for the presence of the string "Cream" in the string returned by the Request object's Form entry for "ingredients." This works fine for the example given, but suppose that the following line were added to the form at some point in the future:

```
<INPUT TYPE="checkbox"NAME="ingredients"VALUE="Ice Cream">Ice
Cream
```

Now, simply testing for the substring "Cream" doesn't seem like such a good idea. This is because it can be set to positive by either "Cream" or "Ice Cream," which are two separate list entries. In this case, you will need to try a different approach.

The following code iterates through each entry in the "ingredients" list individually. If any of them is an exact match for the entry being sought, the test returns true. This approach breaks the list entries into separate strings, so that there is no danger of a false substring match as with the previous approach.

```
<%
    For I = 0 to (request("ingredients").count - 1)

        if request("ingredients")(i) = "Cream"Then
            'Do Whatever
        End If
    Next
%>
```

Talking Back

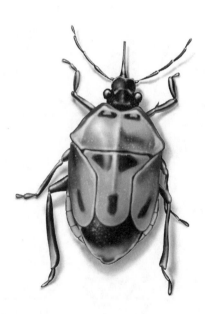

A s you learned in the last chapter, most Active Server Page runs begin with a request from a client browser. The server then loads the page into memory (if it has not already done so) and begins interpreting whatever code is inside the page. After the script has run to completion, the server sends its output across the network, back to the client browser. The complete process is shown in Figure 6-1.

In this chapter, the discussion will focus on the last step in the execution of an Active Server Page: the sending of your script's output back across the network to its client. We'll cover several caveats of which you should be aware when attempting to make your responses. On the other hand, we will also show you a few not widely known techniques that you can use to your advantage.

Redirecting a Request

Sometimes, when a browser requests a certain page in your application, you would like to refer them to a different page. For example, perhaps they are requesting a page that you had to rename, and the page to which you would like

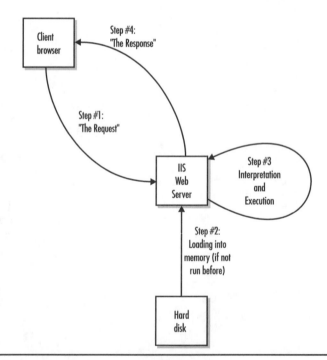

Figure 6.1   Communication between a client and a server

to refer the browser is really just the old page under a new name. Or, perhaps you have created multiple versions of the same script in different languages and would like to refer browsers to the appropriate version for whatever language their users speak.

Regardless of your reasons for wanting to request a browser redirect, there are numerous reasons why such a request might not work as you intended. Sometimes, you might find that your redirection requests fail completely, often producing visible errors. Other times, you might just find that the redirections do not produce exactly the results for which you were hoping.

When Requests Completely Do Not Work

The most embarrassing issues that you are likely to encounter while debugging Active Server Pages are those that produce errors visible to your end users. Unsuccessful attempts at browser redirection often fall into this category. In this section, you will learn the most common causes of such dramatic script failures, as well as how to avoid them.

The Problem with Headers

In order to understand the most common reason for redirection failure, you must first understand how redirection works in general. When a browser first requests a page from your Active Server Pages application, Internet Information Server begins making its response on the very first line in your script that produces output. For example, in the following listing, the first line that produces output is the very last in the script.

```
<%
    Option Explicit
    Dim a
    Dim b
    Dim c

    a = 2
    b = 2

    c = a + 2
    Response.Write "The answer is " & c
%>
```

None of the lines before the one that contains the call to Response.Write produce any kind of output to the browser.

When IIS encounters the first line in a script that produces output, it attempts to decipher the MIME type of the output being produced. Unless you have previously specified otherwise, IIS will always assume a MIME type of text/html.

Before IIS sends a single line of your scripts' output, it will always send a collection of headers. One of the headers that it sends first contains the MIME type of the information that will follow. So, in the preceding example, the response from IIS would consist of a series of headers (one of which would specify a MIME type of text/html) followed by the output of the Response.Write line.

Redirect requests are also specified in the headers sent by IIS. Examine the following modifications to the previous listing:

```
<%
   Option Explicit
   Dim a
   Dim b
   Dim c

   a = 2
   b = 2

   c = a + 2
   Response.Write "The answer is " & c

   if c > 2 then
      response.redirect "biganswer.asp"
   end if
%>
```

Here, we have added an attempt to jump to a page called BIGANSWER.ASP in the event that the value of the variable *c* is found to be smaller than 2. This script would fail every time it was requested!

The reason for this is that by the time that the redirection is attempted, output will already have been sent to the browser. Headers indicating the MIME type of the following content would have preceded this output. Any requests for redirection would also have had to be a part of these headers because a single page is only allowed a single set of headers. For this reason, *you may not request redirection after any point in your script that produces output.* If you do, you will get a screen that looks like Figure 6-2.

Avoiding Unwanted Output

The most basic way to avoid the problem described in the previous section is simply not to send output to clients before attempting a redirect. This is simple in

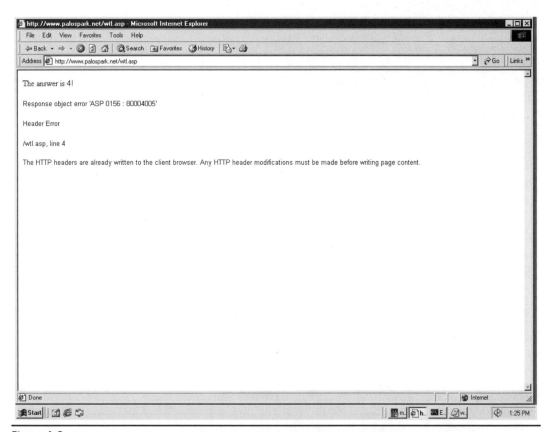

Figure 6.2   An error due to requesting redirection after producing output

the case of intentional output, such as that in the previous example. You could just rewrite such a script to make use of conditional logic flows:

```
If c <= 2 then
    Response.Write "The answer is " & c
else
    response.redirect "biganswer.asp"
end if
```

In this case, you will never get output followed by a redirection attempt. Either the value of *c* will be low enough that a message is produced, or it will be large enough that a redirection occurs—never both. This is an excellent approach to take in simple cases such as the one shown earlier.

What about much more complicated scripts? Take a look at Figure 6-3.

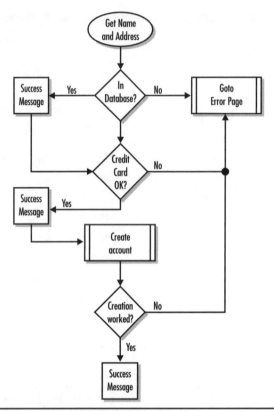

Figure 6.3   The logic underlying a script

First, the name and address of the potential customer are verified against a database of U.S. street addresses. If this test succeeds, a success message is produced. Next, the credit card number for the customer is verified by the credit card clearinghouse. If this test succeeds, a success message is produced. Finally, the account is created in the system. If this creation succeeds, a success message is produced. If an unhandled error occurs at any point in the script, execution skips to a redirection.

Each stage of the flowchart could potentially take several hundred lines of code to program. It would be extremely bad design to embed such large portions of code several layers deep in If-Then-Else logic. It would be better if Active Server Pages provided a way to produce output as your script goes along; if they could then "take it back" if anything required a redirect request.

Fortunately, the buffering mechanism of Internet Information Server provides exactly such capabilities. By turning buffering on for your Active Server Pages, you can request that IIS not actually send any of the output produced by your scripts until those scripts have completely finished executing. This means that you can go ahead and allow your scripts to produce output as they go along. If your script gets to a point where it needs to request a redirection, it can request that the buffer be cleared.

```
Response.Buffer = True

c = a + 2
Response.Write "The answer is " & c

if c > 2 then
   response.clear
   response.redirect "biganswer.asp"
end if
```

Error Watch *Calling Response.Clear without first having enabled buffering will generate a run-time error.*

You can enable buffering for your ASP scripts in two ways. The first is to place the line

```
Response.Buffer = True
```

in your code. The second is via the IIS Management Console. In order to turn buffering on using the Management Console, follow these steps:

1. Select Programs from the Windows Start menu.
2. Open the Administrative Tools program group.
3. Choose the Internet Services Manager.
4. Expand the tree control on the left of the Management Console to display the Web site in which you are interested.
5. Right-click the Web site's icon.
6. Select Properties from the pop-up context menu.
7. Choose the Home Directory tab.
8. Click the Configuration button at the bottom of the tab.
9. Choose the App Options tab.
10. Verify that the Enable Buffering checkbox is checked.
11. Click OK or Apply to confirm your changes.

For pages that take a very long time to finish producing their output, however, you may wish to reconsider turning off ASP buffering. With buffering turned off, your clients should be able to see the output from your scripts as it is produced—so they can be sure that your script is not hung up. On the other hand, with buffering turned off, your clients' browsers will remain completely blank until the end of your scripts' execution. This could make a lot more of them abandon loading your pages before they are finished.

Design Tip *Sometimes, you might absolutely need to display a message briefly before performing your redirect. For example, you might want to warn your client that they are about to be taken to a page that is different from the one they requested. The only problem is, as you have learned in this section, there is no way to perform a redirect from Active Server Pages once output has been sent to a browser.*

A convenient way to overcome this limitation is by using a META tag to instruct the client browser to request a different page shortly after loading the one given to it by your script. In the following listing, the words, "You're about to visit my employer's Website," are displayed on the screen for 12 seconds before the browser navigates to the InterAccess homepage.

```
<META http-equiv="REFRESH"
content="12;url=http://www.interaccess.com">
<%
    Response.Write "You're about to visit my employer's website"
%>
```

When Requests Work Incorrectly

A common mistake that many Active Server Page developers make is thinking that all the code that they put into a given script will be given a chance to execute, even if it occurs after a request for redirection. This is not the case. When an ASP script redirects a browser to another page, it immediately stops its own execution.

This means that a developer has one of two choices in developing an Active Server Page script. On one hand, she can put whatever code she wishes to execute in a script prior to the request for redirection. On the other hand, he might decide to move into whatever script is the target of the redirect exactly that portion of code that should have executed after the redirection.

```
<%
    Option Explicit

    Dim ErrCount

    Response.Redirect "Error.asp"
    ErrCount = Application("ErrorCount")
    ErrCount = ErrCount + 1
    Response.Write "This is the " & ErrCount & " "
    Response.Write "error since this application began!"
%>
```

This script clearly won't work. The first line of the sample terminates the execution of this script and transfers control of the system immediately to the ERROR.ASP script. This means that the total error count is never retrieved from the Application object, incremented, or displayed. Everything stops at the call to Response.Redirect.

```
<%
    Option Explicit

    Dim ErrCount

    ErrCount = Application("ErrorCount")
    ErrCount = ErrCount + 1
    Application("ErrorCount") = ErrCount
    Response.Redirect "Error.asp"
%>
```

This rewrite has used the first methodology suggested earlier to solve half of the problem. It performs the retrieval and increment of the error count prior to requesting a redirect. Unfortunately, it cannot produce output before the redirect because of the limitation on headers that was discussed in the previous section. For this reason, the output must occur in the ERROR.ASP script.

```
<%
    Response.Write "This is the " & Application("ErrorCount") & " "
    Response.Write "error since this application began!"
%>
```

The addition of the preceding code to the ERROR.ASP script would allow the developer to achieve exactly the results for which he or she was looking.

Asking for Permission to Redirect

Consider the following chain of events:

1. An end user requests a page called SURVEY.ASP that contains an HTML form.
2. The end user submits the form (which uses a POST method) to a script named RECEIVER.ASP.
3. RECEIVER.ASP redirects the client to a script named HANDLER.ASP.
4. HANDLER.ASP redirects the client to a script called CONFUSED.ASP.
5. The client browser requests permission to continue.
6. The end user grants permission.
7. CONFUSED.ASP handles the form and returns some output.

You might assume from steps 5 and 6 that CONFUSED.ASP had some special permission requirements associated with it. This is not, however, necessarily the case.

Until its most recent release, Internet Information Server had trouble handling multiple redirections. A *multiple redirection* is any instance when a script requests a redirect to another script that in turn requests a redirect of its own. Figure 6-4 presents this situation graphically.

The issue might arise when multiple redirections are coupled with HTML forms. You might remember from Chapter 5 that forms have two ways of submitting their data to scripts for processing: GET and POST. GET submissions encode form data into the URLs of the pages to which they submit their results. POST

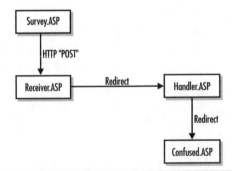

Figure 6.4   A multiple redirection request

submissions pass their data invisibly though a background HTTP process—these submissions may experience problems.

Versions of IIS prior to 5 (which is the version used by Windows 2000) sometimes changed POST submissions to GET submissions during multiple redirects. This was because of obscure requirements in very early versions of the HTTP specification that forbade scripts from redirecting in response to form submissions. This restriction has been lifted in more recent versions of the specification, and similarly this bug in IIS has been resolved.

If you notice this problem arising in your own applications, you have a few options:

- Ideally, you should design your applications not to use multiple redirects. They make your applications harder to follow for developers who may have to maintain them later on. They also waste valuable server CPU cycles.

- Use META tags to achieve client-side script redirection, rather than Response.Redirect. This method is not susceptible to the same bugs in IIS.

- Upgrade to version 5 or later of IIS.

Beyond HTML

HTML has served as the basis for the vast majority of Web conversations since before the very first version of Internet Information Server, much less Active Server Pages. Originally developed by Tim Berners-Lee at the CERN Research Institute in Europe, HTML is a version of SGML (Standard Generalized Markup Language) specially adapted for use on the World Wide Web.

HTML takes an approach to content description that is practically guaranteed to be platform independent. Unfortunately, the price for this platform neutrality has often been a kind of "lowest common denominator" approach to user interface creation. Under standard HTML, for example, it is not possible to resort a list of data once it has been returned to your browser. If you really had to support this capability for your users, you would have to allow them to return all of the data to a script executing on the server, where it would be resorted and returned to them.

It is dissatisfaction with these kinds of limitations that leads many Active Server Page developers into experimenting with data formats beyond simple HTML. Support for such emerging standards as VRML and XML is far from universal, however.

Support for Other Standards

The possibilities are great for sending non-HTML data as part of your Active Server Page applications. When working with Internet Explorer, the transfer of documents using Microsoft Office format is becoming increasingly common. Developers working with these and other non-HTML forms of data often discover that their clients now require special tools and security settings.

Different Forms of Data

Consider the case of an Active Server Pages application that is supposed to sell people life insurance. The pricing on life insurance can vary greatly from one individual to the next based upon a multitude of factors: age, family history, current health, and so on. It is easy to imagine a point in such an application when it could be useful to present the user with a table of values for them to play around with so that they could see how different factors affect their insurance rates.

Variable	Value	Multiplier	Risk Points
Age	24	.5	12
Smoking	0	.25	0
Male	1	.1	.1
Female	0	-.1	0
Drinker	0	.25	0

The simplest way to transmit this information to a Web client would probably be to use a standard HTML table. But, as noted previously, the lack of interactivity inherent in this approach would constitute a considerable bug in your application.

```
<%
Option Explicit

Dim fs, fl
Dim t

Set fs = Server.CreateObject("Scripting.FileSystemObject")
Set fl = fs.CreateTextFile("c:\inetpub\wwwroot\insurance.xls", True)

t = chr(9)

fl.WriteLine "Variable" & t & "Value" & t & "Multiplier" & "Risk Points"
fl.WriteLine "Age" & t & "24" & t & ".5" & t & "12"
fl.WriteLine "Smoking" & t & "0" & t & ".25" & t & "0"
fl.WriteLine "Male" & t & "1" & t & ".1" & t & ".1"
```

```
fl.WriteLine "Female" & t & "0" & t & "-.1" & t & "0"
fl.WriteLine "Drinker" & t & "0" & t & ".25" & t & "0"

fl.close

response.redirect "insurance.xls"
%>
```

This script takes a completely different approach to the problem. Rather than sending the table as HTML, it puts it into a text file named INSURANCE.XLS. Within the text file, the various columns of output are separated with tab characters (assigned to the variable t in the script). The client browser is then redirected to the text file that has been created.

At this point, a truly remarkable event occurs. Assuming that the client computer is using the Internet Explorer browser and assuming that they have installed Microsoft Excel, this page is loaded and displayed within the browser as a Microsoft Excel spreadsheet (see Figure 6-5)!

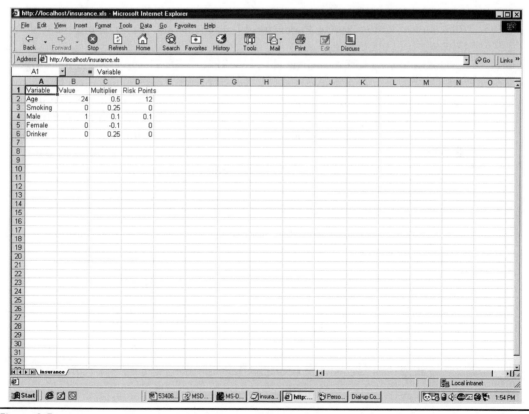

Figure 6.5   Displaying redirected data in another application

This happens because the extension XLS is associated with Excel on machines where Excel is present. Furthermore, Excel's standard behavior when asked to open a file that is in text format (as indeed INSURANCE.XLS would be) is to automatically import it into Excel format. In this state, the end user can play around with the figures as much as he or she cares to in order to gain a better understanding of the prices they are encountering.

Different Tool Requirements

You might have noticed in this discussion that everything rested on two basic assumptions:

- Internet Explorer was being used as the browser.
- Microsoft Excel was installed on the client machine.

Although Internet Explorer's dominance in the market is continuing to grow at the time of this writing, it would probably be a serious bug for any general-purpose Active Server Pages application to make such a gross assumption. Fortunately, Active Server Pages provides a means for you to determine which browser your client is using.

The following script uses the HTTP_USER_AGENT server variable to figure out whether the client browser is Internet Explorer. This usually takes the form of the substring MSIE when it appears in the server variable, so this is what the code looks for. If it finds the substring, it sends the required information to the user in the form of a Word document. If the MSIE substring is not a part of this variable, the client must be some browser other than Internet Explorer, so it is redirected to a simple text version of the required information.

```
<%
    Option Explicit

    Dim ua
    Dim obj

    ua = Request.ServerVariables("HTTP_USER_AGENT")
    If Instr(ua, "MSIE") > 0 Then
        Response.ContentType = "application/x-msword"
        Set obj = Server.CreateObject("BookUtils.BinaryReader")
        Response.Write obj.GetStream("AdvancedText.Doc")
    Else
        Response.Redirect "SimpleText.Txt"
    End If
%>
```

The code responsible for sending the Word document itself deserves a bit more attention. Notice that it begins by declaring a MIME type that Internet Explorer can recognize as Microsoft Word. This tells the browser, "OK, get ready—I'm about to send you a Word document, not HTML." The code then goes on to instantiate a custom component and call the GetStream method on it in order to get output to write to the client. This is needed because the FileSystemObject that is built into Active Server Pages *does not* support binary file types.

In order to build a custom component that fills this gap, all that you really have to do is

1. Figure out how many bytes long the file is.
2. Declare a Byte array big enough to hold all of these bytes.
3. Open the file for binary reading.
4. Retrieve everything from the file into the Byte array.
5. Return the Byte array to the calling procedure.

A simple implementation in Visual Basic might look like this:

```
Option Explicit

Public Function BinaryReader(filename)

    Dim intNumberOfBytes as Integer
    Dim byteArray() as Byte

    intNumberOfBytes = FileLen(filename)
    Redim byteArray(intNumberOfBytes)

    Open filename for binary access read as #1
    Get #1,, byteArray
    BinaryReader = byteArray
    Close #1

End Function
```

Security Concerns

HTML is one of the few forms of data considered truly harmless by most security experts. The reason for this has to do with its lack of interactivity, which you have already heard much about in this section. In short, HTML is capable only of describing how the output should look for your Web pages; it is not capable of accepting user input or responding in any intelligent fashion. Because HTML is incapable of activity, it is considered incapable of taking any actions that would cause harm to computers onto which it is loaded.

Client-side scripts, Java applets, and ActiveX controls are the three most common tools used by Active Server Page developers to add life to their otherwise inactive Web pages. Client-side scripts may be written in either JavaScript (aka JScript or ECMAScript) or VBScript and are typically thought to be the safest of these three from a security standpoint. One of the most compelling arguments in favor of this belief is that their source is completely visible within any page of which they form a part.

Java applets are typically considered only slightly less safe than client-side scripts. Under Java, applets execute in what is referred to as a "sandbox." This means that every action of an applet while it is running in your browser is carefully monitored by the system to ensure that it isn't an attempt to do any of the numerous things that are forbidden for unsigned Java applets to do. Among these forbidden things are

- Making network connections to any computers other than the one from which they were downloaded.
- Directly accessing the native non-Java resources of your operating system (such as Windows API functions).
- Reading from or writing to your local disk storage.

Placing ActiveX controls on your Web pages easily constitutes asking for the greatest degree of trust from those using your Active Server Page applications. There is no inherent limit on the actions of ActiveX controls running within a browser. They may do all the things that are forbidden for Java applets, including reading files at random from your local hard disk and sending their contents to any computer on the Internet! For this reason, you will often find browsers that refuse to use your Active Server Pages if they contain ActiveX controls.

If you have access to the actual browser that is refusing to operate your Active Server Pages, you can work around this kind of issue by reconfiguring the browser's security settings. Under Internet Explorer 5, you would

1. Open the Tools menu.
2. Select Internet Options.
3. Go to the Security tab, as shown in Figure 6-6.

4. Click the Trusted Sites icon.

5. Press the Sites button.

6. Add your site to the Trusted Sites dialog, as shown in Figure 6-7.

If you don't have access to all of the computers and browsers that you want to use your ActiveX controls, you will have to obtain a developer's certificate from a certificate authority and sign your controls. A *certificate authority* is a large corporation, such as Verisign, that is willing to guarantee that whatever controls you sign with their certificates are indeed from you. This would allow anyone whose systems were harmed by your controls to be certain who they should sue for damages. This might seem humorous, but it is 100 percent true.

For more information on signing ActiveX controls, you can visit Verisign's Web site at http://www.verisign.com.

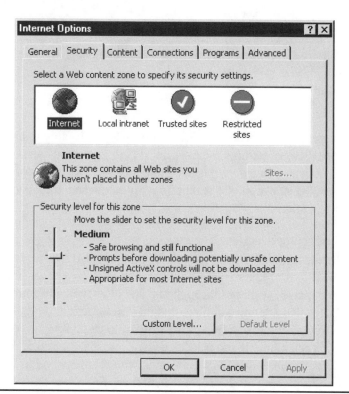

Figure 6.6   The Security tab of the Internet Options dialog

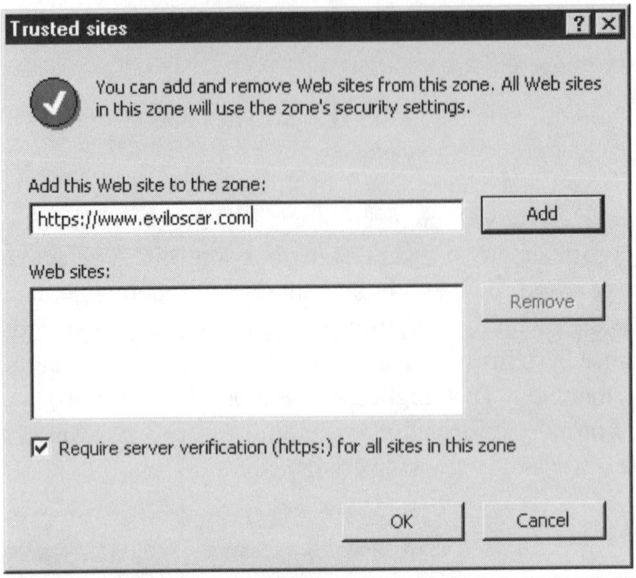

Figure 6.7 Adding a site to the Trusted Sites dialog

Adding Images

Images can often communicate information infinitely more effectively than words alone. Consider how much easier it is to give someone directions from one point to another when a map is available. For this reason, most Active Server Page developers eventually want to incorporate some kind of image into their applications.

Building Scripts That Return Images

Images typically occur as parts of larger HTML pages. It is common to have a great deal of text explaining a concept, such as a news story, accompanied by a few images scattered throughout. The bugs typically found in Active Server Pages that attempt to utilize this mixture of text and pictures all stem from an improper understanding of the flow followed by browsers as they load pages.

When a browser first loads a page across the Internet, it begins by downloading all HTML associated with that page. After this is done, the browser begins parsing the HTML for references to images and other items that need to be downloaded subsequently in order to flesh out the page. As these items are encountered in the HTML, a new and separate connection is established to retrieve each and every one. Each of these items is expected to identify itself with its own set of headers when it is downloaded.

```
<%
    Option Explicit

    If Request("Animal") = "" Then
%>
    Of what animal would you like to see a picture?
    <FORM METHOD="POST">
    <INPUT NAME="Animal">
    </FORM>
<%
    else
        Dim cn, rst

        Set cn = Server.CreateObject("ADODB.Connection")
        Set rst = Server.CreateObject("ADODB.Recordset")

        cn.open "images", "artist", "artpass"
        rst.open "select picture from animals where name = '" & _
            request("animal") & "'", cn

        if rst.eof then
            response.write "No such animal in the database!"
        else
            response.write rst.fields(0)
        end if

        rst.close
        cn.close

    end if
%>
```

This script begins by asking the user to specify the name for an animal he or she wants to view. A connection is then established to a database containing images of many different animals. A recordset is used to try retrieving the picture for the animal specified. If no results are returned, the user is informed that there is no such animal in the database; otherwise the script tries to display the picture.

Error Watch *The most easily avoided mistake in the above script is the use of Response.Write for the transmission of binary data. Response.Write is intended strictly for use with text data. For working with images, which are binary data, you should always use Response.BinaryWrite.*

Besides the use of the wrong Write operation discussed in the Error Watch, there is another glaring problem with this script. Nothing in this code alerts the browser that the content that is about to be returned is of nontext MIME type. Since this is the only material being returned by the script at this point, you can rectify this problem and the previous problem by changing the code as follows:

```
If Rst.EOF Then
    Response.Write "No such animal in the database!"
Else
    Response.ContentType = "image/gif"
    Response.BinaryWrite rst.fields(0)
End If
```

Mixing Images and Text

The example in the previous section was made simple by virtue of the fact that binary data, in this case an image, was the only thing being returned by the buggy section of text. If you ever need to mix text and images in the responses made by your Active Server Pages, you may discover a whole new realm of programming pitfalls. Consider the following overly simplistic approach to incorporating picture captions into the previous example:

```
Dim cn, rst

Set cn = Server.CreateObject("ADODB.Connection")
Set rst = Server.CreateObject("ADODB.Recordset")

cn.open "images", "artist", "artpass"
rst.open "select picture, caption from animals where name = '" & _
    request("animal") & "'", cn

if rst.eof then
    response.write "No such animal in the database!"
else
    Response.Write "This is a " & rst.fields(1)
    Response.ContentType = "image/gif"
    Response.BinaryWrite rst.fields(0)
end if
```

The developer who created this script was hoping that it would display the text "This is a giraffe," for example, followed by a picture of a giraffe from the database. The problem here is the same one-set-of-headers-per-page limitation that you encountered in the section on returning Microsoft Office documents from your Active Server Pages. The only way to work around it in this case is to incorporate the output of another script.

```
rst.open "select caption from animals where name = '" & _
   request("animal") & "'", cn

if rst.eof then
   response.write "No such animal in the database!"
else
   Response.Write "This is a " & rst.fields(0)
%>
<IMG SRC="showpic.asp?animal=<%=request("animal")%>">

<%
end if
%>
```

This revision to the previous examples limits its own output to the display of the appropriate caption. It then uses the standard IMG SRC tag from HTML to redirect the browser to another script *only for the output of a single picture.* It is capable of directing the other script as to which picture it should display by incorporating the name of the animal into the extended URL for the script being called.

The script shown next is the SHOWPIC.ASP page referenced by the preceding code. It makes its own connection to the database and retrieves the binary data for the picture that must be displayed. The test for the existence of this picture is skipped here, because it would have been performed on the previous page. The lines to return the actual picture consist of one line to set the headers properly and another line to send the data.

```
<%
   Dim cn, rst

   Set cn = Server.CreateObject("ADODB.Connection")
   Set rst = Server.CreateObject("ADODB.Recordset")

   cn.open "images", "artist", "artpass"
   rst.open "select picture from animals where name = '" & _
      request.QueryString("animal") & "'", cn

   Response.ContentType = "image/gif"
   Response.BinaryWrite rst.fields(0)
%>
```

Design Tip   *It is important to realize that Access and FoxPro both append OLE headers to images stored within them. It is impossible to display images taken straight out of these databases using the above approach. For appropriate results, you should either store your images in enterprise-level databases, such as SQL Server or Oracle, or you might consider storing your images in regular files and simply referencing them as needed.*

Incorporating Special Strings

A problem that tends to vex novice Active Server Page developers is how to return text without having it interpreted as HTML. This isn't a problem when you want to return a string such as, "Have a nice day, sir." It becomes a problem when you want to return a string that can be interpreted as a special HTML tag, such as "<B>".

A browser would typically interpret the preceding string as a request to switch to bold face type. Nine times out of ten, this is the way that a developer would like it to be interpreted. But, what about the 10 percent of the time that the developer doesn't want this to happen? Suppose, for instance, that the developer were trying to build a Web site to teach people how to use all of the appropriate HTML tags. It would be hard to show people the different tags if every single time the developer uses one, it was interpreted rather than displayed!

```
<%
   Response.Write "The below line demonstrates the use of a hyperlink!<br>"
   Response.Write "<a href=""www.eviloscar.com"">Click me!</a>"
%>
```

This script would like to show the user the proper syntax for building a hyperlink, but all that appears in a Web browser when this page is executed is

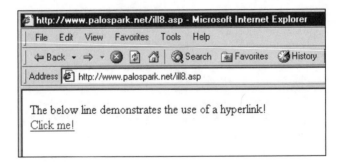

The way to solve this bug is by using the Server.HTMLEncode method. With this method, strings can be converted to contain the special escape sequences needed in order to avoid interpretation by browsers. Without interpretation, they are displayed exactly as received. Rewritten using this technique, the preceding code would become

```
<%

    Option Explicit

    Dim st

    Response.Write "The below line demonstrates the use of a hyperlink!"
    st = Server.HTMLEncode("<a href=""www.eviloscar.com"">Click me!</a>")
    Response.Write st
%>
```

The output looks like this:

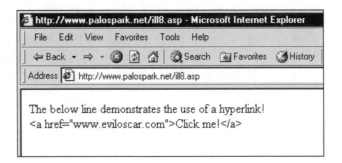

Handling Timeout Errors

Timeouts are errors generated whenever a client or server working within your application gets sick of waiting for a response. When a client generates a timeout response, it is typically because too much time has elapsed without any sign of activity from the server. When a server generates a timeout, it is usually because the currently running script has exceeded the time limit for its completion.

Errors Due to Oversized Content

Trying to send too much content from your script to Web browser clients will often cause those clients to generate timeout errors. The reason for this is that the amount of time it can take to transfer large content over modem connections can be painful. Browsers implement timeout safeguards to prevent their users from having to sit through hours of Internet connectivity while waiting for simple Web pages to load.

The two most common causes of oversized content are graphics and client-side executables. Graphics can be either extremely small or massively large, depending on the number of colors and amount of detail supported. The chief obstacles presented by client-side executables are size and sheer number of files.

Graphics

Graphics shouldn't be a problem for Active Server Page developers. The two leading Internet standards for image transfers, GIF and JPG, are capable of compressing large pictures into relatively trivial file sizes. If you find that any of the graphics on your pages are over a couple of hundred K in size, you definitely have a problem. You should check that these files are in GIF or JPG format.

You can usually determine the format of a picture by examining the extension on its filename. GIF and JPG are the extensions used by file formats that support the kind of image compression you need for transferring files over slow Internet connections. If you discover that your large files are in any other format, follow this procedure to translate them (and shrink them in the process).

1. Choose Programs from the Windows Start menu.

2. Open the Accessories program group.

3. Click Imaging to open Kodak Imaging for Windows.

4. Select Open from the File menu at the top of the screen.

5. Choose the file that needs to be converted to a compressed file standard.

6. Choose Save As from the File menu. Your screen should resemble Figure 6-8.

7. Select JPG File from the Save As Type drop-down list.

At this point, you should have a properly compressed version of whatever graphic you were previously using. If you compare the file size of this new file to the one in the non-JPG or non-GIF format, you should see a marked improvement. Use this on your page instead of the old file and your timeout problems should disappear.

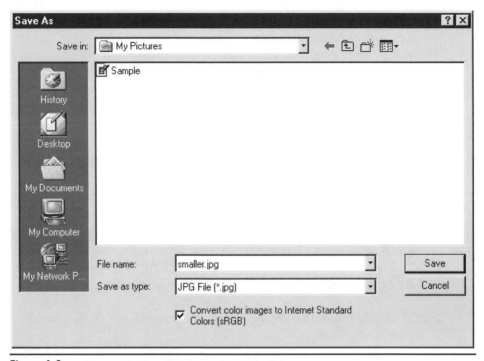

Figure 6.8   The Imaging application's Save As dialog

Client-Side Executables

Active Server Page developers often use client-side executables, such as Java applets and ActiveX controls, to overcome some of HTML's lack of interactivity. The only problem with this approach is that it entails transferring entire mini-applications across the Internet from the Web server to the client browser. This can often involve enough of a delay to cause a client to declare a timeout error.

In the case of Java applets, the issue usually isn't file size. Java applications are not executables in the truest sense of the computer science term but are actually specially compressed code intended for interpretation by programs already located on the client computers. These programs already contain most of the code needed to run the applications, so it takes a considerable drain off the amount of code that needs to be contained in each Java applet.

The real problem with Java applets can be the enormous numbers of supporting files that must be transferred in order for them to work. This is a problem because every file that must be transferred requires that an additional network connection be established and maintained. This is a very time-consuming task that can quickly overload many clients and servers alike.

ActiveX controls also require a host of supporting files in order to operate. In the case of controls created with Visual Basic, one of these files may be the Visual Basic Runtime library, which is well over 1MB in size! So, in addition to sheer number of files, the size of files is also of great concern when working with ActiveX controls.

Fortunately, both of these client-side executables support the ZIP archiving format under Internet Explorer and Netscape.

A ZIP file is a specially compressed file that can contain any number of other files. The advantages of putting your files in a ZIP are that only one file then needs to be transferred from server to client and that this one file is usually much, much smaller once it has gone through ZIP compression.

You can obtain software for creating ZIP files from http://www.winzip.com. Follow these steps to put your files into a ZIP archive:

1. Right-click the desktop or folder where you would like the new ZIP file to be located.

2. From the pop-up context menu, choose New.

3. From the New pop-up context menu, choose WinZip File.

4. When the WinZip icon appears, type the name of the new ZIP file.

5. Hold down the Ctrl key and select every file that you would like to be a part of the new ZIP file.

6. Drag any one of the selected files to the new ZIP file.

7. When the + sign appears over the highlighted ZIP file, drop the file.

Your files will now be added to the ZIP file for use in your Active Server Pages.

Errors Due to Long-Running Tasks

The Web is the ideal platform for many kinds of applications. Systems that must be accessed simultaneously by multiple users, for example, can benefit greatly from the Web's inherent client-server architecture. Systems that must operate on a wide variety of platforms are also natural candidates for Internet deployment.

Sometimes as a developer, however, you are asked to shoehorn an application into a situation that is less than ideally suited for it. Active Server Pages that take a long time to return their responses are a case in point. Browsers are typically configured to expect responses from Web servers within a generally short time after making their requests—30 seconds or less is quite common. If your scripts take longer than this to produce their output, you run the serious risk of encountering browser timeout errors.

Similarly, Internet Information Server will usually allow only a single script to execute for a certain amount of time. If a script exceeds this time limit, IIS has the power to terminate it and generate an ASP timeout error.

24x7 Increasing IIS's ASP Script Timeout

The best way to avoid ASP timeouts is to design your applications in such a way that they do not exceed IIS's time limits. However, sometimes the difficulties involved in such a redesign are not warranted by the benefits. In these cases, you may wish to consider simply raising IIS's ASP script timeout to a level high enough to allow your scripts to finish running without interruption.

1. Select Programs from the Windows Start menu.
2. Open the Administrative Tools program group.
3. Choose the Internet Services Manager.
4. Expand the tree control on the left of the Management Console to display the Web site in which you are interested.
5. Right-click the Web site's icon.
6. Select Properties from the pop-up context menu.
7. Choose the Home Directory tab.
8. Click the Configuration button at the bottom of the tab.
9. Choose the App Options tab.
10. Type your desired timeout value (in seconds) into the ASP Script timeout blank.
11. Click OK or Apply to confirm your changes.

Using the Shell Command

Consider the following request for the development of an Active Server Pages application:

> "The first page of the application should display a list of all the products and services offered for sale by our firm. The user should be able to select one or more of these products and services. Upon submission of this form, the application should collect the e-mail addresses and telephone numbers for all of our customers who have ever purchased these products and services. It should return a list of all the unique telephone numbers in this list to the end user. It should also send a 50%-off coupon to every customer on the list."

Whether this application is really an ideal candidate for Active Server Page development depends largely on the size and organization of the company's sales database. For a very small company, such as a newly established consulting firm with only a few customers, it might be possible to both return the list of telephone numbers and generate all the required e-mails before facing the prospect of a browser timeout. For a slightly larger company, such as a local record store, retrieving the list of telephone numbers might still be possible, but sending even 100 e-mails within the required time frame is unrealistic.

One way that a developer might circumvent such time limitations is by using a COM component to kick off a standalone process that will actually complete the bulk of the work. Because the call to the standalone process executes asynchronously, the COM component's method is able to return immediately. This allows the ASP application to quickly respond with a message to the user stating that their requested work is under way.

```
<%
    Option Explicit

    Dim strQry
    Dim obj

    strQry = "SELECT email FROM customers " & _
            "WHERE product in " & _
            "(SELECT product FROM target_products)"

    Set obj = Server.CreateObject("ASPBook.CouponMailerObject")
    obj.SendMails(strQry)

    Response.Redirect "status.html"
%>
```

This code snippet assumes the execution of some prior code. This prior code would be responsible for populating the target_products table with the names of all the products whose purchasers are to be targeted by our e-mail campaign. The preceding script instantiates a COM component and passes it a SQL statement that can be used to retrieve the list of e-mails to which coupons should be sent. It finishes by directing the client to a page called STATUS.HTML.

```
Option Explicit
Public sub SendMails(strQry)
    Dim g

    Open "c:\instructions.txt" for output as #1
    print #1, strQry
    close #1

    g = shell("c:\spammer.exe", vbHide)
End sub
```

This is the subroutine that would have to exist in the COM component instantiated here. This code begins by saving whatever SQL query was passed to it into a simple text file. It then requests that the program SPAMMER.EXE be started in its own process and in a state that is completely invisible to the user interface on the server where this component is running. This last bit is a requirement for any component that wants to run in the process space of the Internet Information Server.

```
Option Explicit

Sub main()
    ' Declare objects for access to the email address database
    Dim cn as New ADODB.Connection
    Dim rst as New ADODB.Recordset
    ' Declare a counter for the number of emails sent
    Dim intEmailCount as Integer
    Dim strQry as String

    ' Open the email address database
    cn.open "salesdb", "manager", "pencil"

    ' Retrieve the SQL query generated by the Active Server Page
    ' and stored in this file by the COM component
    Open "c:\instructions.txt" for input as #1
    Line Input #1, strQry
    Close #1

    ' Retrieve the actual list of email addresses
    rst.open strQry, cn
```

```
' Loop through every single address on the list
Do until rst.eof
    DoEvents
    ' This routine would be defined elsewhere and would
    ' take care of the details of actually sending Email
    Call SendCoupon(rst.fields(0))
    ' Increment the count of emails sent
    intEmailCount = intEmailCount + 1

    ' Update the status page on the web so that the end-user can be
    ' kept abreast of their job's progress
    Open "c:\inetpub\wwwroot\status.html" for output as #1
    Print #1, "We have sent " & intEmailCount & " emails so far..."
    Close #1
Loop

' Close database resources before terminating
rst.close
cn.close

End sub
```

Here you see the main routine for the SPAMMER.EXE application. Documentation has been added to the code itself to help you understand exactly what is going on here. Two points deserve additional mention: the text file that this process read from, and the HTML file to which it writes. The text file was originally created by the COM component in order to store the SQL query created by the Active Server Page. This is one way you can pass parameters and instructions between COM components and the standalone processes that they instantiate. It should be noted that this approach is safe for use only in situations where simultaneous access by multiple users is unlikely, if not impossible.

The HTML file is the page to which the client was originally redirected at the end of the first script. It is overwritten every time that a new e-mail is sent out. This would allow the end user to check on the status of their e-mailing project simply by refreshing their browser display. It should be noted that this is also a workable solution only in situations where multiuser access is unlikely or impossible. If several e-mail jobs were started simultaneously, they would overwrite each other's status pages, and this would render this information highly unreliable.

Creating Work Orders for the Scheduler
The previous section showed you how to kick off a standalone process via a COM component instantiated in your Active Server Pages. This had the

advantage of providing constant feedback to the end user through a status page that was constantly rewritten by the standalone process. It had the considerable disadvantage, however, of not working under multiuser scenarios.

There is a variation on the above approach that sacrifices the benefits of the status page's feedback in exchange for multiuser support. Rather than spawning standalone processes at the time of your ASP scripts' execution, you can create little "work orders" for a process that will run on schedule at some point in the future. Each of these work orders are put in the same directory, but in different files with random (or sequential) numbers for their names.

When your standalone process executes later on, it will go through every file in the chosen directory. It will open files, read their contents, execute their directives, and then delete them from the system so that they don't get executed again. Feedback to the user regarding the state of their request may be accomplished by an e-mail at the end of execution.

```
<%
    Option Explicit

    Dim fs, fl
    Dim LastFileNumber, NextFileNumber
    Dim NextFile
    Dim strQry

    LastFileNumber = Application("LastFileNumber")
    NextFileNumber = LastFileNumber + 1
    Application("LastFileNumber") = NextFileNumber

    NextFile = NextFileNumber & ".txt"

    Set fs = Server.CreateObject("Scripting.FileSystemObject")
    Set fl = fs.CreateTextFile(NextFile, True)

    strQry = "SELECT email FROM customers " & _
            "WHERE salesperson = '" & request("salesperson") & "'"

    fl.WriteLine (strQry)
    fl.WriteLine (request("salesperson"))
    fl.Close

    Response.Write "Your emails will be sent out later tonight!"
%>
```

This is a variation on the script from the previous section. This application would e-mail all the customers associated with a given salesperson, rather than a certain set of purchased products. All of the files created by this application are numbered sequentially, and this is supported by the code at the start of this script that retrieves the last number used from the Application object. The code goes on to write the appropriate SQL into the work order file, followed by the name of the salesperson (so the standalone process knows who to notify when the work is finished).

24x7 Importance of Creating Log Files to Track Progress and Problems

Notice that the Active Server Page listed earlier ends with a simple declaration that the user's e-mails will be sent out sometime later tonight. This is considerably less interactive than the approach shown in the previous section, where the end user was redirected to a constantly updated status page.

It is important to counter this loss in interactivity by logging all the actions taken by your scheduled processes. This way you can later check to ensure that all your jobs have run to completion. If not, you will at least be able to determine exactly where they failed.

```
Option Explicit

Sub main
    Open "log.txt" for output as #1
    Dim x as OrgUtils.EnviroMaster
    Set x = new OrgUtils.EnviroMaster
    Print #1, "Successfully instantiated the EnviroMaster component..."
    x.IdentifyPollutedCreeks
    Print #1, "Successfully identified polluted creeks..."
    x.CleanWaterSources
    Print #1, "Successfully cleaned water sources..."
    Set x = Nothing
    Print #1, "Run finished!"
    Close #1
End sub
```

This example uses a fictional environmental application to demonstrate a simple approach to maintaining a log file. The file is opened at the start of the program's execution. From that point on, every major action of the application is logged in the file. If any step were to cause a catastrophic failure of the application, it would be clear from the log files afterward exactly where execution had terminated. In the next example, you can see that trouble was encountered after the identification of polluted creeks and before the cleaning of the water sources:

```
Successfully instantiated the EnviroMaster component...
Successfully instantiated polluted creeks...
```

Using COM Objects with Active Server Pages

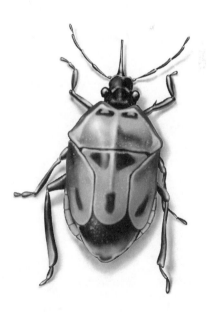

The first tool for executing custom code on a Web server in response to client requests was the Common Gateway Interface (CGI). One drawback to this approach was its Unix-centric reliance on the concepts of *standard input* and *standard output*—which didn't fit well into the model of GUI-based environments (such as Windows). Another problem was the fact that each new CGI request resulted in the creation of an additional process on the server. This severely limited the scalability of applications using CGI.

Active Server Pages address both of these issues. By providing the intrinsic objects Request and Response, the means of input and output are made completely at home in a Windows environment. And by allowing you to create and execute your own COM components within the same process space as Internet Information Server itself, if you like, ASP has also managed to avoid the one-process-per-request resource requirements of CGI.

Installing COM Components

In order to use a COM component as a part of your script, you must first ensure that the COM component in question has been *registered* with the operating system on your Web server's computer. When a component is registered, entries are made within the Windows registry to tell the system where it can find the code corresponding to your component's name. Without registration, IIS will return an error whenever you attempt to use your component.

Consider the following script:

```
<%
    Option Explicit

    Dim obj

    Set obj = Server.CreateObject("StarTrek.TransporterControl")

    if not(obj.BeamUp("Spock")) then
        response.write "He's shown up with a beard!"
    else
        response.write "Spock transported successfully."
    end if
%>
```

If you enter this code onto your computer and try to run it right now, you will almost certainly get the following error:

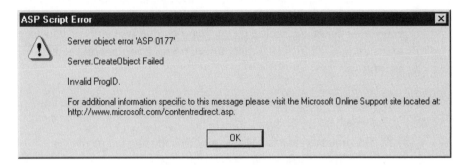

This is just ASP's way of telling you, "Either you don't have on this system the component that you are trying to use, or you have it, but you haven't registered it—which makes it impossible for me to find it."

Registering a Component

For every COM component in existence, there is a 128-bit number that uniquely identifies it. This number is known as a Globally Unique Identifier (GUID) because the number that represents one component is guaranteed to be unique from the number identifying every other COM component throughout time and space.

A typical GUID might look like the following:

```
4abf2131-27c8-00bd-79fc-11bb114e8441
```

The developers who first designed COM could have decided to burden us with the task of typing in such codes every time that we wanted to instantiate a given COM component. In this case, a common object creation might look like this under ASP:

```
Set obj = _ Server.CreateObject("4abf2131-27c8-00bd-79fc-11bb114e8441")
```

Common sense should tell you, as it did them, that this approach would be loaded with hardships for the average programmer. Not only would developers need to remember long strings of arcane characters just to make use of simple objects, but the slightest typo would cause the complete failure of their applications.

For this reason, COM includes routines that can look up the GUIDs associated with various components based on the shorter, more natural names developers choose for them. So, in the preceding example where the developer is attempting to instantiate a StarTrek.TransporterControl component, the flow of events is as follows:

1. ASP interprets the request for creation of the StarTrek.TransporterControl object.

2. IIS requests that COM instantiate one instance of the StarTrek.TransporterControl class.

3. COM searches the Windows registry for an entry for this class.

4. If it finds an entry, it gets the GUID for the class; otherwise it returns an error.

5. COM uses the GUID to search the registry for the filename and location of the code for this class.

6. If it finds an entry, it creates the object from the file; otherwise it returns an error.

7. If the file contains an appropriate COM object, the new instance is passed back to IIS; otherwise an error is generated.

8. IIS passes a handle to the new object instance back to ASP.

A naïve Active Server Pages developer might believe that simply copying a given DLL, OCX, or EXE file onto their Web server will be sufficient to allow their scripts on that server to use whatever COM components those files contain. This thinking is wrong. If you examine the steps outlined above, you can see that having the required files on a machine is sufficient to satisfy only the requirements of step 7. But to get to step 7, COM must first pass through steps 3, 4, 5, and 6. These are the steps on which instantiation will fail unless you first register your COM components.

Registering with RegSvr32

Registering a component with Windows creates the required entries in the Windows registry in order for the lookups described above to succeed. The simplest way to register the components in a given file is often to use the command-line tool known as RegSvr32. This tool is included as part of Windows 2000.

To begin learning about RegSvr32, first start the Windows command interpreter. If you aren't sure how to do this, just choose Run from the Windows Start menu and enter **cmd**, as shown here:

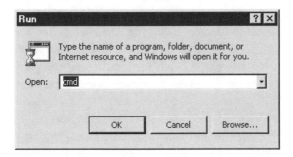

Once you are at a command prompt, just type **regsvr32**, and you should be presented with this dialog box:

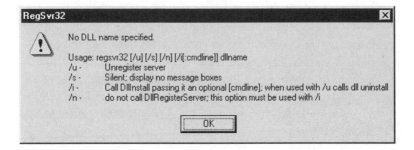

(If your system complains that it can't find this file, search your hard disks for an executable named REGSVR32.EXE. Typically, it is found in the Windows system directory.)

The most basic use of RegSvr32 occurs without any options at all. In order to register the COM components in a given file on your system, run the following command:

```
Regsvr32 <filename>
```

For example, in order to register whatever components were in a file called STRTRK.DLL, you would enter

```
Regsvr32 strtrk.dll
```

One option on the list that might prove particularly useful is */s*. Using this switch, you can suppress the generation of any Windows dialog boxes in response to your registration attempts. This would be particularly helpful if you ever wanted to create a batch file to automate the registration of several COM components on multiple machines. If dialog boxes were generated after every registration attempt, a batch file would pause at each point and wait for user input. Using the /s option, however, you can prevent this and keep your batch jobs rolling.

Error Watch *If you think that a particular COM component may already have been registered on a system, you should always first call RegSvr32 with the /u option to unregister it before attempting to register it again. This way, you can prevent duplicate (often mangled) entries in the Windows registry. To unregister the COM components in the file STRTRK.DLL, enter **Regsvr32 /u strtrk.dll**.*

Registering via Visual Basic

You can also register COM components on your system directly from Visual Basic, if you're building your components in this development environment. Visual Basic automatically registers the COM components in ActiveX DLL and ActiveX EXE projects whenever those projects are compiled. Therefore, all you have to do to register your components from Visual Basic is to compile successfully.

To compile an ActiveX DLL or ActiveX EXE under Visual Basic, follow this procedure:

1. Start Visual Basic.
2. Open the Project or Project Group containing the components you wish to register.
3. If you have opened a Project Group, select the specific Project containing your components from the Project Navigator.
4. Open the File menu.

5. Select Make.

6. Choose an appropriate location for the EXE or DLL file.

7. Choose an appropriate name for the EXE or DLL file.

Following these steps creates your DLL or EXE file and registers your components. The name that you use to access your components is not related to the filename you have chosen. Instead, it will be the name of the project followed by the name of the class within that project. So, in the case of the component StarTrek.TransporterControl, we can deduce that *StarTrek* is the name of the ActiveX DLL or EXE project that was compiled under Visual Basic. *TransporterControl* is the name of one class within this project.

Figuring Out Component Dependencies

It is very rare in the world of modern software design for any piece of code to exist and function in complete isolation from all other software. Many applications exist almost entirely as loose associations of several independent components, using the distributed capabilities of DCOM to glue themselves together into a useful whole. Most nondistributed applications feature at least one central executable, regardless of how many libraries might be supporting it.

Active Server Page developers often think of DLL and OCX files as being self-contained and incapable of having their own dependencies. For this reason, they often copy such files from their development to production Web servers and assume that they will be able to use them as soon as they have properly registered them on their target systems. This is often not the case, however.

Components such as those found in DLL and OCX files are designed to run within the process space of whatever executable loads them into memory. Other than this, they are much the same as standalone executables. They are completely capable of requesting that other components be loaded into memory in order to provide functionalities that they require.

If you move a component to another computer and register it without bringing across all of the components that it relies on and registering them as well, you will get an error. The most common message produced by Active Server Pages in this situation is the rather cryptic declaration shown in Figure 7-1.

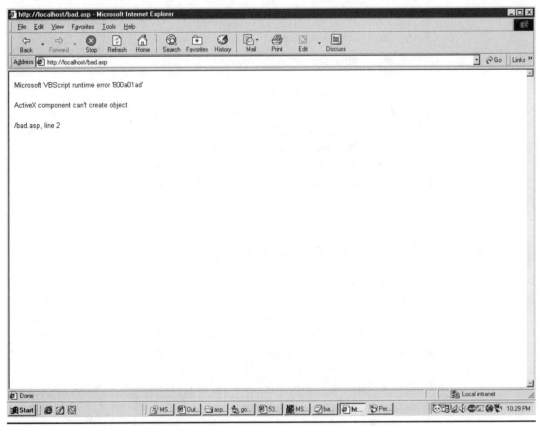

Figure 7.1 A missing dependency error

Source Code Inspection

In order to properly move a component from one system to another, you must make sure to move all of the components that a component is itself dependent on. If you are the author of the component that must be moved, this process might be relatively straightforward. You can begin by examining the source code to see what components you have referenced.

For example, under Visual Basic, many of the components that are required by your custom components will be listed under the References dialog, as shown in Figure 7-2.

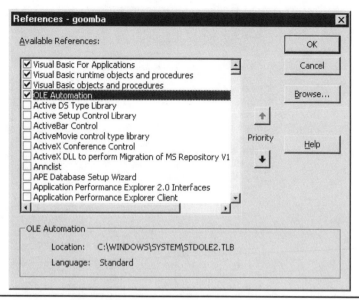

Figure 7.2   The Visual Basic References dialog

The list at the top of the dialog shows many of the components on your system that are available for use within your own creations. The ones with checkmarks next to them (usually at the top of the list) are those currently being used by your application. The exact paths to the physical files that contain these components appear at the bottom of the dialog whenever you highlight their entries in the list at the top. This information can be useful for gathering all the files that you need to distribute with your components.

Whereas the References dialog focuses on components in DLL and EXE files, the Components dialog tends to revolve more around controls found in OCX files. These are the visible ActiveX controls that are typically placed directly onto forms for interaction with end-users. Figure 7-3 shows what the Components dialog looks like.

Like the References dialog, the components with checkmarks next to them here are the ones that are actually being used by your current project.

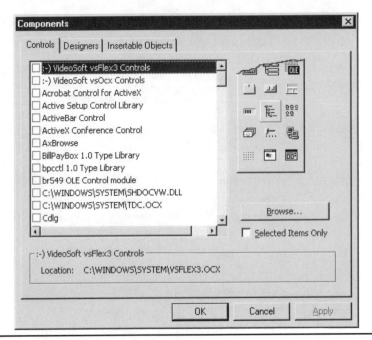

Figure 7.3   The Visual Basic Components dialog

The Dumpbin Tool

What happens when you need to use a component in your Active Server Pages for which you don't have the source code? This situation is increasingly likely due to the profusion of third-party components for COM-enabled applications. It is not uncommon to purchase components intended to serve single, small functions (such as sending e-mails) and receive nothing with their purchase in the form of either source code or documentation.

In these instances, the best course of action is to always install whatever components you have purchased by using their own custom setup applications. These are typically furnished to you at the time of component purchase and are usually (but not always) named SETUP.EXE. Other variations on this name are INSTALL.EXE, WINSTALL.EXE, and SETUP32.EXE.

Installation programs typically know about all of the files that their components depend on. When these programs aren't available, however, you must resort to the use of additional tools to try to discover what these dependencies are. The oldest, simplest, and most established of these tools is Dumpbin. It is included as part of the Windows Platform SDK and comes on the CD for Visual C++.

Using Dumpbin is particularly easy:

1. Locate DUMPBIN.EXE on your local drive system (usually, it is at Program Files\Microsoft Visual Studio\vc98\bin).

2. Locate the physical file containing the component for which you wish to locate dependencies.

3. Enter the following command:

```
Dumpbin /imports <filename>
```

4. Examine the output generated for the phrase, "Section contains the following imports…" Each section marked by this phrase should contain a list of DLL files required by your component to execute

The Depends Tool

With a utility like Dumpbin, you might think that the days of missing dependencies are completely over. Unfortunately, as good as the Dumpbin utility is, it still falls short of showing the complete dependency information for the components used by your Active Server Pages. In order to understand why this is, you must first understand the difference between staticly and dynamically linked components.

A staticly linked component is joined with the code for your own components when they are compiled. The advantage to this is that these kinds of files always show up in the output of Dumpbin. The disadvantage is that they can dramatically increase the memory requirements of your own components. This is because they are always loaded along with your components at the start of your own components' life cycles.

Dynamically linked components offer much greater flexibility because they are not loaded into memory until your own components specifically request them. This dramatically reduces the memory requirements for your components, because not all the components on which they depend need to be in memory at the same time. The down side to this, however, is that dynamically loaded components are *not* included in Dumpbin's output.

For this reason, Microsoft has created an additional utility known as Depends. Depends is a GUI application included with the Microsoft Platform SDK and Visual Studio. Using it is a little different from using Dumpbin. The following steps describe how to use the Depends tool.

1. Locate DEPENDS.EXE on your local drive system (it is usually at Program Files\Microsoft Visual Studio\Common\Tools).

2. Execute the program.

3. From the File menu, choose Open.

4. From the Profile menu, choose Start Profiling. Your screen should look like Figure 7-4.

5. Under Program Arguments, enter whatever command is required in order to start software that can use your component.

6. Choose the correct Starting Directory for this component.

7. Click OK.

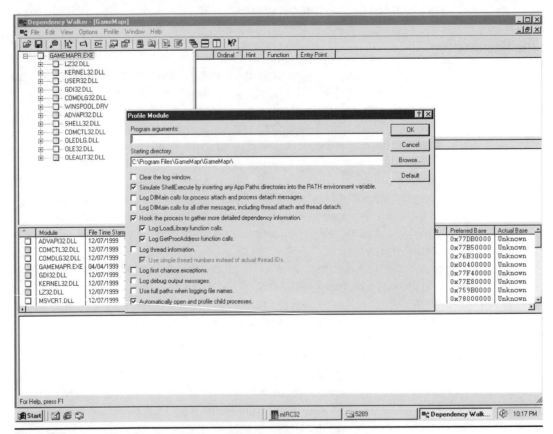

Figure 7.4 Using the Depends tool to gather dependency information

8. Use your application in every way imaginable, so that you can be sure every action that might request the loading of a dynamic component has been called.

9. As you use your component, notice the list of events generated at the bottom of the window.

10. If any error messages pop up regarding missing components, note that these dynamic files must be installed for your component to operate correctly

The Package and Deployment Wizard

The absolute best way to distribute components from one computer to another is through the use of Visual Studio's Package and Deployment Wizard. The Package and Deployment Wizard is capable of using the information stored in your projects to build lists of every component required in order for them to continue functioning. It is able to do this partially through the data contained in your References and Components dialogs, but also through the use of dependency files.

Dependency files are specially formatted text files that are capable of telling development environments (such as Visual Basic) what components are required by components being used in projects. In order to see what some dependency files looks like, just search your hard drives for files ending in .DEP. There are typically several of them in the Windows system directory. Once you have a few, open one inside of Notepad. It looks something like this:

```
[StarTrek.Dll]
Dest=$(WinSysPath)
Register=$(DLLSelfRegister)
Version=1.0.32.44
Uses1=BuckRodgers.dll
Uses2=OuterLimits.Dll
Uses3=
CABFileName=Startrek.cab
CABDefaultURL=http://www.eviloscar.com/fake/controls
CABINFFile=StarTrek.inf
```

This file is basically telling any development environment that uses the components in StarTrek.DLL all about where they would like to be placed in the file system and what other files they require in order to operate. If you ever got a dependency error under Active Server Pages and had access to this dependency file, you could immediately see that the two files required for successful operation are BUCKRODGERS.DLL and OUTERLIMITS.DLL.

Binding Support

The basis for all of Microsoft's COM technology is the requirement that every COM-compliant object implement an interface known as IUnknown. Using just the methods in the IUnknown interface, a client application can discover all information necessary about the methods offered by a COM component, the parameters taken by those methods, and the types of data that they return.

Accessing the features of IUnknown requires that an application support many of the low-level pointer manipulations typically associated with languages such as C++, however. Active Server Pages cannot achieve this by itself. The COM specification therefore also stipulates that components may choose to offer support for another interface called IDispatch, which can offer the same kinds of run-time discovery of methods and their parameters.

Late Binding Versus Early Binding

Applications that can access COM components through the IUnknown interface can make use of what is known as *early binding*. Under early binding, the specific types of objects that variables will hold can be declared at the time a script is written. This allows the development environment to check at the time of a program's compilation to ensure that

- The type of object being declared is already registered on the system where it will be used.

- The code in the application doesn't do anything obvious to assign an improper object type to this variable.

By way of contrast, late-bound components are complete mysteries to the compiler until runtime. This is because the variables used to contain them are not declared to be of any specific type. Because Active Server Pages only support the Variant, non-specific data type, ASP applications cannot directly use early-binding and must instead use late-binding.

An Active Server Pages developer who attempted to use early binding in his application might write code that looked something like the following:

```
<%
   Option Explicit

   Dim obj as StarTrek.TransporterControl

   Set obj = new StartTrek.TransporterControl

   if not(obj.BeamUp("Spock")) then
      response.write "He's shown up with a beard!"
   else
      response.write "Spock transported successfully."
   end if
%>
```

Unfortunately, Active Server Pages do not support the IUnknown interface directly. The preceding script is, therefore, full of errors from start to finish. This is partially because, without support for the IUnknown interface, it would be impossible for ASP to correctly restrict the kinds of objects available for use with variables .

The other errors in this script involve the use of the keyword *new* in the lines that set the objects to point at new instances of their objects. Under Visual Basic, the keyword *new* is offered for use with components that offer early binding via IUnknown. Under Active Server Pages, this support is not available, so all new objects must be instantiated using the Server object's CreateObject method.

IDispatch

Without the ability to make use of the IUnknown interface, you are left with a development environment where you can only late-bind to your components. This means that there will be no way for your code to restrict at compile time the kinds of objects that might be assigned to any given variable. This is true of Active Server Pages, which neither support IUnknown nor compile scripts prior to their first use.

The solution to ASP's lack of support for IUnknown and early binding is usually reliance on the IDispatch interface and its late-binding capabilities. The preceding script sample, rewritten to utilize these technologies, might look something like this:

```
<%
   Option Explicit

   Dim obj
```

```
Set obj = Server.CreateObject("StarTrek.TransporterControl")

if not(obj.BeamUp("Spock")) then
    response.write "He's shown up with a beard!"
else
    response.write "Spock transported successfully."
end if
%>
```

As luck would have it, however, not all COM components support the IDispatch interface. Some COM components offer only the IUnknown interface and can, therefore, be used only with development environments where early binding is available. If you attempt to instantiate such a component from Active Server Pages using just the Server object's CreateObject method, you will get an error (refer to Figure 7-1).

If you see this error, you should try to verify that support for IDispatch is truly lacking from the component that you are trying to instantiate. The reason why it is important to determine this is because there are numerous other things that can produce the error message under Active Server Pages. If you have access to technical support or documentation for the component, you may refer to these sources for your answer. Otherwise, if you have access to the Visual Basic development environment, you can perform a simple test on your own.

To test a component under Visual Basic to determine whether it supports the IDispatch interface, first try declaring and instantiating the object using early binding.

```
Dim z as StarTrek.TransporterControls
Set z = new StarTrek.TransporterControls
```

If this works, you can be certain that the control has been properly registered, as some interaction with it via the IUnknown interface is possible. Now, change your code (as shown here) to utilize late binding and, therefore, IDispatch:

```
Dim z as Object
Set z = CreateObject("StarTrek.TransporterControls")
```

If the code now fails, you have conclusively proven that the problem with your component under Active Server Pages is the component's lack of support for the IDispatch interface.

24x7   Overcoming Lack of IDispatch Support

The most desirable course of action for an Active Server Pages developer is to avoid any components that don't support the IDispatch interface. Sometimes, though, a certain component provides a functionality that is just too valuable to pass up. In these cases, you might consider writing wrapper components that can be instantiated from ASP scripts and used to drive components that can't be instantiated from ASP.

Under Visual Basic, a short wrapper class for the Star Trek component used in the preceding examples might look like this:

```
Private z As StarTrek.TransporterControls

Private Sub Class_Initialize()
   Set z = new StarTrek.TransporterControls
End Sub

Public Function BeamUp(name As Variant) As Variant
    BeamUp = z.BeamUp
End Function
```

The "initialize" event of the Visual Basic component creates one instance of whatever object doesn't support the IDispatch interface. A procedure is then added to the Visual Basic object for each procedure in the component being wrapped. These procedures take whatever parameters are needed in order to invoke the wrapped component's procedures and return the appropriate results to the ASP script.

Java Objects as COM Components

The use of Java objects as COM components in your Active Server Pages presents several potential benefits to you as a developer. To begin with, the encapsulation of code within Java objects can facilitate the migration of those components to non-Windows platforms, should the need ever arise. Also, Java's heritage in the world of C++ has given it more of a true object-oriented nature than can be achieved through the use of Visual Basic or similar platform. Finally, Java objects operating as COM components can usually be recompiled and tested on the fly, without the need to restart the entire applications under which they operate.

The Microsoft Java SDK

The problems that most Active Server Page developers first encounter when attempting to use Java objects with their scripts are due to nonconformity between the Microsoft Java SDK and the rest of the Java tools available. In general terms, the Microsoft Java SDK and Visual J++ (the Java-creating portion of Visual Studio) both allow for the easy creation of Windows GUI applications using Java as a language rather than as a platform. The disadvantage is that it is very easy for a developer to create an application that uses Windows-specific features without even realizing that they are doing so. Often this isn't discovered until everything falls apart the first time someone tries to use such an application on a different platform, such as Unix.

The specific errors that developers often must deal with when using Java in ASP pages involve the proper compilation and testing of their Java code. Consider the following snippet:

```
public class UseMeWithASP
{
    public boolean isThisAlwaysTrue()
    {
        return true;
    }
}
```

In most Java documentation available in books and on the Internet, you would be instructed to place this class in a file named UseMeWithASP.java and compile it with the statement

```
Javac UseMeWithASP.java
```

Under Windows, things typically aren't case-sensitive. Creating this file as USEMEWITHASP.JAVA, therefore, might not seem to make much of a difference. Unfortunately, in this case it would. This bug can be extremely difficult to track down, because Windows developers are unaccustomed to looking for differences in the cases of filenames. Just remember this: Whenever the Java compiler complains that it can't find your source file, check that the capitalization of your class name, filename, and command-line parameter all match *exactly*.

The other error in the command is that Microsoft has chosen not to refer to their Java compiler as JAVAC. Instead, they have named it JVC. The preceding command should, therefore, be

```
Jvc UseMeWithASP.java
```

Similarly, Microsoft has created a Java run-time application that is a little different from the standard Java execution environment with which you may be familiar from Sun and other vendors. To execute a standalone Java program under Windows, you should type

```
Jview UseMeWithASP
```

This will only work, as with all implementations of Java, provided that the public class within the named file contains a public method named MAIN.

Design Tip *It is a very good idea to put a MAIN method inside every public class that you intend to use with Active Server Pages. The actions taken by any such method should provide a good test for every other method in every other class contained in the same file. The value of this is that, in the event something in the future should break, you have a quick and easy way to test every bit of this file's functionality without having to create a separate test application.*

The JavaReg Tool

After an ASP developer finally manages to get their Java component compiled and tested properly, they often attempt to jump right into using it with their scripts. In the case of the UseMeWithASP object described earlier, this might amount to dropping the .class file for it into the same directory as the following script and trying to execute it:

```
<%
   Option Explicit

   Dim obj

   Set obj = Server.CreateObject("UseMeWithASP.class")
   If obj.isThisAlwaysTrue() Then
      Response.Write "I guess it really *is* always true!"
   End If
%>
```

Trying to run this script will generate an error like this:

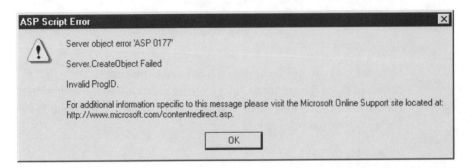

You might recall from previous discussions in this chapter that every COM component must first be registered on a system before it can be instantiated and used by Internet Information Server. The problem is that simply compiling a Java program and copying it to the same directory as your ASP scripts is not sufficient to register it as a COM component on your system. The only way to do this is through the JavaReg utility that is included as a part of the Microsoft Java SDK.

To use JavaReg to register the UseMeWithASP object as a COM component, you would enter something like this:

```
Javareg /register /class:UseMeWithASP /progid:UMWA.One
```

In this case, the UseMeWithASP.class file must be present in the directory where this command is executed. The /register option tells JavaReg that you wish to register any public classes in the file as COM components. If you wanted to remove their registry entries, you could use /unregister instead.

The final option, /progid, addresses the second problem with the ASP script shown earlier. The problem is that the developer has tried to instantiate the object by passing the name of the file containing it to the Server.CreateObject method. This is not what is expected by this method. Instead, the CreateObject method expects the ProgID of a registered COM component. In this case, that ProgID would now be UMWA.One.

```
<%
    Option Explicit

    Dim obj

    Set obj = Server.CreateObject("UMWA.One")
```

```
If obj.isThisAlwaysTrue() Then
    Response.Write "I guess it really *is* always true!"
End If
%>
```

Installing Class Files

To this point, everything has been done correctly in terms of coding your Java and ASPs and registering the proper Java objects as COM components. Frustratingly, if you attempt to run your script at this point, you will produce exactly the same error message as before. It is as if Windows were purposefully refusing to acknowledge the existence of your Java class files.

In fact, this is close to the truth. What is actually happening is not that Windows is specifically hiding these files, but that Internet Information Server just doesn't know where to look for them. Usually, Java files need to be on the classpath for a given system in order for them to be recognized and used by the Java runtime environment. In this case, however, it is not as clear—because it is not the standard Java runtime that will be executing your components.

IIS requires that any Java class files be in the trustlib directory if they are going to be called from Active Server Pages. This directory is typically found at \winnt\java\Trustlib on Windows 2000 machines. Once your class files are copied here, you should finally be able to run your ASP scripts without further difficulty.

Error Watch   *It is important that every .class file generated and/or needed by your Java components be positioned properly within the trustlib directory and/or its subdirectories. Developers often move over the main .class file for a component and forget the many other .class files on which it depends. If you make this mistake, you will continue to get errors until all of the required .class files are arranged appropriately under the trustlib directory.*

COM Component Security

Security concerns generally intensify as soon as COM components become a part of any Active Server Pages solution. For one thing, COM components can exert a much greater degree of control over the systems on which they run than any ASP page by itself. The Active Directory Services components, as an example, can alter user permissions and completely modify entire Windows directory structures. You have to be concerned about any technology that empowers developers at this level.

The security settings associated with COM components under Active Server Pages can be grouped into two large segments: those for in-process components and those for out-of-process components. Both of these groups have their own set of default permissions, which determine what components of their kind are typically allowed to do, barring further instructions. They also have identity settings, which determine who (in terms of Windows users) they look like to various and sundry security-monitoring mechanisms as they execute.

In-Process Components

An *in-process* component is a COM object that runs entirely within the process space of another application. Usually, the application within which it executes is the application that first requested its instantiation. Sometimes, though, an object can be configured to run within the Microsoft Component Services process. You will learn more about Microsoft Component Services in Chapter 9.

The default permissions for COM components that run in-process are typically the lightest in terms of Active Server Pages. On the other hand, their default identity is usually one of the least powerful.

Default Permissions

By default, every in-process COM component on a given system may be instantiated by every Active Server Page script running on the same system. This means that, as an administrator, unless you take specific measures to the contrary, any component that you register for use with one application may also be used by every other application on the same server. This may not be a good idea in all cases.

Imagine the following scenario:

```
<%
   Option Explicit
   Dim doomsday
   Set doomsday = Server.CreateObject("doomsday.bomb")
   doomsday.explode
%>
```

This script is imagined as a way of automating the process of starting a full-scale thermonuclear war. Under proper password protection, it should be accessible only to the president of the United States, so that if anything went horribly wrong while he (or she) was away from the office, he (or she) could always use it remotely. Unfortunately, without further administrative action, the doomsday.bomb component would be just as accessible from every other script on the same server.

To prevent this, follow this procedure:

1. Find the DLL or OCX file containing the component that you would like to secure.

2. Bring up the properties for this file and select the Security tab.

3. Limit the Read & Execute permissions for this component so that it matches the list of users allowed to execute the appropriate ASP application shown earlier.

Identity

In the absence of instructions to the contrary, in-process components executed under Active Server Pages will operate under the special System account. The System account has full access to all the resources of a given machine, such as the entire file system. It does not, however, have access to any network resources, such as drives shared from other computers. This can, in many cases, be too much freedom in some ways and too little freedom in other ways.

The best way to change the identity of an in-process component is to configure it to run under Microsoft Component Services. The procedure for doing this is described in detail in Chapter 9.

Out-of-Process Components

An *out-of-process* component is a COM object that runs entirely within its own process space. This may mean that a new process is created for each instance of the same COM component instantiated by Active Server Pages. For this reason, ASP developers tend to regard out-of-process components as resource hogs and to shy away from their use.

However, components run out-of-process are less likely to cause disruption to other pieces of your system in the event of their failure. This is because they execute in their own process spaces, almost completely isolated from the process space where your scripts execute (Internet Information Server).

There are some special permissioning issues surrounding the use of out-of-process components in Active Server Pages. There are also some special restrictions on out-of-process components that can make it very difficult to change the identity under which they execute.

Default Permissions

By default, you cannot use out-of-process components from Active Server Pages. This is because of the way that IIS comes configured to run out of the box. As I alluded to earlier, many system administrators feel that out-of-process components can place too great a performance burden on their servers. One reason for this is the tendency for out-of-process components to create one new process for every instance of their objects in use. On an ASP application with several hundred users and many pages, this can become far to great a load for most servers to sustain.

Even on relatively low-traffic servers, the nature of out-of-process components will always cause them to exert more of a drain on system resources than similar components that are used in-process. This is because, with out-of-process components, procedure calls and other messages must be passed between the IIS process and the process space of the component in question. This cross-process communication is very resource-intensive and costly to performance.

On the other hand, passing messages between IIS and components running in-process is relatively straightforward and painless. This is because whatever components are running in-process are actually running as a part of IIS itself. Therefore, any messages that need to be passed can be handled within the same process space and do not need to pass through process barriers.

If, even in consideration of all this, you still want to use out-of-process components as a part of your Active Server Pages solution, you may at first need to set the AllowOutOfProcCmpnts registry setting to reflect this fact. This is because, prior to Windows 2000, IIS restricted the use of out-of-process components. If you are using IIS 3 or IIS 4 and do not first set this registry setting, you will get an error from IIS suggesting that you do so the first time that you try to use an out-of-process component in your scripts.

To change this registry setting

1. Choose Run from the Windows Start menu.

2. Type **regedt32** to invoke the Registry Editor (see Figure 7-5).

3. Select the Window labeled HKEY_LOCAL_MACHINE.

4. Expand the SYSTEM node in the tree control to the left.

5. Expand the CurrentControlSet node.

6. Expand Services.

7. Expand W3SVC.

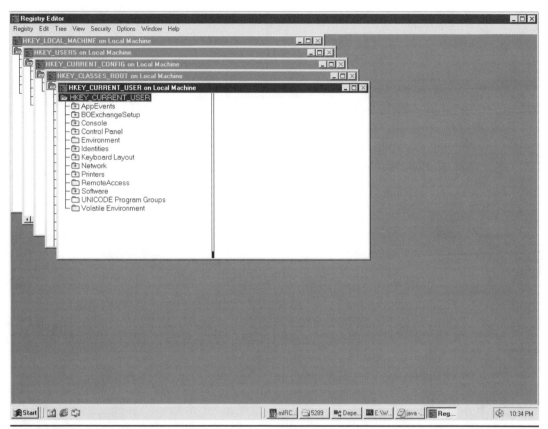

Figure 7.5 The Registry Editor

8. Expand ASP.

9. Expand Parameters.

10. On the right-hand side of the window, double-click the entry for AllowOutOfProcCmpnts.

11. Type **1** in the Data text field.

12. Click OK.

13. Close the Registry Editor.

14. Restart your computer.

Identity

Components running out-of-process under Active Server Pages typically execute as the user IWAM_<machine>. For example, on a machine known as BEEFJERKY, an out-of-process component would usually execute under the IWAM_BEEFJERKY user account. Anything that this user was allowed to do by the permissions of the system where IIS was running would be allowed for this component. Anything that this account was not allowed to do would be forbidden for this component.

For example, consider this script:

```
<%
   Option Explicit
   Dim fs, fl
   Set fs = Server.CreateObject("Scripting.FileSystemObject")
   Set fl = fs.GetFile("e:\blah.txt")
   fl.close
%>
```

This script would fail with a security error if the IWAM_BEEFJERKY account lacked access to the BLAH.TXT file on its local disk storage. One way to address this might be to add the IWAM_BEEFJERKY account to the list of accounts with access permissions for this file. But perhaps you don't want this to happen. Perhaps there are other things that run under this same account that you *don't* want to be able to access this file. What can you do now?

The obvious answer is to change the account under which your component is executing to something other than IWAM_BEEFJERKY. In the section on in-process components, we suggested that you do this by configuring your component to run under Microsoft Component Services, which is explained fully in Chapter 9. Unfortunately, out-of-process components can't run under Microsoft Component Services, so we will need to find another way to achieve our goals.

The simplest way to make this happen is to use the dcomcnfg utility that is built into Windows 2000. Usually, this is used to set up components for remote access. Fortunately, it happens to provide exactly the kind of identity-switching capabilities that we need for components, whether they run remotely or locally.

1. Choose Run from the Windows Start menu.

2. Type **dcomcnfg** to invoke the Registry Editor and open the Distributed COM Configuration Properties dialog (see Figure 7-6).

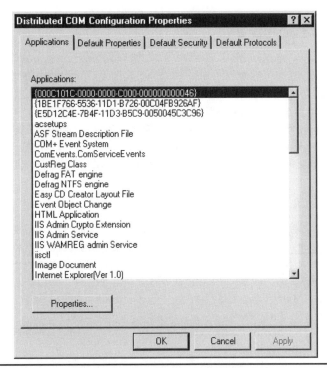

Figure 7.6   The Distributed COM Configuration Properties dialog

3. Select your component on the scrollable selection list.

4. Click Properties.

5. Go to the Identity tab.

6. Select This User.

7. Enter the user's name (with domain) in the User field. Use the Browse button if you'd like to make sure that you have formatted everything correctly.

8. Enter this user's password into the Password and Confirm Password fields.

9. Click OK to confirm your changes.

Your component will run under the account you have chosen from now on.

Invoking Procedures

COM components are often best thought of in the context of object-oriented programming and design. Like objects, COM components feature interfaces that are composed of numerous methods for effecting changes upon the internal state of the component. A COM component that represents a bank account, for example, might feature an interface called ITransactions. The various methods upon this interface would all change the data stored inside of the component in different ways: withdrawal, deposit, overdraft, and so on.

Type Conversions

Although COM components features interfaces and methods just like regular objects, the exact way in which these methods are called is slightly unusual under Active Server Pages. The main reason for these differences is the lack of support for specific data types under VBScript. This typically causes errors for ASP developers when they attempt to use their scripts with components that expect specific data types.

Standard Data Types

Most advanced development platforms, such as Java or Visual Basic, support the concept of specific data types. This means that variables are declared as storing information only of a specific kind. Any attempt to store data of a different kind into these variables results in a trappable run-time error.

```
Public Function addNumbers(a As Integer, b As Integer) As Integer
    addNumbers = a + b
End Function
```

This function is written in Microsoft Visual Basic. It takes two parameters, both of which must be integers, and returns a single integer as a result. You can tell from the single line of code that constitutes the body of this procedure that the result returned is the sum of the two parameters.

Under Visual Basic, you can write code like this to utilize a method like this on a COM component:

```
Option Explicit

Sub main()
   Dim ans as Integer

   Dim obj as Mathematics.SimpleComponent
   Set obj = new Mathematics.SimpleComponent

   ans = obj.addNumbers(2,2)
   msgbox "The answer is " & cstr(ans)
End Sub
```

When Everything Is a Variant

The preceding code would not function under VBScript because, as discussed earlier, VBScript supports only the Variant data type. This can lead to serious errors if Variant data is passed to the component, rather than integers.

```
<%
   Option Explicit
   Dim ans, obj
   Set obj = Server.CreateObject("Mathematics.SimpleComponent")
   ans = obj.addNumbers(2,2)
   response.write "The answer is " & ans
%>
```

This code will work, because automatic casting allows the integer returned by the component to be contained by the Variant variable *ans*. The two parameters being passed to this function are both constants (2 and 2), and they are therefore completely capable of being treated as integers.

The only problem is that most Active Server Page scripts don't run based on constants that are defined at the time they are written. Most require and operate on input from end-users, which is where it all starts to collapse.

```
<%
   Option Explicit
   Dim a, b, ans, obj
   Set obj = Server.CreateObject("Mathematics.SimpleComponent")
   a = Request("FirstNumber")
   b = Request("SecondNumber")
   ans = obj.addNumbers(a,b)
   response.write "The answer is " & ans
%>
```

This rewrite will fail on the line that invokes the addNumbers function with this error:

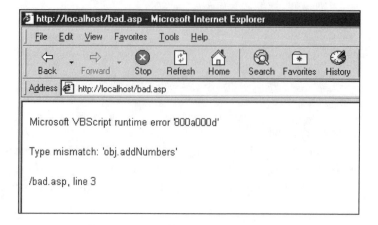

The reason for this is that the input received from the Response object has been stored in Variant variables and has, therefore, already been cast as a Variant when it is passed to the COM component. This is different from the Integer data type that the component is expecting. The only solution is to rewrite the component's method in a way that doesn't expect specific data types.

```
Public Function addNumbers(a As Variant, b As Variant) As Variant
    addNumbers = a + b
End Function
```

Mutability

When writing Active Server Pages that invoke methods on COM components, you should be mindful of design decisions that can adversely affect your applications' performance. The decision of whether to pass parameters to these procedures "by value" or "by reference" is key to many of these performance optimizations.

ByVal

Whenever you work with a COM component that is either out-of-process or remote, you should try to make every parameter passed "by value." Under VBScript (and Visual Basic) this is accomplished by adding the keyword ByVal in front of the parameters in your method declarations.

```
Public Function addNumbers(ByVal a As Variant, ByVal b As Variant) As Variant
    addNumbers = a + b
End Function
```

The benefit to using a ByVal declaration with a remote or out-of-process component is that it causes actual copies of the data to be sent across the process (and/or network) boundaries, rather than specialized pointers to the data that remain within the client application. Because of the effort involved in maintaining such pointers across process (and/or network) boundaries, it actually winds up being easier to transmit the entire set of parameter data.

ByRef

Whenever you work with a COM component that is in-process, you might want to consider passing parameters "by reference." Under VBScript (and Visual Basic) this is accomplished by adding the keyword ByRef in front of the parameters in your method declarations.

```
Public Function addNumbers(ByRef a As Variant, ByRef b As Variant) As Variant
    addNumbers = a + b
End Function
```

The benefit to using ByRef declarations with in-process components is that they only transmit pointers to the data within the client application, rather than all of the data itself. Because it is easy to maintain pointers within a single process space, it winds up being much less resource-intensive than passing all the data itself.

Design Tip   *In general, it is a bad idea to pass any more parameters "by reference" than your code absolutely requires. The reason for this is that, if an error were to arise in your code resulting in improper values being stored in a given variable, it would be nice to have limited the number of places where this error might occur. The more procedures you have passed this variable to "by reference," the more procedures need to be checked for errors.*

Storing COM Objects

Three main kinds of storage are available under Active Server Pages. *Page-level storage* is the sort that can be accessed by dimensioning a variable within your script and assigning a value to it. This value can be a simple data type or an instance of an object.

```
<%
    Option Explicit
    Dim x, obj

    x = 32
    Set obj = Server.CreateObject("Pully.Harness")
%>
```

Session-level storage is the sort that can be accessed via the methods and properties of the intrinsic Session object. There is one Session object for each unique client accessing your ASP application at any given point in time.

```
<%
    Session("FavoriteColor") = "Blue"
    Set Session("ToolObject") = Server.CreateObject("Pully.Harness")
%>
```

Application-level storage is the sort that can be accessed via the methods and properties of the intrinsic Application object. There is only one Application object for an entire ASP application, so data stored into this object can be read and overwritten by all the different clients and scripts in an application.

```
<%
    Application("NumberOfVisits") = Application("NumberOfVisits") + 1
    Set Application("DBConn") = Server.CreateObject("ADODB.Connection")
%>
```

There are various pros and cons to using each of these kinds of storage with COM components. The following table compares them:

	Positives	Negatives
Page-Level Storage	Less storage required than at Session levels	Frequent instantiations.
Session-Level Storage	Less frequent instantiations	Most storage required—one object for every client using your application. Apartment-threaded components can only be handled by the thread that made their Session.
Application-Level Storage	Least storage required; very few instantiations	Apartment-threaded components can only be handled by the thread that made the Application. Only one instance of any component is available for the entire application.

The general impression this table should give you is that Page-level storage for your objects is generally a good choice with few drawbacks. In the special case of a single object that is likely to be shared by every script in an application, such as a database connection, it might make more sense to put your objects in Application-level storage. Because of the restrictions on Apartment-threaded components, however, you should try to avoid their use with either Session- or Application-level storage.

Creating COM Objects for Active Server Pages

In Chapter 7, you learned about some problems that many developers get into when they first start using COM objects in their Active Server Pages. We assumed in that chapter that these components already existed when the ASP developer first decided that he or she wanted to use them. Perhaps, for example, the components were available for purchase from a third party component vendor, or maybe the creator of the components was simply another developer working for the same organization.

Often, however, the task of building such components falls upon the same developer who is building the ASP scripts to use them. In this scenario, the construction of the COM components becomes an issue of direct relevance to the creation of bug-free Active Server Page applications. For this reason, in this chapter you will learn about some of the most common mistakes ASP programmers make when creating COM components for use with their scripts.

Component Locking

Active Server Page applications come in a form that is one of the easiest to modify in the whole world of computers: simple text. Often, developers create their ASP scripts in a simple text editor such as Notepad. You can then load these pages immediately into a Web browser in order to verify that they are operating as expected. No compilation is even required, because Active Server Pages are interpreted as they are loaded into Internet Information Server.

All this can change, however, when you begin making COM components a part of your ASP solutions. In the case of in-process components, making modifications can be complicated by the location of your code within the process boundaries of other applications. It is common to find that components in use by other applications are "locked," preventing you from making any changes to their code!

DLL Files

In-process COM components are most often contained within dynamically linked library (DLL) files. The locking problems that developers typically encounter when working with these files are distinct and differ somewhat from those encountered when working with executable (EXE) files.

First, we'll cover the major symptoms of the problems typically associated with DLL locking. Then you will learn possible ways in which you can circumvent such problems.

Consider the following sequence of events:

1. A developer constructs a COM component and compiles it to a dynamically linked library called COMP3.DLL.

2. The developer now writes a script in Active Server Pages that instantiates and uses a COM component from the COMP3.DLL. file.

3. The ASP page is executed once, and it is discovered that the COM component is not acting exactly as required.

4. The developer modifies the code for the COM component and attempts to recompile it.

5. The developer receives this error:

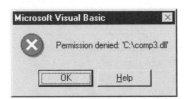

The reason for this error is that the components found in a DLL or OCX file are loaded into the memory space of their client process the first time that they are instantiated. This is why they are known as in-process components. The catch is that the code for these files may remain loaded into the memory space of the client process long after their components have ceased being used.

This is usually highly advantageous from a performance perspective. By retaining DLLs and OCXs in its memory, IIS saves itself a lot of work. If it didn't do this, it would have to load and unload entire files every time a client requested a page that used COM components. Instead, IIS loads these files only the very first time a script is executed that requires the COM component(s) within them. The process is shown in Figure 8-1.

Although this strategy is much better for performance, it complicates the work of Active Server Page developers trying to write COM components for use in their scripts. Many programmers come to the conclusion that they must either

- Get their COM components to function perfectly the first time they write them, or

- Restart their servers every time that they want to modify a COM component.

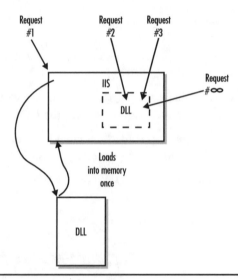

Figure 8.1   IIS loads a DLL into memory only once

Fortunately, there are better ways...

Testing Your COM Components outside of ASP

It is unrealistic to expect developers to get their COM component code 100 percent correct the very first time they write it. Anyone who has done even the slightest bit of programming should be able to understand this instantly. For this reason, the first possibility suggested earlier can be largely discounted. It raises one interesting point, though: How can ASP developers test the functionality of their COM components without going through the hassle of having them loaded into IIS?

If your COM component has been written in Java or C++, a good approach might be to add a *main* method to each of your classes. Properly written, this main method should attempt a wide variety of actions on the methods and properties of the object. If you output the results of these attempts to standard output, then this method can be executed from the command line if you ever need to test the component.

```
public class Car
{
    public static void main(String args[])
    {
        Car x = new Car();
        x.honkTheHorn();
        if (x.wipeTheWindshield())
```

```
        {
            System.out.println("Windsheild wipers working well!");
        }
    }

    public void honkTheHorn()
    {
        System.out.println("BEEP! BEEP, I tell you!!");
    }

    public boolean wipeTheWindshield()
    {
        return true;
    }
}
```

This is one example of how you might implement such a test harness using Java. Notice that the main method calls every public method available within the class. The honkTheHorn() method produces output on its own which is sufficient to verify that it is functioning correctly. For wipeTheWindshield(), however, a specific console output has been added to the main routine to let the user know that everything is working okay.

Unfortunately, in-process COM components created under Visual Basic do not support the concept of a main procedure. The reason for this has to do with the nature of the files where such components are stored. Historically, DLL files have been used for the storage of function libraries that could be called from separate applications, typically written in C or C++. The concept of a main routine occurring within a function library is not supported under either of those languages. It was not, therefore, supported when Visual Basic began working with these types of files, either.

Fortunately, Visual Basic does allow for the creation of multiple projects within a single project group. This means that you may choose to create an ActiveX DLL project for use with your Active Server Pages. In order to test this component, you could then add a Standard EXE project that instantiates objects from your DLL project and puts them through their paces. In order to do this, follow these steps:

1. Start Visual Basic.

2. Either create a new ActiveX DLL project or open an existing one.

3. If you are creating a new ActiveX DLL project, add whatever code to it you would like to call from your Active Server Pages.

4. Select Add Project from the Visual Basic File menu.

5. Choose Standard EXE from the Add Project dialog.

6. In the Project Explorer window, right-click the icon representing your new project.

7. Click Set as Start Up.

8. Select References from the Visual Basic Project menu.

9. Locate the entry corresponding to your ActiveX DLL project and make sure that it is checked. (It should appear close to the top of the list.)

10. Add code to your Standard EXE project that instantiates objects from your DLL project and tries out all of their methods and properties.

Error Watch   *If you compile your DLL project, you may find more than one entry for your COM components in the References dialog for your EXE project. This is because one set of references will be pointing to the set of objects contained within the DLL project in the Visual Basic IDE. The other set of references will be pointing to the objects stored within the compiled DLL file. For testing purposes, you will always want to use the references that point to the Visual Basic IDE's objects. This will make it much easier to test your changes and follow your code's execution in the Visual Basic debugger!*

Unloading an Application

The testing just described can best be thought of as *unit testing*. This means that all you have really proven by completing the steps successfully is that your component functions appropriately in almost complete isolation. This is a good first step toward keeping your code bug-free, but more testing is required.

The next phase of testing in the construction of any information system is usually integration testing. Integration testing is the first point in the debugging of a system where all of the components must be shown to function correctly in cooperation with each other. Given the nature of this testing, you really can't consider it complete until you have successfully used your components extensively within your Active Server Pages themselves. This, of course, means that your components will be loaded into IIS's memory and process space.

If anything goes wrong at this point, you will need to unload your components from the IIS process space. The best way to do this depends upon the exact version of IIS that you are running.

Under IIS 4, follow this procedure to unload your DLLs from the server's process space:

1. Open the Internet Services Manager.

2. Locate the icon for the Web site using your DLLs and right-click it.

3. Choose Properties from the pop-up context menu.

4. If the box marked Run in Own Process Space is checked, uncheck it. If it is unchecked, then check it.

5. Click OK to close the dialog.

6. Repeat steps 2–5.

7. Unregister the component from your Web server using this console command:

   ```
   regsvr32 /u filename
   ```

8. Make your modifications to the code of the in-process component.

9. Recompile the component and copy it to your Web server (if it isn't already there).

10. Reregister the new copy of the component using this console command:

   ```
   Regsvr32 filename
   ```

Under IIS 5, follow this procedure to unload your DLLs from the server's process space:

1. Open the Internet Services Manager.

2. Locate the icon for the Web site using your DLLs and right-click it.

3. Choose Properties from the pop-up context menu.

4. Click Unload.

5. Unregister the component from your Web server using this console command:

   ```
   regsvr32 /u filename
   ```

6. Make your modifications to the code of the in-process component.

7. Recompile the component and copy it to your Web server (if it isn't already there).

8. Reregister the new copy of the component using this console command:

   ```
   Regsvr32 filename
   ```

Restarting IIS Service

In some very rare cases, the procedures just described may fail. For example, a component may become involved in a circular reference that prevents it from being unloaded by IIS. In a *circular reference*, a COM component (call it component A) creates an instance of another COM component (call it component B). The newly created component (B) is capable of obtaining a reference back to the first component (A), usually by having it passed as the parameter on some method call:

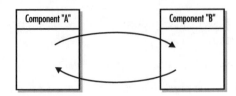

The problem becomes that component A can't be unloaded until B is unloaded (because of the open reference), and B can't be unloaded until A is unloaded (for the same reason). This creates a no-win situation leading to complete stalemate and no component unloading.

In such cases, the only way to regain control is often to completely stop and restart Internet Information Server. The mistake that Active Server Page developers often make in doing this is to only stop the Web server. This seems logical at first, since it is the Web server that runs Active Server Pages. In such a situation, however, matters cannot be rectified and components unloaded until the entire IIS application is restarted.

To restart IIS, follow this procedure:

1. Open Settings on the Windows Start menu.

2. Select Control Panel.

3. Double-click the Administrative Tools icon.

4. Double-click the Services icon.

5. Right-click the icon labeled IIS Admin Service.

6. Choose Stop from the pop-up context menu.

7. Unregister the component from your Web server using this console command:

   ```
   regsvr32 /u filename
   ```

8. Make your modifications to the code of the in-process component.

9. Recompile the component and copy it to your Web server (if it isn't already there).

10. Reregister the new copy of the component using this console command:

    ```
    Regsvr32 filename
    ```

11. Right-click the icon labeled IIS Admin Service.

12. Choose Start from the pop-up context menu.

If you get an error message at any point during the above process, it typically means that the damage inflicted by your component is too great for IIS to be restarted by itself. At this point, your best bet is simply to restart the entire server. This is one of the strongest arguments in favor of having at least one computer dedicated solely to serving as an Active Server Page development box. For more information, refer to Chapter 1.

EXE Files

In Chapter 6, you learned about some of the limitations of the ASP Response object. One of these limitations was, in fact, a limitation of the entire HTTP protocol: It is stateless. Because of its inherently stateless nature, Web servers and clients have placed limitations on the amount of time that they are willing to wait to receive responses to their requests. On clients, this is typically called a response timeout. On servers, this is usually a script-execution time limit.

Either of these limitations may become a problem if you have a COM component that takes a particularly long time to finish its work. One way to circumvent such limitations is to write your components in such a way that they accomplish most of their work under separate executables that they spawn off. Your components can then return their method calls immediately while their work is carried on under different processes.

Here is the listing for a small Active Server Page that instantiates a database maintenance COM component. It requests that all records from the start of 1997 to the end of 1999 be deleted.

```
<%
    Option Explicit
    Dim obj

    Set obj = Server.CreateObject("DBUtil.Kille")
    Call obj.delete(#1/1/1997#, #12/31/1999#)
    Response.Write "Deletion finished!"
%>
```

Now, on a system with many records, it is easy to imagine this process taking a very long time. So the method in the DBUtil.Killer component that implements the deletion calls another process to perform the task and return immediately.

```
public sub delete(startdate as date, enddate as date)
    Open "c:\instructions.txt" for output as #1
    Print #1, format(startdate, "MMDDYY")
    Print #1, format(enddate, "MMDDYY")
    Close #1

    g = shell("c:\deleteall.exe", true)
end sub
```

This is all good so far. The Active Server Page properly instantiates and invokes the object, which then creates instructions for a standalone process before kicking it off with the shell command. The component then returns control to the ASP, which prints out a message telling the user that their wishes have been fulfilled and the data is gone.

Imagine, however, if the actual standalone executable were coded in this fashion:

```
Sub main
    do until (false)
        ' Vital work goes on here
    loop
end sub
```

This is a problem because the loop described will never reach its end. Instead, the process will hang forever. You will notice this, because it will be listed on the Processes tab of the Windows Task Manager (see Figure 8-2).

The Processes tab of the Task Manager shows you every process currently executing on this Windows 2000 system. The best way to use this dialog to find hung processes is to click the top of the column labeled Image Name so that the Task Manager will sort all the entries this way. You can then quickly scan the rows for instances with Image Names that match the name of your programs' executables.

Over time these processes will accumulate. You will be able to see this because there will be many rows in the Task Manager that share your programs' executable names as their Image Names. The load on your Web server will become worse and worse until eventually the entire system will lock up. This is a very serious bug in the design of your ASP application!

Eliminating Hung Processes

The main difficulty in getting rid of these hung processes is that they belong to a different user. The exact user that they belong to is determined by the identity

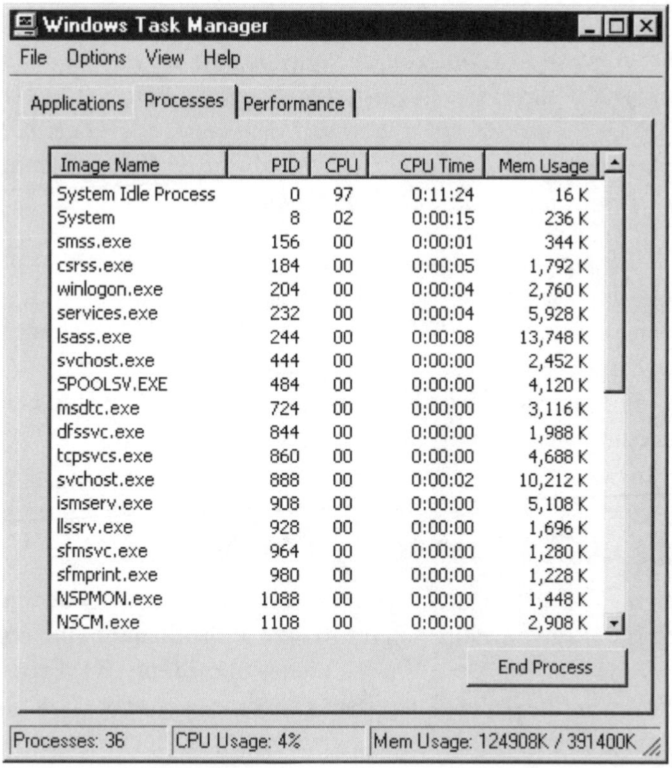

Figure 8.2 The Windows Task Manager

under which your COM component was running when it first spawned them. Unless you have taken steps to the contrary, in-process components will default to running under the identity of the System account. For more information on this, see the previous chapter on using COM components in your Active Server Pages.

There are two possibilities for eliminating hung processes:

- Make sure that your in-process component will run as a user account under which you can log in, or

- Restart your entire computer.

The second option is a no-brainer. It will, however, make you extremely unpopular with your system administrators. Once again, this is a strong argument in favor of reserving a box specifically for use in debugging your Active Server Page applications. See Chapter 1 for details.

Design Tip *Sometimes, COM components crash due to low-level problems with system libraries and other pieces of code that are not necessarily under the control of an ASP developer. A particularly good tool to use in sorting out these kinds of Access Control errors is WinDBG. You can learn all about this tool and download the latest version for free from the Microsoft Web site at http://msdn.microsoft. com/downloads/sdks/platform/windbg.asp.*

Getting your component to run under a different user account is a more interesting proposition. It is required because there is no way to log in to a Windows computer under the System account. This special account is used to represent the operating system as a whole, not any individual user.

For information on how you can get a component to execute under a user account other than System, see Chapter 9.

Resolving COM Dependency Problems

In the previous chapter, you learned about the many dependency issues Active Server Page developers have to deal with when moving components from one computer to another. When it comes to creating COM components from scratch, however, the dependency issues become even more complicated and difficult to debug. Some of these issues involve the nuances of resolving the references in your component projects. Others arise because of inappropriate choices in a project's compatibility settings.

Unrecognized References

Sometimes, as you create COM components for use with your Active Server Pages, you will encounter errors that complain about unrecognized references in your code. These errors typically refer to inconsistencies between the settings in your projects' References dialogs and their code. Sometimes these inconsistencies are conflicts between the names of multiple classes. Other times, the classes required by your components are missing from your projects' References dialogs altogether.

In this section, you will learn the details of both these kinds of problems and how you can resolve them to keep your Active Server Page applications bug free.

Conflicting Class Names

Under Active Server Pages, every COM component that a developer wants to instantiate must be referred to using a combination of its library and object names. In the following code snippet, the developer is requesting the creation of a Recordset object from the ADODB library:

```
<%
   Option Explicit
   Dim obj
   Set obj = Server.CreateObject("ADODB.Recordset")
%>
```

When ASP programmers move into creating their own COM components, they must completely relearn their approach to requesting object instantiations. Under Visual Basic, the intrinsic Server object is not typically part of creating new objects. Instead, VB developers use the keyword *new*.

```
Option Explicit

public function getRecordset()
   Dim obj as ADODB.Recordset
   Set obj = new ADODB.Recordset
   set getRecordset = obj
end sub
```

Assuming that the appropriate references have been set in the Visual Basic Reference dialog, the preceding code should compile and operate perfectly. However, many ASP programmers coming to Visual Basic for the first time fall into the very bad habit of dropping their library names altogether! This probably seems like a luxury under Visual Basic, since Active Server Pages would not tolerate this behavior for a second.

```
Option Explicit

public function getRecordset()
   Dim obj as Recordset
   Set obj = new Recordset
   Set getRecordset = obj
end sub
```

This code will compile and work appropriately if—and only if—an object named Recordset is contained within exactly one library referenced by the current Visual Basic project. So, if the project containing the above code had a reference set to the ActiveX Data Object library everything would work fine. And if the project instead had a reference to the Data Access Objects library, it would also work fine.

But if this project held references to both the ActiveX Data Object (ADO) library and the Data Access Object (DAO) libraries, then the COM object produced would be extremely dangerous to use in your ASP applications. The reason for this is that both of these libraries contain Recordset objects. Just by looking at the code, you have no way of knowing which kind of recordset is being instantiated, ADO or DAO.

You can figure out the answer to this question by looking at the specific ordering of the references in your COM component projects (see Figure 8-3).

When objects occur in more than one referenced library, the library that is highest on this list is the library referred to by any otherwise ambiguous references. So, in this case, the recordset would be an ADO recordset. This could cause very difficult-to-find bugs in your Active Server Pages if you ever tried to use the recordset returned from such a method *as if it were from a different library!*

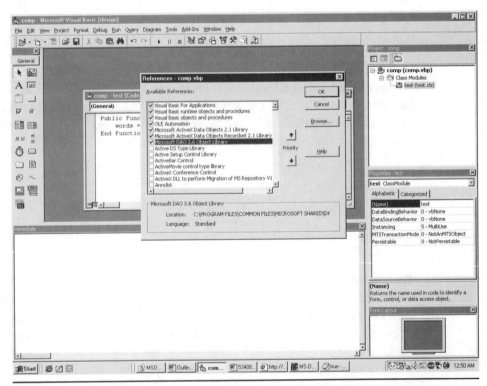

Figure 8.3   Using the References dialog to determine the order of references in your COM component projects

```
<%
  Option Explicit
  Dim obj, rst

  Set obj = Server.CreateObject("Custom.RecordsetMaker")
  Set rst = obj.getRecordset()
  if rst.connection is null then
     response.write "No connection!"
  end if
%>
```

The problem with this code is that it is trying to use the connection property that is found on DAO recordsets. Unfortunately, because of the way that the ambiguous reference was resolved, the recordset that has been returned is an ADO recordset. This would be largely impossible to troubleshoot just by looking at the code for the getRecordset method. Therefore, when writing COM components for use with Active Server Pages, you should always use the full library and class name combinations when instantiating objects.

Missing References

Missing references are another problem that many ASP programmers encounter when they first begin writing their own COM objects. Fortunately, although this problem will stop your development dead in the water, it is relatively easy to recognize and resolve.

To continue with the example started in the previous section, what would happen if neither reference had been set? What if the Recordset object being instantiated did not occur as a member of any of the libraries listed in the References dialog for your VB project? In this case, Visual Basic would generate an error the first time you tried to compile your project:

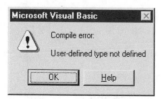

All you need to do to resolve this situation is add a reference for the library containing the class from which you would like to create objects.

Compatibility Settings

It is the rare COM component that spends its entire life in exactly the same state. COM components that are poorly designed and/or implemented usually prompt requests for patches, maintenance, and other kinds of code changes. However, components that are well thought-out and written tend to be very popular and spawn numerous requests for enhancements and extensions.

Developers used to working with Active Server Pages are typically unfamiliar with the myriad issues that can arise when creating new versions of existing component software. In this section, you will learn about a few of the options Visual Basic provides to assist ASP developers in this way.

Consider the case of a simple Active Server Page using a very simple COM component.

```
<%
    Option Explicit
    Dim obj
    Set obj = Server.CreateObject("Messages.Happy")
    Response.Write obj.Greeting
%>
```

This code creates an instance of an object from the Messages.Happy class and sends the data returned by its Greeting method to the intrinsic Response object's Write method.

```
public function Greeting()
    Greeting = "Yay!!"
end function
```

As you can see, the code contained within the component for this method is really nothing special in its current state. It simply returns the constant text "Yay!!" every time that your ASP scripts call it.

Visual Basic supports a number of compatibility options to support the ongoing evolution of components such as this. In order to take a look at these options, follow this procedure:

1. Open your ActiveX DLL project under the Visual Basic IDE.

2. At the bottom of the Project menu, select Properties.

3. Select the Component tab on the Project Properties dialog (see Figure 8-4).

4. Examine the three options located in the Version Compatibility frame at the bottom of the dialog. The following sections describe these options.

No Compatibility

If you haven't compiled your project yet, the option you'll most likely select here is No Compatibility. If you use this option, then Visual Basic will offer no special assistance in preparing new versions of your software component. This option may be fine for many ASP developers, depending on how you plan to test new versions of your component.

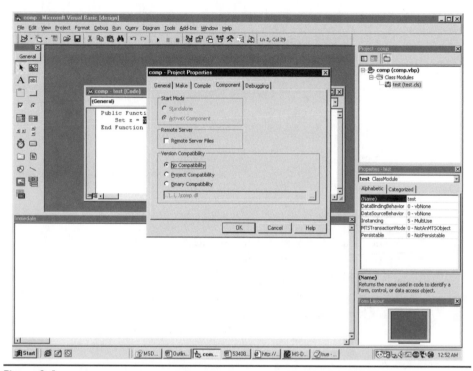

Figure 8.4   The Project Properties dialog

Earlier in this chapter, you learned about the locking difficulties that often accompany the use of in-process components with Active Server Pages. If you compile a component, load an ASP that uses it into your browser, and discover that it hasn't performed exactly the way that you would like, you must first unload the component from IIS before you can recompile it. If you can do this conveniently (probably meaning that you have set up a dedicated ASP testing server), the No Compatibility option should work fine for you.

Project Compatibility

Most developers feel that the burden of unloading COM components from IIS every time that they want to modify them is simply too great. The quickest alternative for many of these developers is simply to test their components thoroughly under the Visual Basic IDE before they ever attempt to use them within their Active Server Pages. You learned earlier in this chapter that the quickest way to accomplish this is by making use of VB's capability to bring EXE and DLL projects together within the same project group. The appropriate compatibility option for this approach to COM development is Project Compatibility.

To see why, suppose that you added a Standard EXE project to a Visual Basic IDE that already contained the component shown above. This EXE might start off looking similar to the Active Server Page code within which you would ultimately like the component to run.

```
Option Explicit

sub main()

    Dim obj as Messages.Happy
    Set obj = new Messages.Happy
    Debug.Print obj.Greeting

end sub
```

The idea is that you would execute the code in this project to verify that the appropriate message was generated by your component. Eventually, you would be satisfied that this was the case and might want to move on to adding new methods and properties to your component. How about something for when a visitor leaves your Web site?

```
public function Farewell()
    sad = "Boooo!!"
end function
```

Once you have entered the code for this method and gone back to your EXE project, you would expect the method to be available for your use. If you have selected No Compatibility, however, new methods will *not* become available for your immediate use! In order to make this new method appear, you must follow this procedure:

1. Open the References dialog under Visual Basic's Project menu.

2. Remove the reference to your ActiveX DLL project.

3. Close the References dialog.

4. Reopen the References dialog.

5. Add back the reference to your ActiveX DLL project.

6. Close the References dialog.

At this point, the new Farewell method should be available for testing from your Standard EXE project.

This is obviously not the ideal way to test your in-process components before adding them to your Active Server Page applications. To remedy the situation, simply change your version compatibility to Project Compatibility. Once this has been done, Visual Basic will automatically ensure that new methods are available immediately for use by Standard EXE projects within the same project group.

Binary Compatibility

The final option Visual Basic makes available for maintaining compatibility between versions of your components is Binary Compatibility. This option truly presents absolutely no benefit to ASP developers, and it should therefore never be used on components for use with ASP scripts.

Binary compatibility is intended to prevent the following scenario: A developer creates a component that features just a few methods. Client application developers then use this component as a part of their compiled applications, and these applications are installed on numerous computers. Then the original component's developer adds a number of methods, properties, and events. The new version of the component is installed on some machines where the old client software is present, and the old client software breaks on computers where the new component is installed.

Without the Binary Compatibility option, installing a new version of a component may cause older client applications to break. This is because, without binary compatibility, the GUID that uniquely identifies a component may change with any modification that alters the component's interface. Examples of such changes would be the addition and removal of object methods or alterations in the parameter lists for those methods.

This is only a problem for applications that use early binding, because only these applications store the GUIDs for their components referenced internally. Since Active Server Pages are strictly late bound, there is no reason to worry about new versions of your components causing your ASPs to break—unless you change their interfaces in ways that should legitimately cause your pages to fail.

An example of a change that should legitimately cause your pages to fail would be the deletion of a method on an object that is called from ASP. Obviously, if the method no longer exists, there isn't much that ASP can do about it. In these cases, you will receive this error:

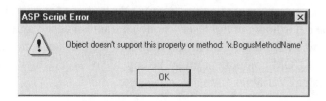

IIS Versus the Desktop

Most COM components are initially designed, created, and tested under a desktop execution environment. A desktop execution environment under Windows means any situation in which a specific user is logged into the console of a machine and personally executing code. In contrast to this, Internet Information Server drives most COM components running under Active Server Pages, and the user (if any) who happens to be logged into the console while this is occurring is usually completely irrelevant.

Environment Variables

Environment variables can sometimes be a convenient way to store configuration information between user sessions. For example, the setting that determines which directories are searched for executables (and in what order they are searched) is usually stored under Windows and Unix in an environment variable known as PATH.

On the Desktop

When a COM component runs in a desktop setting, it is allowed access to the environment strings for whatever user is currently executing its client application. If this user has sufficient access, the component may also be capable of accessing the System variables for a given computer. If you aren't familiar with the kinds of data typically stored in these variables, execute the following steps on the computer on which your COM component(s) will be running:

1. Open Settings from the Windows Start menu.
2. Select Control Panel.
3. Double-click the System icon.
4. Choose the Advanced tab of the System Properties dialog.
5. Click Environment Variables. Your screen should resemble Figure 8-5.

In a desktop application, your COM component will always be able to access the data shown in the User Variables frame. These values vary from one user to another. Depending on the privileges of the user account running your application, your COM component might be capable of accessing the values shown in the System Variables frame.

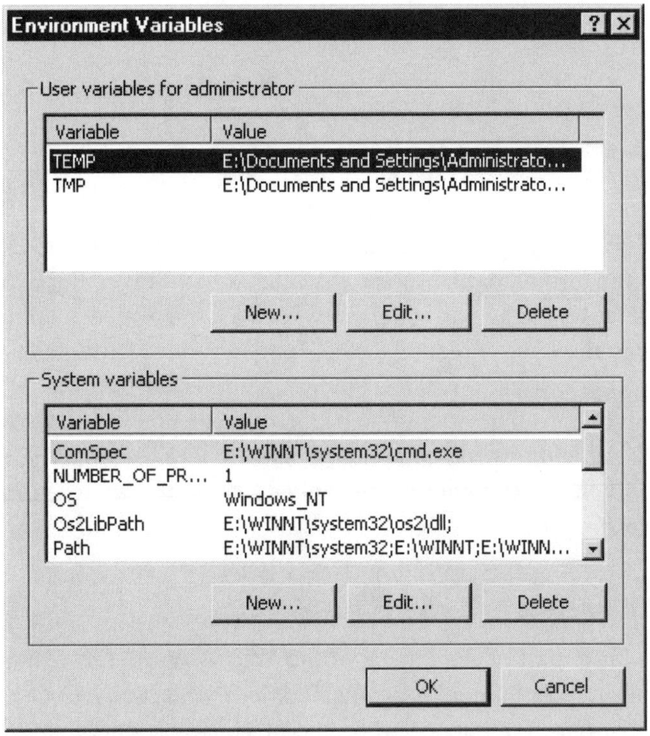

Figure 8.5   Environment variables

In Active Server Pages

When your COM components run under Active Server Pages, they typically execute under the identity of the System account. For more information on this, refer to the previous chapter. Suffice it to say here that the System account is not a regular user account because it cannot be used by anyone to actually log into your computer's console. Instead, it is a special account reserved for the internal workings of the Windows operating system.

For this reason, the only environment variables that your COM components will usually be able to access under Active Server Pages are system variables. Consider the following code:

```
Option Explicit
public function returnEnvironmentVariables()
   Dim temp as String
   Dim I as Integer

   I = 1
```

```
    do
        temp = Environ(I)
        returnEnvironmentVariables = returnEnvironmentVariables &
        vbCrLf & temp
        I = I + 1
    until temp = ""
end function
```

This function is intended to iterate though every environment variable on a given computer and return it to the Active Server Page from which it was called. What would actually happen whenever this was run under ASP, however, is that only the environment variables under system variables would be returned.

If you want to add the environment variables for a specific user to this list, you might consider running your components under Microsoft Component Services. Under Microsoft Component Services, you can specify the identity under which a given COM component should execute. For more information about this, consult Chapter 9.

User Interface Access

A large part of the appeal of the Windows operating system is its highly intuitive, graphical user interface. The interactivity of this interface is, for the most part, not supported by the platform-independent facilities of the World Wide Web. In previous chapters, you learned about how the output of your scripts could be affected by such limitations. In this section, you will learn about restrictions on your COM components that arise from the nature of the Active Server Page environment.

Limitations of Active Server Pages

COM components that execute under Active Server Pages are absolutely forbidden from accessing the user interface on the computers where they execute. This means that they cannot prompt the currently logged-in user for input of any kind. They also may not display any forms, even as pop-up dialogs.

Active Server Page developers often interpret these simple restrictions in terms that are far more restrictive than they actually are. Although COM components may not display UI components during their execution, they may still leverage many kinds of functionalities that may be packaged within UI components.

For example, many common functions and routines are sold by third-party software vendors in the form of OCX controls rather than DLLs. OCXs typically contain ActiveX controls that must be placed on forms in order to be accessed. You can still use OCXs on forms in COM components that are running under Active Server Pages; you just can't make the forms visible on the UI of the computer running IIS.

24x7 Adapting UI Components for Use under IIS

Although you can continue to use forms and ActiveX controls as a part of your COM components under Active Server Pages, your exact approach to doing so will typically require some modifications. Here is a bit of code that could easily be found in many Visual Basic projects:

```
Private Sub Form_Load()
   CustomOCX.MakeComputations
End Sub
```

There is absolutely nothing wrong with any of this code from the standpoint of Active Server Pages. You can use forms in your COM components just as you might use any other class; you just can't make them visible. The same holds true for OCXs like the one named CustomOCX in this example.

There are two problems with this example that would, however, cause it not to function as intended. The first is the fact that all of the code is contained with the Load event. Under standalone Visual Basic applications, this is pretty standard because many applications begin with the automatic loading of a prespecified form. This is not, however, how COM components ever begin their execution.

The other problem with this code is that it makes use of the implicit form that exists in standard executables but not in COM components. It is understood above that the CustomOCX control referred to in the code is the one on the implicit form, but this has no meaning in a COM component where such a form doesn't exist. You must explicitly instantiate every instance of a form that you plan on using in a COM component under Active Server Pages.

```
Option Explicit

Public Sub workWithTheForm()
   Dim frm as FormWithinCOMforASP
   Set frm = new FormWithinCOMforASP
   frm.CustomOCX.MakeComputations
End Sub
```

If you call this routine from your Active Server Page, it will perform exactly the same duties as the code shown earlier would perform under a standalone Windows application. The bulk of the work has been removed from the Form_Load event so that it occurs even in the absence of a default application startup event. Furthermore, this code explicitly creates an instance of the form, which we have called FormWithinCOMforASP, so that we can then work with the specific instance of CustomOCX that is located on this form.

Getting Around the Limitations

There are a couple of extra steps that you should take regarding the UI of COM components that you intend to use under Active Server Pages. One of these is intended to ensure that your components can never, ever become stalled waiting for interaction with the currently logged-in user. The other is intended to ensure that your components will still have the capacity for telling you or your system administrators when they experience problems.

If you can design your COM components in such a way that they do not require the use of any user interface objects, whether displayed or not, you should always mark them for unattended execution. By marking a component for unattended execution, you guarantee that any message boxes or other dialogs that might otherwise be generated by your code will be ignored when the component operates under Internet Information Server. This increases the reliability of your component, but means that your project cannot include

- Forms
- MDI forms
- User controls
- Property pages
- User documents
- Data reports

To mark a component for unattended execution, follow these steps:

1. Open your COM component's project under the Visual Basic IDE.
2. Choose Properties under the Project menu. You'll see the dialog shown in Figure 8-6.
3. Make sure that Unattended Execution is checked. (If the checkbox is grayed out, it is because there are UI components still within your COM component's project.)

Once you have removed all capability from your COM component for producing output through the standard user interface, make sure you compensate by generating sufficient log files from your components. A simple text file that can be read after the fact to let you or a system administrator know what a component was doing at every given point in time should be sufficient.

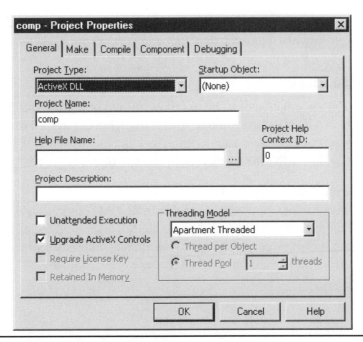

Figure 8.6   The Project Properties dialog

Printing

You have learned that COM components usually run under the System account when executing under IIS. If they are running out-of-process, they may run as the IWAM_<machine> account. Printing is not possible in either of these cases, however, because printers are stored within the user profiles for "real" users only—that is, accounts that can actually log in to the console of the machine. Neither of these accounts fit this description.

If you really must print from your Active Server Pages, consider loading your component into Microsoft Component Services. Under Microsoft Component Services, you can assign your components to execute under a specific user account. For more information, see Chapter 9.

Code Issues for COM Components in ASP

There are a couple of things that you should know about the nuances of writing code for COM components that will be used with Active Server Pages. One of them has to do with the way that your code instantiates COM components. The other involves the way that your components use data.

Instantiation Issues

The instantiation of COM components into objects of specific classes happens at two levels when working with Active Server Pages: There are the objects that your components create for their own internal use and the instancing of your own COM components by their ASP-client scripts.

CreateObject and GetObject

The absolute most reliable way to use COM components within your own COM components is to early-bind with them. This means declaring variables to be of the specific type that is capable of holding them, their library, and class. It also means adding appropriate references to your projects.

```
Option Explicit

Public function bestApproach()
    Dim obj as ADODB.Connection
    Set obj = new ADODB.Connection
end function
```

The second best way to use COM components within your own COM components is to late-bind with them using the CreateObject keyword. The problem with this is that you are not given the same assurances at compile time that the objects requested by your code really exist on the system. The one slight benefit is that you can gain some flexibility in what objects are stored in which variables.

```
Option Explicit

Public function okApproach()
    Dim objA as Object
    Dim objB as Object

    Set objA = CreateObject("ADODB.Connection")
    Set objB = CreateObject("CDONTS.NewMail")

    Set objA = Nothing
    Set objB = Nothing

    Set objA = CreateObject("CDONTS.NewMail")
    Set objB = CreateObject("ADODB.Connection")
end function
```

This code leverages the flexibility of late binding to swap the kinds of objects that are stored in two variables at runtime.

The absolute worst choice for using other COM components within your own COM components is the GetObject keyword. GetObject theoretically supports attaching the variables in your code to already running instances of COM-enabled applications (such as Excel) at runtime. This way you can avoid starting many instances of large applications simply to support multiple instances of your own components. This almost never works under Active Server Pages, however, because of the identity issues described earlier in this chapter. So, as a general rule, you should *never* use GetObject in COM components designed for use with Active Server Pages.

Instancing Settings

There are several choices of support for various instancing models available to your COM component projects under Visual Basic. Some of them are acceptable choices for objects that you will use with Active Server Pages, and some of them are not. In order to change the instancing properties of your COM component, follow these steps:

1. Open your ActiveX DLL or ActiveX EXE project under the Visual Basic IDE.
2. In the Project Explorer, double-click the class you want to set instancing properties.
3. In the Properties frame, locate the row labeled Instancing.
4. Expand the drop-down list to the right of this label, as shown in Figure 8-7.

Private   You cannot directly instantiate objects of this type from Active Server Pages. In fact, you can't use them at all directly from Active Server Pages. The only use for objects of this sort is as helper objects for other objects within your COM component.

PublicNotCreatable   Like Private objects, these objects can't be instantiated from Active Server Pages, either. Unlike Private objects, however, you may create functions in other objects that can be created by ASP scripts, and these functions may return instances of these objects to your scripts for further use. This is rather a specialty kind of instancing.

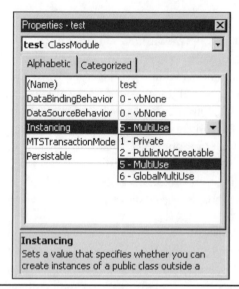

Figure 8.7 Expanding the list in the Properties frame

SingleUse   This form of instancing is available for use only with out-of-process COM components (ActiveX EXE projects). If you set your instancing this way, every new instance of this object that is created will spawn a new EXE process on your Web-serving machine. This can be great from a reliability standpoint because a crash in one object will not affect the other objects on your system. It can be a nightmare from a performance standpoint, however, because of the enormous numbers of processes that can result.

GlobalSingleUse   From an Active Server Pages standpoint, this choice is exactly the same as SingleUse.

MultiUse   This should be your choice for in-process components (ActiveX DLL projects) 99.99 percent of the time. COM components used by ASP scripts that have this kind of instancing will share their code among however many instances your scripts request. This is extremely efficient both in terms of load times and memory consumption.

GlobalMultiUse   From an Active Server Pages standpoint, this choice is exactly the same as MultiUse.

Improper Internal Use of Data

The ways that your components manipulate their data internally can also have profound impacts on the correct operation of your Active Server Pages.

BAS Modules

It is possible to store public variables in BAS modules within your COM components. These variables can then be shared between all of the objects existing within the same component. This can be useful in the creation of desktop applications, where there is typically only a single thread of execution at any point in time. Unfortunately, under Active Server Pages, you stand to have many threads working at different places within the same components at exactly the same point in time.

What will happen in this situation is that client browser requests that happen to execute on the same thread will share the same copies of these global BAS variables. You might design your COM components based upon this information in such a way that you actually leverage it to share information between various browser clients.

Unfortunately, this approach would be wrong also. Client requests that are handled by different threads will have completely different copies of these variables and completely different sets of information. You will, then, have arbitrary groupings and regroupings of the browsers and sessions that are currently using your Active Server Page applications.

For this reason, you should avoid the use of public variables in BAS modules in your COM components if you plan to use those COM components with Active Server Pages.

User-Defined Types

Under VBScript, all data is treated as a Variant. You have already seen that this forbids you from ever using data of specific types in the values returned by your COM components. User-defined types (UDTs) are no exception to this rule. In fact, UDTs are even worse in some cases because VBScript lacks any facility for describing such custom data-storage structures.

If you have a COM component that uses UDTs to store information, and you absolutely must use it with Active Server Pages, you should consider encapsulating all your custom data structures within their own objects. This way you can retain your own way of organizing your data, but you don't lose the ability to share that data with your ASP scripts.

Consider this:

```
Option Explicit

public function returnCustomer()
    Dim obj as UDTWrappers.Customer
    Set obj = new UDTWrappers.Customer

    obj.AccountNumber = "4125995573241111"
    obj.Name = "Marcia Baca"
    obj.Balance = 43.25
    obj.Address = "1313 Mockingbird Lane"

    Set returnCustomer = obj
end function
```

This function beautifully sidesteps the issue of using UDTs with Active Server Pages by placing all of the data that would normally fall into UDT fields into properties on a special COM object instead. The COM object is then returned by the function for further processing by the ASP that originally invoked the returnCustomer method.

Using Transactions with ASP

One of the most important things you can do, as a developer, is safeguard against failures in your applications. Fundamentally, you should carefully design and debug your Active Server Pages in a way that limits the number of potential errors as much as possible. At a slightly more advanced level, you can "bullet-proof" your scripts in such a way that you can be reasonably sure that any errors that *do* arise will be dealt with swiftly and effectively, without causing a general failure of your ASP application.

The most sophisticated and foolproof approaches to bullet-proofing your Active Server Pages all revolve around the use of transactions. A *transaction* is a structure used to group otherwise separate activities into a single unit. This single unit must either completely succeed or completely fail. In the event of a failure, all changes made by the unit are undone or *rolled back* (to use the proper terminology).

What makes a transaction special and useful in protecting your Active Server Pages from errors is the bit about complete success or complete failure. In order for a transaction to succeed, every single step within that transaction must succeed. If even one of the steps fails, all the work done by all of the other steps in the transaction gets rolled back. To see the usefulness of this, imagine the following sequence of events, shown in Figure 9-1:

1. A customer gives a construction company a down-payment of $50,000 to build a house.

2. The construction company lays the foundation.

3. The construction company builds the structure.

4. The customer pays the construction company the remaining $250,000.

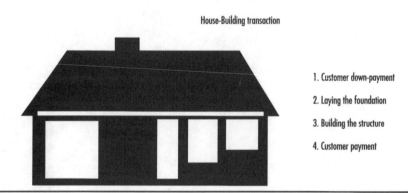

House-Building transaction

1. Customer down-payment

2. Laying the foundation

3. Building the structure

4. Customer payment

Figure 9.1　Every part of a transaction must succeed, or the transaction fails

All these events constitute a single transaction. If failure occurs at any point within the list of steps, it would never be satisfactory to leave matters where they stand. The customer will want back their down payment if the process stops anywhere short of completing step 3. On the other hand, the builder will want to take back all of the building if the customer can't come up with the remaining $250,000 at the end of everything. For this reason, the capability to roll back all work done so far in the event of failure at any point is essential in the construction and use of transactions.

Fundamentals of Transactional Pages

The most basic way to incorporate transactions into your Active Server Pages is through the use of transactional pages. In this section, you will learn how transactional pages can help you lessen the consequences of potential errors in your ASP scripts.

The newest version of Microsoft Component Services allows ASP developers to make the code in their scripts transactional. What this means is that, as your scripts execute, you can evaluate circumstances to determine whether everything is proceeding the way that your business logic requires. If not, you can request that Active Server Pages undo all the changes made by your scripts up to that point in time.

Error Watch *It is important to realize that the only changes currently supported by Component Services roll-back are those changes made to databases. Any other changes, such as modifying flat-text files or sending out e-mails, are completely irrevocable under current technologies and should be treated as such.*

Single-Page Transactions

The following listing shows a page that attempts to automate the house construction process described earlier. In real life, of course, houses can't be built anywhere near this fast—so perhaps the page is talking about simulated houses that exist only within the framework of the computer's own memory. Whatever the case, the developer has tried to provide some degree of resistance to errors without resorting to the use of transactions.

```
<%
   Option Explicit

   Dim cn
```

```
Dim builder

Set cn = Server.CreateObject("ADODB.Connection")
Set builder = Server.CreateObject("Construction.Builder")

cn.open "homedb", "builder", "hammer"

if builder.takeMoney(50000) then
    cn.execute "update jobs set status = 1"
    if builder.layfoundation() then
        cn.execute "update jobs set status = 2"
        if builder.buildstructure() then
            cn.execute "update jobs set status = 3"
            if builder.takemoney(250000) then
                cn.execute "update jobs set status = 4"
            else
                cn.execute "update jobs set status = 0"
            end if
        else
            cn.execute "update jobs set status = 0"
        end if
    else
        cn.execute "update jobs set status = 0"
    end if
end if
```

This code is, of course, a complete and utter nightmare! In order to support the idea that all the steps must be completed in order for any changes to remain in effect at the end of the script, the developer has had to construct an elaborate If-Then-Else hierarchy. In this case, the changes that are being verified involve the recording of status codes in the database. If any of the steps fail at any point, the status of the database is set back to 0.

This logic is far more elaborate and difficult to follow than it would be if the developer had simply made use of transactional Active Server Pages. Compare the preceding listing to this rewritten version:

```
<%@ Transaction=Required %>
<%
    Option Explicit

    Dim cn
    Dim builder

    Set cn = Server.CreateObject("ADODB.Connection")
    Set builder = Server.CreateObject("Construction.Builder")

    cn.open "homedb", "builder", "hammer"
```

```
    if not(builder.takeMoney(50000)) then
        ObjectContext.SetAbort
    End If
    cn.execute "update jobs set status = 1"

    if not(builder.layfoundation()) then
        ObjectContext.SetAbort
    end if
    cn.execute "update jobs set status = 2"

    if not(builder.buildstructure()) then
        ObjectContext.SetAbort
    end if
    cn.execute "update jobs set status = 3"

    if not(builder.takemoney(250000)) then
        ObjectContext.SetAbort
    end if
    cn.execute "update jobs set status = 4"
%>
```

Notice how much easier it is to read this code. Each step exists at exactly the same level in the code's flow of logic—no nested If-Then-Else structures. Furthermore, there is no need to specifically track the original state of the database, which is why the original code continually referred to setting the status field back to 0. If this script calls the SetAbort method on the intrinsic ObjectContext object at any point in time, all changes made to databases by this script will immediately be rolled back.

All this was made possible by the addition of the <% @Transaction=Required %> directive at the top of the script. It tells Active Server Pages to treat all the rest of the code in this file as a single transaction.

Multiple-Page Transactions

You have now seen how to use ASP's transactional capabilities within a single page to ensure that all the database modifications made by a script either succeed or fail as a single unit. But how can you leverage this technology for procedures that span the course of several pages? The previous example is a perfect case in point: It is highly unlikely that an entire home-construction process could be fit into the context of a single Active Server Page!

A naïve approach to this problem might look something like this:

```
<%@ Transaction=Required %>
<%
    ' VARIOUS CODE GOES HERE
```

```
Response.Redirect "moneytaker.asp?amount=50000"
Response.Redirect "foundationlayer.asp"
Response.Redirect "structurebuilder.asp"
Response.Redirect "moneytaker.asp?amount=250000"
%>
```

The assumption here is that the transaction declared at the start of this page might be passed on to all the pages that this page calls. This is close to the truth, but the methodology suggested earlier would never work. Recall from Chapter 6 that as soon as you redirect a client to another Active Server Page, the page currently executing ceases operation. For this reason, the preceding script would never get further than the first redirection to MONEYTAKER.ASP.

The full truth of multipage transactions under ASP is that a single transaction may be shared by multiple pages if

- Every page in a given group includes an appropriate @Transaction directive, and

- The pages are linked via calls to Server.Execute from a single, central page, or

- The pages are linked via calls to Server.Transfer at the end of each page

The first rule is relatively simple to understand. Every page in your transaction group must have an @Transaction directive at the very top. If it doesn't have this line, your transaction will automatically be committed as soon as this page is executed. If the next page executed after this page has an @Transaction directive itself, a completely new transaction will be created when it is executed.

Error Watch   *If you choose to include an @Transaction directive in your Active Server Page, it must always occur on the first line of the file containing your script. If it occurs at any other point in the file, an error will be generated.*

The next rule introduces the concept of the Server.Execute method. In short, calling this method will ask Active Server Pages to run another script as if it were a part of the currently executing script. When the other script is finished, control is returned to the script that called Server.Execute. The entire flow looks like Figure 9-2.

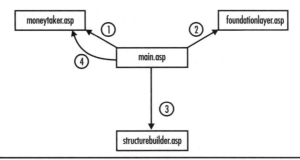

Figure 9.2 The flow of the Server.Execute method

Using Server.Execute, you could easily rewrite the code example from earlier in this section.

```
<%@ Transaction=Required %>
<%
   ' VARIOUS CODE GOES HERE
   Server.Execute "moneytaker.asp?amount=50000"
   Server.Execute "foundationlayer.asp"
   Server.Execute "structurebuilder.asp"
   Server.Execute "moneytaker.asp?amount=250000"
%>
```

The other option you have for connecting multiple pages under a single ASP transaction is to use the Server.Transfer method. This is a little like Server.Execute except that control is completely transferred to the page being invoked by the method call. In order for this to work in a situation such as the one in the previous code sample, each script must end with a Server.Transfer to the next script on the list. Graphically, it might look like Figure 9-3.

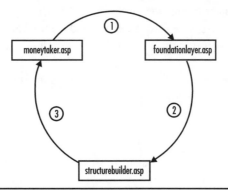

Figure 9.3 The flow of the Server.Transfer method

As a further illustration, some sample code for FOUNDATIONLAYER.ASP might look like this:

```
<%@ Transaction=Required %>
<%
   ' VARIOUS CODE GOES HERE
   Server.Transfer "structurebuilder.asp"
%>
```

The "meat" of whatever this page is intended to accomplish goes where the comment is in the above listing. And then, at the very end, you can see the call to Server.Transfer that causes the server to jump to the next page in the series of pages that are intended to participate in the same transaction.

Microsoft Component Services

Arguably one of the most significant pieces of software to come out of Redmond in the last few years is Microsoft Component Services. Microsoft Component Services offers much more than transaction support for your applications. When COM components are run under Component Services, they benefit from some of the most advanced middleware-enabling technologies currently available in the marketplace. Connection pooling, object serialization, and caching are just a few of the services provided by Microsoft Component Services to COM components running within its process space.

Adding Components to the Server

To facilitate extended support for transactions to the COM components in your Active Server Pages, you must first load these components into Microsoft Component Services. In order to load your components, you must first create a new COM+ application in which they may reside. To do this, follow these steps:

1. Open Settings from the Windows Start menu.
2. Click Control Panel.

3. Double-click Administrative Tools.

4. Double-click Component Services.

5. Expand the Component Services tree node.

6. Expand Computers.

7. Expand the computer where you wish to install your component.

8. Right-click COM+ Applications.

9. Choose New from the pop-up context menu.

10. Click Application. Your screen should look like Figure 9-4.

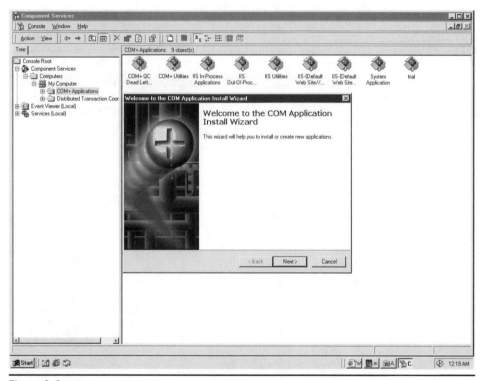

Figure 9.4 The COM Application Install Wizard

11. Click Next to go to the second screen of the COM Application Install Wizard (see Figure 9-5).

12. Choose Create an Empty Application.

13. Enter the name of your choice for your new application (we used **TestApp**) and click Next. You'll see the screen shown in Figure 9-6.

14. Click Next to allow your application to run as the user currently logged on.

15. Click Finish.

At this point, you have created a completely new COM+ application that is empty and waiting for your components. There are two ways that you can add them. If your component has not yet been registered on this computer, the

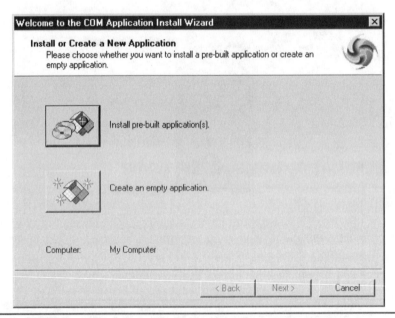

Figure 9.5   Preparing to create a new application

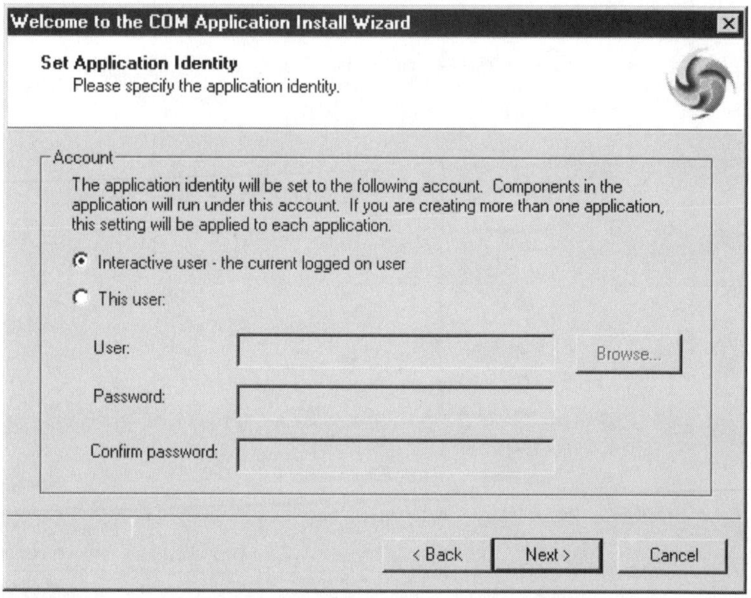

Figure 9.6   Setting the application's identity

simplest way is to drag your .DLL file(s) from the Windows Explorer onto the icon representing your new application.

The second approach is good for situations where your component has already been registered. If you find yourself in this situation, append the following steps to the previous ones:

1. Expand the COM+ Applications node.

2. Expand the node for your newly created application.

3. Right-click Components.

4. Choose New from the pop-up context menu.

5. Click Component.

6. Click Next. You'll see the screen shown in Figure 9-7.

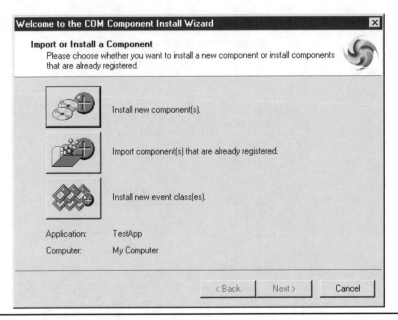

Figure 9.7 Adding a component to a registered application

7. Choose Import Component(s) That Are Already Registered.

8. Select the correct component from the resulting scrollable list.

9. Click Next.

10. Click Finish.

Verifying That a Component Is Being Used

As soon as you have loaded a component into Component Services, you have gained the ability to attack one of the most common bugs under Active Server Pages. Sometimes, your scripts refer to components other than the ones that you intended to use. Other times, your scripts refer to the correct components, but problems with the registry under Windows prevent your requests from ever actually reaching the component.

Until the graphical interface for Component Services (and before this, Microsoft Transaction Server) came along, it was very difficult to tell if COM was even trying to talk to your components. Messages passed between client applications and server components without any visible signals on the desktop of your computer. This is no longer the case.

Using the Components view of Components Services, you can tell whether any client applications are currently using your components by the state of the applications' icons. If their icons seem to be spinning, they are currently talking to client applications that would like to use their services. If they appear to be completely static and motionless, they are not involved in any conversations with any client applications.

To put this into real terms, you could create the following test script:

```
<%
   Option Explicit
   Dim obj, i
   Set obj = Server.CreateObject("Utilities.Widget")
   for i = 1 to 25
      obj.test()
   next I
%>
```

The purpose of the loop that calls the same method 25 times is to make sure that you have plenty of time to open up the Component Services application and check for spinning icons. Otherwise, if you only called the test method once, it might finish before you ever even got to see the icon spinning. This way, if you are running the preceding script, and your component is not spinning in the management console window, you know that one of two things are true:

- There is some problem with the way that your component is registered.

- The component being called by your script is not the same as the one you have loaded into Component Services.

Getting the ObjectContext Object

The ObjectContext object is the main "life line" between the internals of your COM components and the services provided by Microsoft Component Services. It is through ObjectContext that you declare whether a transaction should be completed or aborted.

Under Visual Basic and other COM component development platforms, ObjectContext is not an intrinsic object. This is important to understand because it is a source of frequent errors when Active Server Pages developers first begin writing their own COM components.

```
public function takeMoney(dollars as Variant) as Variant
   if dollars > 0 then
      ObjectContext.setMyTransactionVote TxCommit
```

```
    else
        ObjectContext.setMyTransactionVote TxAbort
    end if
end function
```

This is a fairly straightforward attempt at implementing a simple rule as a method on a COM component. In short, it says, "As long as the guy is trying to give us a legitimate sum of cash, pass the transaction along; otherwise vote to abort it." If any component within a transaction votes to abort, the transaction is aborted. This makes perfect sense in the context of what you saw previously in ASP transactions.

The problem with the preceding code is that it never goes through any of the steps needed in order to actually obtain a proper ObjectContext object. First, the developer should have declared variable storage for objects of both the ObjectContext and IcontextState varieties. Then, she should have called the GetObjectContext method, storing its results in the ObjectContext variable before passing it to the IcontextState variable.

```
Option Explicit

public function takeMoney(dollars as Variant) as Variant
    Dim oc as ObjectContext
    Dim ics as IcontextState

    Set oc = GetObjectContext
    Set ics = oc


    if dollars > 0 then
        ics.setMyTransactionVote TxCommit
    else
        ics.setMyTransactionVote TxAbort
    end if
end function
```

Using the ObjectContext Object

Earlier you learned how to create COM components that vote on whether to complete transactions under Active Server Pages. You saw that this was accomplished primarily through the features and functions of the ObjectContext object. It is also through ObjectContext that you can gain access to the intrinsic objects bundled into Active Server Pages.

For example, suppose that you wanted to accept input from a user though a standard HTML form and then have it all processed by a COM component running under Microsoft Component Services. If the input is properly formatted, then various actions are taken. If the input is not even formatted correctly, however, the entire transaction is aborted.

You can achieve these results under Microsoft Component Services by accessing the Item collection on the ObjectContext object. The Item collection contains entries for every intrinsic object running under Active Server Pages, so it should be completely possible to read directly from the Request object or write output directly to the Response object.

Design Tip *Although you can do all of the preceding, it is generally considered very bad form for COM components to interact directly with an application's input/output streams. The input and output, the theory goes, should be handled by the client application based on results returned by the logic components. This way, you can achieve a true three-tier architecture where your scripts handle the user interface, your components handle the "business logic," and your databases handles the data storage.*

If you decide that this approach is appropriate for the design of your applications, you can use code like this to achieve your aims:

```
Option Explicit

public function takeMoney(dollars as Variant) as Variant
    Dim oc as ObjectContext
    Dim ics as IcontextState

    Set oc = GetObjectContext
    Set ics = oc

    if dollars > 0 then
       ics.setMyTransactionVote TxCommit
       ics("Response").write "That seems like a fair price!"
    else
       ics.setMyTransactionVote TxAbort
       ics("Response").write "What are you trying to pull, buddy?!"
    end if
end function
```

Applications

There are two main kinds of COM+ applications under Microsoft Component Services. The first of these is the library application. The other is the server application.

Library Applications

You can create a library application to hold your COM components as follows:

1. Choose Programs from the Windows Start menu.
2. Open the Administrative Tools program group.
3. Click Component Services.
4. Find the COM+ Applications node for your computer in the tree control on the left and right-click it.
5. Choose New from the pop-up context menu, and then click Application.
6. Click Next.
7. Click Create an Empty Application.
8. Make sure the radio button labeled Library Application is selected.
9. Be sure to enter a name for the new application.
10. Click Next.
11. Click Finish.

Benefits

The main benefit to putting your COM components in library applications is that their performance will be much improved. The reason for this is that library applications execute under the process of their client applications. In terms of Active Server Pages, this means that every component you instantiate would become a part of the IIS process.

This helps performance because messages between components do not have to cross as many process boundaries. It is, in fact, a little like the difference between in-process components and out-of-process components. The only difference is that under Component Services, all the components run in-process—just possibly not within the process of the client application!

Drawbacks

The problem with putting all of your components into the same library application is that a catastrophic failure in one component can easily bring down all your other components. It could even bring down the entire Internet Information Server (IIS)!

As to why this is the case, consider the following code listing:

```
<%
   Option Explicit

   Dim obj
   Set obj = Server.CreateObject("Factory.Widget")

   obj.Construct(24)
   Response.Write "Done building 24 widgets!"
%>
```

This script creates an object from the Factor.Widget class and calls a Construct method on it to generate 24 widgets (whatever those may be). The code is pretty straightforward and should have no relationship to the next listing.

```
<%
   Option Explicit

   Dim obj
   Set obj = Server.CreateObject("Garden.Flower")

   obj.Plant("Daisy")
   Response.Write "I planted a daisy!"
%>
```

This script creates an object from the Garden.Flower class and calls a Plant method on it to plant a daisy. This could not possibly have any less to do with creating widgets. You should imagine both of these listings occurring on completely different ASP pages. In fact, you should imagine them occurring on completely different ASP applications. Graphically, their work looks like Figure 9-8.

As you can see, they are completely separate in every way, except for the fact that both of their components exist within the same process space. Now, if you

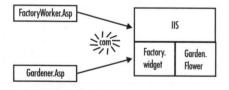

Figure 9.8   Two different ASP applications can share the same process space

imagine the Factor.Widget class exploding in some way (an Access Control error, for example), it becomes easy to see why the Garden.Flower component would no longer work effectively (see Figure 9-9).

Server Applications

With server applications, all failures within the application are encapsulated. You can create a server application to hold your COM components as follows:

1. Choose Programs from the Windows Start menu.

2. Open the Administrative Tools program group.

3. Click Component Services.

4. Find the COM+ Applications node for your computer in the tree control on the left and right-click it.

5. Choose New from the pop-up context menu, then click Application.

6. Click Next.

7. Click Create an Empty Application.

8. Make sure the radio button labeled Server Application is selected.

9. Be sure to enter a name for the new application.

10. Choose an identity under which you would like your components to execute. For more information on this, see the section "Identity Issues" later in this chapter.

11. Click Next.

12. Click Finish.

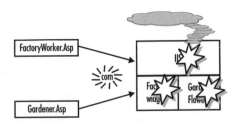

Figure 9.9   How an error in one library application affects another library application

Benefits

Since server application errors are encapsulated, all of the components for such an application run within the same process space—but not the process space of the client application. Within the context of Active Server Pages, this means that you never have to worry about your code causing IIS to completely stop running.

Figure 9-10 shows the new situation in which the two components discussed in the previous section on library applications would now exist.

In the figure notice that, although the Factory.Widget class is exploding, the debris is contained by the boundaries of its own process. For extra safety, in this example we have created two COM+ applications, one for each component. Both of these applications are server applications.

The other advantage to running your components under server applications is that you may then assign them to execute under specific identities. This has been referred to as one of Component Services's greatest strengths in several chapters, as it can allow you to work around limitations on printing, accessing network resources, and a variety of other user-level issues. You can learn more about exactly how this works in the next section "Identity Issues."

Drawbacks

The main drawback to server applications is the decrease in component performance. Shut out of the client application's process space, server application components must communicate using the Windows crossprocess communications mediums. This can be one of the most resource-intensive things your components must ever do.

For this reason, you might want to consider using server applications primarily for testing purposes. Whenever you have a new component that you are not completely sure about, you can begin it in its own server application and leave

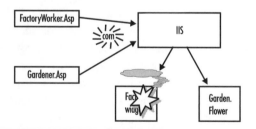

Figure 9.10　A server application encapsulates errors

it there for a while. During this period, you could make sure to let lots of client application processes access it to thoroughly test all its methods and behaviors in many different situations.

Once you are convinced that a component is free of any bugs that may cause IIS (and all your Active Server Pages) to crash, you can put it in a library application along with all your other components. This way, you can get the performance benefits of a library application without the risks.

Identity Issues

In several previous chapters, you have learned about limitations on what Active Server Page scripts might ask COM components to do. For example, printing documents from ASPs that call COM components will typically fail. The reason for this and many other similar limitations is that in-process COM components under ASP run as a part of the IIS server process. This means that instead of running as specific users' accounts on your Windows computer they run under the peculiar System account.

The System account has no true existence as a Windows user, however. It cannot access any resources that are earmarked specifically for logged-in users. Printers and shared drives are two examples of such resources.

Administration

Setting the identity for a COM component under Component Services is relatively straightforward.

Interactive User

The Microsoft Management Console makes it easy to create new server libraries that will operate under a specific user account. The steps for doing this were covered earlier in this chapter in the section "Server Applications." In this section, you are most concerned with the step in which you are asked to choose an identity for your components (see Figure 9-11).

The main option in the Identity dialog is Interactive User. If you choose this option, the COM components in your COM+ application will always run as whatever user currently happens to be logged on to your Windows server's console. This could be useful in the case of ASP scripts that you intended to run *only at the console of the Web server's machine!*

```
<%
  Option Explicit

  Dim obj
  Set obj = Server.CreateObject("AdminObjects.DriveFormatter")

  obj.Reformat("e:\")
%>
```

The object in this script would be an excellent choice to run under the permission of whichever user happens to currently be logged in. If you restricted this script to local use (by using an IP restriction of 127.0.0.1—if you don't remember this, review Chapter 1), you could make sure that only Administrators were able to use the power of such a script. This would be an excellent idea, because the preceding script is designed to completely reformat a system's hard disk.

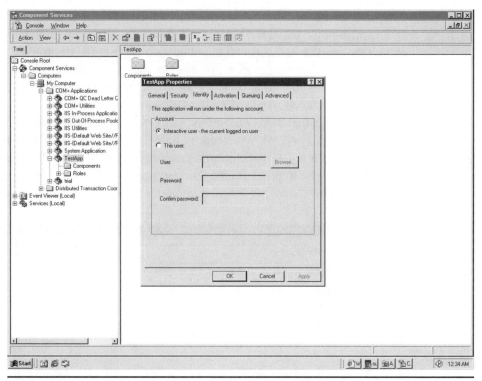

Figure 9.11   Choosing an identity for your components

The This User Option

It is more common to want to use an Active Server Page script in Web clients on many different remote computers, however. In cases like this, if you want your scripts to do things that would ordinarily require a logged-in user with a console application, you should probably choose the This User option.

Once you have enabled the This User radio button, three text boxes become available to take your entries. The first of these is labeled User, and it should be the full login name of the user account under which you would like your COM+ application to operate.

The most common mistake Active Server Page developers make when filling out this text field is to neglect the domain name of the user they wish to use. This is important, because most Windows boxes support the concept of multiple domains with overlapping user names. If you don't specify a domain name, Windows has no way of knowing where to find the correct user.

The best way to avoid making this error is to avail yourself of the Browse button on the dialog. You'll then see the dialog shown in Figure 9-12.

The drop-down list at the top of the Select User or Group dialog allows you to choose the specific domains that might contain the user for whom you are looking. As you change the value selected in this list, the exact list of available users will change. To make your final user selection, double-click the row containing the user under which you would like your COM+ application to run.

If this were all that there was to this dialog, this feature of Component Services would represent a pretty major security hole in Windows 2000. Anyone would be able to have their components running as if they were anyone else. This would make it impossible to prevent unauthorized personnel from achieving major security breeches by asking for their components to run as Administrator, for

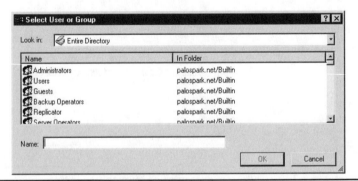

Figure 9.12   The Select User or Group dialog

example. The dialog protects against this by forcing you to enter the password for whatever user account you select.

To prevent having to echo the password that you enter to standard output, the dialog asks you to enter the password for a second time. If the two passwords you entered don't match, the program realizes that you have made a typo and asks you to re-enter. If they match, they are accepted—but will only work if they are correct!

Coding Components

In the previous section, you saw many ways to use the Microsoft Management Console interface to assign identities to your COM+ applications. Sometimes, though, you might not know what identity you want for your COM component until your Active Server Page is actually running. Under these circumstances, you can usually change the identity of your components using code.

The Win32 API provides a series of calls designed to allow your components to impersonate various users as you see fit. In order to make this happen, you first must know the username, domain, and password for any user that you want to impersonate. Once you know this, you can begin writing an Active Server Page that uses impersonation in order to achieve its aims.

Suppose, for example, that you wanted to write an Active Server Page that would copy a file to shared drive on your server's local area network. You might write something that looks like this:

```
<%
    Option Explicit

    If Request("Filename") = "" Then
%>
<FORM METHOD="POST">
Filename: <INPUT NAME="Filename"><br>
<INPUT TYPE="Submit">
</FORM>
<%
    Else
        Dim obj
        Set obj = Server.CreateObject("NiftyUtils.NetworkAccess")
        obj.changeToUser("jeeves", "granite", "maraca")
        obj.copyFile(request("filename"))
        response.write "File copied to the network drive!"
    End If
%>
```

This Active Server Page relies on the services of a custom component known as NiftyUtils.NetworkAccess. In order for this component to access a network drive, it must impersonate a specific user account. In order to do this, it must avail itself of three Win32 APIs:

- LogonUse
- ImpersonateLoggedOnUser
- RevertToSelf

LogonUser

The first API that a component must call in order to impersonate a Windows user is the LogonUser API. This function essentially takes a username, domain, and password as parameters and returns either a zero to indicate that the login attempt failed, or a nonzero value to indicate that it has succeeded. More useful than the return value, however, is the handle to a Windows session running under the given user that a successful execution will also produce. This handle is stored in the final parameter passed to the function and is later used with the ImpersonateLoggedOnUser API.

If you are unfamiliar with the use of the Windows API, you should be aware that the Private function declaration that follows should be placed in a standard BAS module. It should occur outside the boundaries of any procedures, therefore, becoming global to the entire project in which it is located.

```
Option Explicit

Const LOGON32_LOGON_BATCH = 4
Const LOGON32_PROVIDER_DEFAULT = 0

Private hndl as Long

Private Declare Function LogonUser Lib "kernel32" (ByVal lpszUsername _
as _String, ByVal lpszDomain as String, ByVal lpszPassword as String, _
ByVal _dwLogonType as Long, ByVal dwLogonProvider as Long, phToken _
as Long) as Long

public function changeToUser(username, domain, password)
    Dim u as String, d as String, p as String

    u = username
    d = domain
    p = password
```

```
      If LogonUser(u, d, p, LOGON32_LOGON_BATCH, LOGON32_PROVIDER_DEFAULT, _
      hndl) _
          <> 0 Then
          ' INSERT REST OF CODE HERE
          changeToUser = false
      else
          changeToUser = true
      end if
  end function
```

This code begins by storing the three Variant parameters in Strings, to ensure that they will work correctly with the API invocation. It then invokes the API with the parameters described above, plus a couple of constants. The first constant, LOGON32_LOGON_BATCH, tells Windows that the kind of login being attempted is actually just a process trying an impersonation, not a real, "flesh and blood" user sitting at the console. The second constant, LOGON32_PROVIDER_DEFAULT, tells Windows to use whatever system is the default on this server for authenticating user login attempts.

The final parameter is a holder for the handle to the Windows session that will be created for this user in the event that this API call succeeds. This handle must be used with the ImpersonateLoggedOnUser API in order for the component to work under the requested user's account.

ImpersonateLoggedOnUser

If you examine the listing in the previous section closely, you will find a commented line that reads INSERT REST OF CODE HERE. Once your code reaches this point, it will have a handle to a valid Windows session under the desired user account, but it won't be able to use it yet. In order to do this, you must first call the ImpersonateLoggedOnUser API.

```
Private Declare Function ImpersonateLoggedOnUser Lib "kernel32"
(phToken as_ Long) as Long

public function changeToUser(username, domain, password)
    ' ... SEE PREVIOUS LISTING FOR CODE HERE
    If ImpersonateLoggedOnUser(hndl) <> 0 Then
        ' INSERT USEFUL CODE HERE
        changeToUser = true
    Else
        changeToUser = false
    End If
    ' ... SEE PREVIOUS LISTING FOR CODE HERE
end function
```

This listing should be envisioned as laying over the same code in the previous listing. Essentially, we have just added the Win32 API declaration for ImpersonateLoggedOnUser that is required by Visual Basic, as well as the code to make use of it. Notice that the hndl variable, which was declared in the previous listing and used as a parameter for the LogOnUser function call, has reappeared here. It is the sole parameter for the ImpersonateLoggedOnUser function.

When you call this function, you are essentially telling Windows, "Please start running this thread under the following session…" If this function call succeeds, everything you do in your code after this will run as if it were executing under the desired user's account. This lasts until your code either ends or calls the RevertToSelf API function.

RevertToSelf

The third, and final, API call that your component should make when impersonating a Windows user is RevertToSelf. It should make this call after it is finished impersonating the requested user and is ready to go back to executing under the identity with which it was first instantiated. The call is particularly easy to use, as it requires no parameters of any kind. It simply returns a nonzero value to indicate success, or a zero value to indicate failure.

```
Private Declare Function RevertToSelf Lib "kernel32" () as Long

public function changeToUser(username, domain, password)
    ' ... SEE PREVIOUS LISTING FOR CODE HERE
    If RevertToSelf() <> 0 Then
       changeToUser = true
    Else
       changeToUser = false
    End If
    ' ... SEE PREVIOUS LISTING FOR CODE HERE
end function
```

Once again, this code should be seen as an overlay for the code from the previous two sections. The call to RevertToSelf should only occur if both the call to LogOnUser and ImpersonateLoggedOnUser have already both succeeded.

Database Rollbacks

There is possibly no greater need for transactions than when it comes to database technologies. To many people, the whole idea of a database server is that it is guaranteed to reliably and effectively store their applications' data. Without support for the concept of transactions, the reliability of the data stored in a database can easily be brought into question.

As one example, a database might contain two tables: one named Deposits and one named Withdrawals. In the event of a transfer between a customers accounts, you would never want a modification to be made to Withdrawals without a corresponding modification to Deposits, and vice-versa. Otherwise, money could easily get lost and data corrupted. This is why virtually every enterprise-level database supports the concept of transactions.

Native Transaction Support

The easiest way to prevent data corruption from your Active Server Page applications is to leverage the native support for transactions available through your database server. The most effective way to gain access to such native support is by using the Active Data Objects collection of data access objects with the OLEDB drivers for your databases.

Consider the problem described earlier. You want to write your Active Server Page in such a way that a transfer always entails a withdrawal and a deposit; never just one. How can you be sure that if one action fails, the other is rolled back? Examine the following code:

```
<%
  Option Explicit

  Dim cn, rst

  Set cn = Server.CreateObject("ADODB.Connection")
  Set rst = Server.CreateObject("ADODB.Recordset")

  cn.open "bankaccounts", "teller", "toughjob"

  cn.BeginTrans
  cn.execute "update customers set balance = 234.50 where custid = _
  4314"
  rst.open "select balance from customers where custid = 4314"
  if rst.fields(0) <> 234.50 then
     cn.RollbackTrans
  else
     rst.close
     cn.execute "update customers set balance = 44.25 where custid = _
     8152"
     rst.open "select balance from customers where custid = 8152"
     if rst.fields(0) <> 44.25 then
```

```
        cn.RollbackTrans
    else
        cn.CommitTrans
    end if
end if
%>
```

There are three things that you should notice in the example, and they are all methods of the Connection object.

Method	Purpose
BeginTrans	Call this at the beginning of a series of database activities that you want to exist within a single transaction.
RollbackTrans	Call this if you want to undo all the changes made to your database since the last call to BeginTrans.
CommitTrans	Call this if you want to lock in all of the changes made to your database since the last call to BeginTrans.

Cross-Database Rollbacks

This approach works fine when all your database operations work on a single database server. Sometimes, however, you want to group actions into transactions that span several database servers. In order to make this work, you must leverage the transactional capabilities of Microsoft Component Services.

At the time of this writing, SQL Server and Oracle (versions 7.3.3 and later) are the only databases that support transactions under Microsoft Component Services. This means that you can group together activities on multiple SQL and Oracle servers into a single transaction, but any activities that work against other databases will exist outside of such transactions.

To use Component Services as the basis for your DB transactions strategy, you simply write your code as you normally would, and use the ObjectContext's setMyTransactionVote property to register whether your transactions should be completed.

```
Option Explicit

public function transferMoney(dollars as Variant) as Variant
    Dim oc as ObjectContext
    Dim ics as IcontextState
    Dim cn as ADODB.Connection
    Dim rst as ADODB.Recordset

    Set oc = GetObjectContext
    Set ics = oc
    Set cn = oc.CreateInstance("ADODB.Connection")
    Set rst = oc.CreateInstance("ADODB.Recordset")
    cn.open "bankaccounts", "teller", "toughjob"

    cn.execute "update customers set balance = 234.50 where custid = _
    4314"
    rst.open "select balance from customers where custid = 4314"
    if rst.fields(0) <> 234.50 then
        ics.setMyTransactionVote TxAbort
    else
        rst.close
        cn.execute "update customers set balance = 44.25 where custid = _
        8152"
        rst.open "select balance from customers where custid = 8152"
        if rst.fields(0) <> 44.25 then
            ics.setMyTransactionVote TxAbort
        else
            ics.setMyTransactionVote TxCommit
        end if
    end if
end function
```

Notice that this code is almost identical to the code used in the Active Server Page example that used Active Data Object to enforce database transactions. The main difference is that the power of Component Services is being used to enforce transactions via the ObjectContext reference. This allows you to open connections to as many different SQL Server and Oracle databases as you like, and they all must be bound by the limits of this transaction.

24x7 The Importance of ObjectContext

Whenever you want to use Component Services to enforce your database transactions, you must be sure to instantiate all your ADO objects using the ObjectContext's CreateInstance method. If you create your objects in any other fashion, for example by using Visual Basic's *new* keyword, your databases will not be a part of your Component Services transactions.

The reason for this is that Component Services needs some way of keeping track of all the databases that your transactions use. If you create all your ADO objects through the method that it provides, it is able to keep a record of every ADO connection that it sees. This is useful when you eventually want to commit or roll back a transaction, because Component Services then knows all the connections that must be updated.

However, if you instantiate all your objects outside of the ObjectContext, there is no way for Component Services to keep track of them. When the time comes for a commit or rollback, Component Services doesn't know anything about your databases and completely passes over them.

Connecting to Your Data

O ver the course of the next few chapters, you will learn about debugging errors in Active Server Pages that involve databases. In this chapter, you'll learn about the difficulties of establishing connections to databases from ASP scripts.

SQL Server

Microsoft's SQL Server database is arguably the most popular source for data under Active Server Pages. Part of the reason for its popularity amongst ASP developers is its tight integration with the Windows operating system. Another factor weighing heavily in its favor is its highly intuitive graphical user interface (GUI).

On the other hand, it is SQL Server's tight integration with the Windows operating system that causes problems when you attempt to form connections using platform-independent Web technologies such as Basic authentication. In this section, you will take a look at connecting to SQL Server databases on both local and remote machines.

SQL Server on the Local Machine

Connecting to a SQL Server running on the same machine as your Active Server Page scripts typically involves establishing a data source name (DSN) and choosing and installing an appropriate driver.

Establishing a DSN

There are two ways to refer to your SQL Server database from an ASP script:

- Data source name (DSN)
- DSN-less connection string

You can establish a DSN for your SQL Server by following these steps:

1. Choose Settings from the Windows Start menu.
2. Open the Control Panel.
3. Open Administrative Tools.
4. Double-click the icon labeled "Data Sources (ODBC)." You'll see the dialog shown in Figure 10-1.
5. Select the User, File, or System DSN tab. For more information on the differences between these three kinds of DSN, see the section later in this chapter on DSN selection.

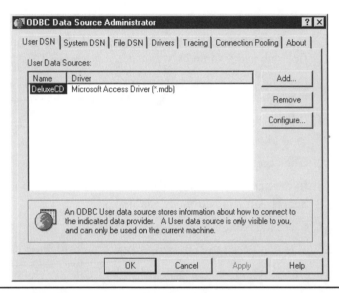

Figure 10.1   The ODBC Data Source Administrator dialog

6. Click the Add button. The dialog shown in Figure 10-2 will appear.

7. Choose "SQL Server" from the list box.

8. Click the Finish button.

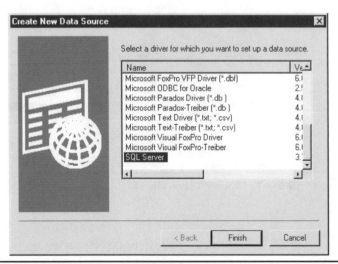

Figure 10.2   The Create New Data Source dialog

9. In the next screen of the Wizard, enter the name by which you would like to refer to your SQL server from your Active Server Pages into the text field labeled "Name."

10. Optionally, enter a description for your SQL Server data into the field labeled "Description." It will *not* be used in any way by Active Server Pages.

11. Choose "(local)" from the "Server" drop-down list. Your screen should look like Figure 10-3.

12. Click the Next button.

13. In the next screen, make sure that the radio button labeled "With SQL Server Authentication" is enabled.

14. Click the Next button.

15. You don't need to make any changes to next button, so just click Next again.

16. Confirm that your screen looks like Figure 10-4, and then click Finish.

At this point, you will be given the opportunity to test your new DSN to make sure that it will really let you connect to your SQL Server (see Figure 10-5).

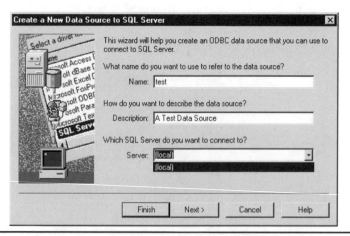

Figure 10.3   The Create a New Data Source to SQL Server dialog

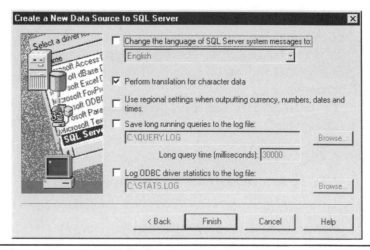

Figure 10.4   The last screen of the Create a New Data Source to SQL Server Wizard

Figure 10.5   Testing your DSN

If you click the button labeled "Test Data Source," you should see a brief pause followed by a message box confirming your ability to connect to SQL Server. If your system hangs at this point or if you get an error message, it means there is a problem either with SQL Server itself or some of the configuration settings you have chosen.

To verify that SQL Server is operating correctly, you can perform the following steps:

1. Choose Programs from the Windows Start menu.

2. Open the Microsoft SQL Server 7.0 program group.

3. Choose Query Analyzer. You'll see the dialog shown in Figure 10-6.

4. Unless you have changed the password for your "sa" login, press OK to accept all the defaults in the Connect to SQL Serve dialog. If you have changed your "sa" password, enter the new one before clicking OK.

5. If your SQL Server is operating correctly, you will see the screen shown in Figure 10-7. If your SQL Server is not working right, you will see a screen that looks similar to the one in Figure 10-8.

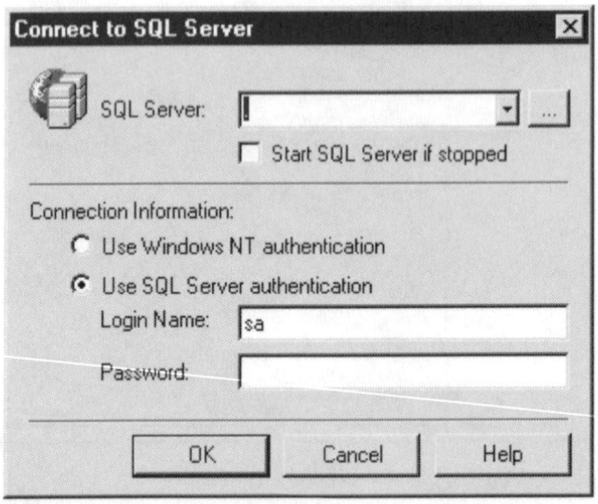

Figure 10.6   The Connect to SQL Server dialog

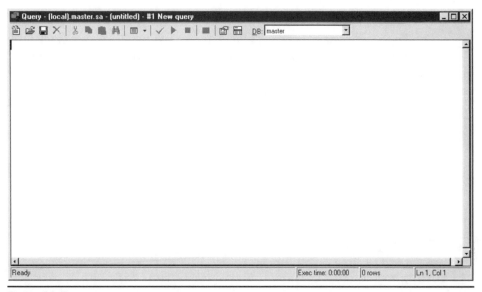

Figure 10.7   SQL Server is operating correctly

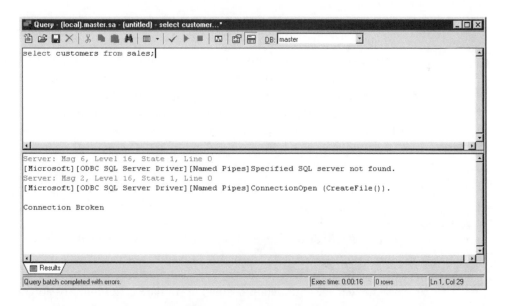

Figure 10.8   SQL Server is not operating correctly

Using the OLEDB Driver

The best driver currently available for use with SQL Server is the OLEDB driver provided by Microsoft. Here is an example of code that uses the OLEDB driver:

```
<%
   Option Explicit

   Dim cn
   Dim rst

   Set cn = Server.CreateObject("ADODB.Connection")
   Set rst = Server.CreateObject("ADODB.Recordset")

   cn.provider = "MSDASQL"
   cn.open "sales", "sa", ""

   rst.open "SELECT name FROM salespeople", cn

   do until rst.eof
      response.write rst.fields(0) & "<br>"

      rst.movenext
   loop
%>
```

OLEDB drivers are typically referred to as "providers" because they provide your applications with the data they need. The relevant line in the preceding script, therefore, is the one that sets the connection's Provider property equal to the string MSDASQL. This string is Microsoft's shorthand name for their OLEDB provider for SQL Server. If you do not set the Provider property, ADO will assume that you want to use the default ODBC provider.

24x7 Data Providers

It is worth noting that Windows doesn't necessarily come with the SQL Server OLEDB provider already installed. If you try to run the preceding script on a computer where the provider has not been installed, you will get a runtime error.

The best way to keep all your data providers up-to-date is to regularly download and install the latest Data Access Components from Microsoft. For more information, refer to http://www.microsoft.com/data.

SQL Server on a Remote Machine

Working with a remote SQL Server can be a little trickier than working with one located directly on the Web server running your ASP scripts.

Establishing a Remote DSN

In the previous section on working with local SQL Server databases, you learned how to set up and configure a DSN for your data access scripts to use. Many of these steps are the same when you want to set up a DSN for a remote SQL Server, but there are a few differences.

1. Open the ODBC Data Source administrator.

2. Add a user, file, or system DSN for the SQL Server. For more information on the differences between these three kinds of DSN, see the section later in this chapter on DSN selection.

3. Enter a name and description for your DSN.

4. Enter the name or IP address of your SQL Server into the box labeled "Server." *This is an entirely different concept from the name of the machine on which your SQL Server is running!* If you have any doubts, consult your SQL Server administrator.

5. Click the button labeled Next.

6. If your ASP application will be using Anonymous or Basic authentication, make sure that the radio button labeled "With SQL Server Authentication" is enabled. Otherwise, choose "With Windows NT Authentication."

7. Click the button labeled "Client Configuration." You'll see the screen shown in Figure 10-9.

8. In the frame labeled "Network Libraries," choose the protocol by which you intend to communicate across the network with your SQL Server. If you are unsure about this, consult your SQL Server administrator.

9. In the frame labeled "Connection Parameters," enter any data specific to the protocol you have chosen for your networked SQL Server access.

10. Click OK.

11. Click Next.

12. Click Next.

13. Click Finish.

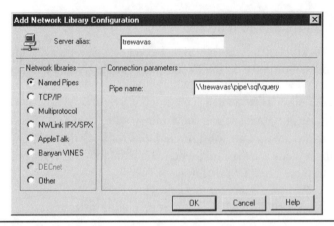

Figure 10.9   The Add Network Library Configuration dialog

If you click the button labeled "Test Data Source," you should see a brief pause followed by a message box confirming your ability to connect to SQL Server. If your system hangs at this point or if you get an error message, it means that there is a problem with SQL Server itself, with some of the configuration settings you have chosen, or with the network connection between your computer and the one on which SQL Server is running.

You can begin testing the network connection between your computer and the one running SQL Server simply by using the Ping command. Ping sends several blocks of data to a remote computer on a prespecified port and waits for that remote computer to echo them back. If the blocks aren't echoed back, the other computer either is not receiving the blocks or is unable to respond.

To use Ping to test a remote computer's network connectivity, type

```
ping <computer name>
```

at the Windows command prompt. If there is a problem connecting to the target computer, you will see a screen that looks more like Figure 10-10.

If Ping works and you are certain that SQL Server is running properly on the remote computer, but you still can't connect, your choice of networking protocols is the most likely culprit. You can change your protocol selection by clicking the "Client Configuration" button during DSN setup. SQL Server supports several different protocols out-of-the-box.

Named Pipes   This is usually the default option when establishing a new DSN for SQL Server. Named pipes are one of the lowest-level communications

```
E:\WINNT\System32\cmd.exe                                    _ □ ✕

E:\>ping www.yahoo.com

Pinging www.yahoo.akadns.net [204.71.202.160] with 32 bytes of data:

Hardware error.
Hardware error.
Hardware error.
Hardware error.

Ping statistics for 204.71.202.160:
    Packets: Sent = 4, Received = 0, Lost = 4 (100% loss),
Approximate round trip times in milli-seconds:
    Minimum = 0ms, Maximum =  0ms, Average =  0ms

E:\>
```

Figure 10.10   Cannot connect to your target computer

mechanisms provided by the Windows operating system. For this reason, you should choose this protocol if *and only if* the computer running your SQL Server and all its clients are all running the Windows operating system. Named pipes are an ideal choice when the performance of your connection is of the utmost importance.

TCP/IP   The Internet runs on this protocol, therefore it is an ideal choice for connecting computers across the Internet. TCP/IP is also arguably the most platform-neutral and widely available networking protocol.

Multiprotocol   The multiprotocol setting allows your client to try several different protocols for connecting to SQL Server until it finds one that works. This should be your choice whenever you aren't sure about the specifics of your connection.

IPX   IPX is the native protocol spoken by systems such as NetWare, and it was the industry standard before the rise of the Internet to prominence during the mid-1990s. If your organization still uses such a network, this may be your only option for connecting to SQL Server.

Security Settings

In order for Windows authentication to operate properly between Active Server Pages and SQL Server, your scripts must be permissioned in a way that requires your users to identify themselves. The standard way to do this is to enable

Windows authentication for whatever ASP applications you intend to use with SQL Server. To do this, follow these steps:

1. Choose Programs from the Windows Start menu.
2. Open the Administrative Tools program group.
3. Select Internet Services Manager.
4. Right-click the icon for your application in the left-hand tree view.
5. Choose Properties from the pop-up context menu.
6. Select the Security tab.
7. Click the Edit button in the "Anonymous Access and Authentication Control" frame.
8. Make sure that "Integrated Windows Authentication" is enabled.
9. Click OK to confirm your changes.

Error Watch *It is important that, besides turning on Windows authentication, you also turn off anonymous authentication for any ASP application that will use Windows authentication to connect to SQL Server. The reason for this is that, with anonymous authentication available, it is typically possible for users to connect to your application without being forced to identify themselves. They are then operating under the default IUSR_<machine name> account, which typically lacks permissions on SQL Server databases.*

Accounts

Once you have enabled Windows authentication for your Active Server Pages application and configured your DSN to connect using Windows authentication, you might expect everything to be smooth sailing. You would, of course, be mistaken. Consider the following code listing:

```
<%
    Option Explicit

    Dim cn
    Dim rst
```

```
    Set cn = Server.CreateObject("ADODB.Connection")
    Set rst = Server.CreateObject("ADODB.Recordset")

    cn.provider = "MSDASQL"
    cn.open "operations", "sa", ""

    rst.open "SELECT software FROM inventory", cn

    do until rst.eof
        response.write rst.fields(0) & "<br>"

        rst.movenext
    loop
%>
```

The main problem with this listing is that it still explicitly requests the use of the SQL Server system account, "sa." This completely defeats the purpose of enabling Windows authentication. The idea is that the login used to connect to the SQL Server should be the same as whatever login is used to connect to your ASP application. In order for this to happen, the line in the preceding code should read

```
cn.open "operations"
```

There are three kinds of accounts that might try to run this script:

OK to Run Scripts	OK to Access SQL Server	Results
No	No	Refused access
Yes	No	Error
Yes	Yes	Success

It is normal for users to be refused access when they don't have permissions on your ASP scripts, so this is acceptable. It is also normal for users to successfully use your scripts when they have the required permissions, so there is no need to discuss this. Allowing users to access your pages without granting them access to the required databases will generate the run-time error shown in Figure 10-11, however.

Users typically find this confusing, so it is better to prevent users from accessing any ASP scripts that might perform data access that you want to

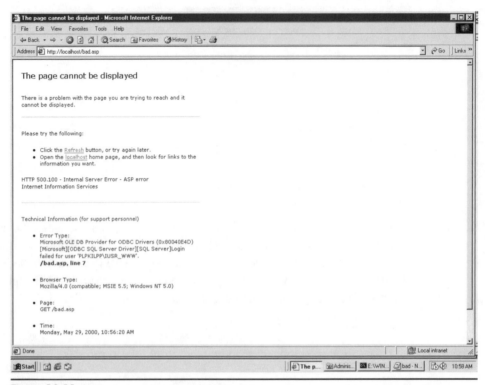

Figure 10.11 An access error

restrict. If you get the error shown in Figure 10-11, and you would like for the user in question to be able to access your SQL Server, you must add an entry for them into the SQL Server users' database.

1. Select Programs from the Windows Start menu.

2. Open the Microsoft SQL Server 7.0 program group.

3. Select Enterprise Manager.

4. Locate the SQL Server in question in the tree view on the left.

5. Double-click the icon to start the SQL Server Taskpad. You'll see the screen shown in Figure 10-12.

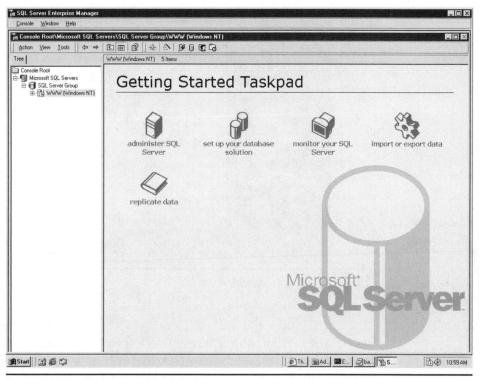

Figure 10.12   The Taskpad opening screen

6. Click the icon labeled "Administer SQL Server."

7. Click the icon labeled "Create a Login." You should see the Create Login Wizard, shown in Figure 10-13.

8. Click Next.

9. On Select Authentication Mode screen, make sure that "Windows NT Account Information" is selected.

10. Click Next.

Figure 10.13 The Create Login Wizard

11. On the Authentication with Windows NT screen, enter the domain and login for the user to whom you would like to grant access in the text box labeled "Windows NT Account" (see Figure 10-14).

12. Make sure that "Grant Access to the Server" is selected.

13. Click Next.

14. On the Grant Access to Security Roles screen, if you would like this user to be able to participate in the administration of this SQL Server, select the appropriate roles from the list of checkboxes.

15. Click Next.

16. On the Grant Access to Databases screen, select all the databases to which you would like to give this user access.

17. Click Next.

18. Click Finish. Your screen should resemble Figure 10-15.

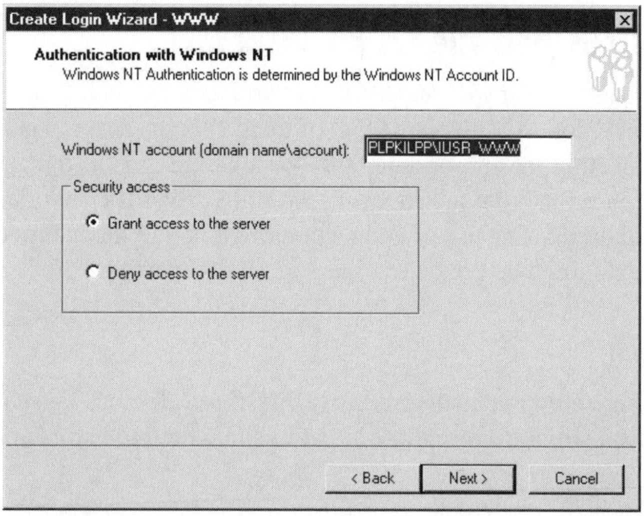

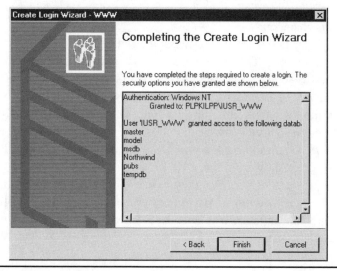

Figure 10.14   Granting a user access

Figure 10.15   The Create Login Wizard completed

Data Sources and the ODBC Interface

There are many data sources that you can use with Active Server Pages besides Microsoft SQL Server. Most of them support access via the ODBC interface. Selecting the appropriate DSN for an ODBC data source is very important to its proper functioning. Choosing the right driver for your database is also extremely important. The use of connection pooling and the nature of the code itself are the remaining two big determiners of ODBC performance.

DSN Selection

There are three main kinds of DSNs: user, file, and system. In this section, you will learn the appropriate situations in which to use each of them.

User DSNs

Data sources listed under the User DSN tab of the ODBC Data Source Administrator are available only by the account under which they are created. Configuration of user DSNs is essentially the same as for system DSNs, which you have seen earlier in this chapter.

User DSNs are typically not a good choice for use with Active Server Page applications. This is because ASP scripts typically execute under the identity of the IIS server process, which is the elusive system account. Because there is no way to log in under the system account, there is no way to create a user DSN while logged in under this account. This means, essentially, that there is no way to create a user DSN for direct use by your Active Server Pages.

If you try to access a user DSN from an Active Server Page script, you will get the error shown in Figure 10-16.

This can be confusing to novice ASP developers who insist, "But I *do* have a DSN named this!" Always remember: If your scripts complain about a missing DSN, check to see if it is a user DSN. If it is, consider switching to a file or system DSN.

File DSNs

File DSNs are similar to system DSNs, with the added benefit that they are saved to files that can then be exchanged between computers. This is useful in cases where you believe that you may have to run multiple instances of the same ASP

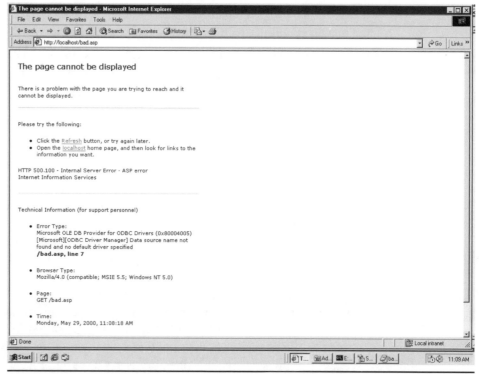

Figure 10.16   Trying to access a user DSN from an ASP generates this error

application on multiple machines, such as in a "Web farm" setting. After copying the files for your application and installing any necessary COM components, you could simply copy over the files for your DSNs and begin using them.

You can establish a DSN for your SQL Server by following these steps:

1. Choose Settings from the Windows Start menu.

2. Open the Control Panel.

3. Double-click the Data Sources (ODBC) icon.

4. Select the File DSN tab.

5. Click the Add button.

6. Choose the appropriate driver from the list box.

7. Click the Next button. You'll see the screen shown in Figure 10-17.

8. Choose a filename under which you would like to store your DSN configuration and place it in the text field on the Create New Data Source dialog.

9. Click Next.

10. Click Finish.

At this point, you may finish configuring your DSN according to the procedures for configuring a DSN outlined at the start of this chapter. All the remaining screens should be familiar to you if you have already read the section on configuring SQL Server for local use.

If you should ever need to use this DSN on another machine, the first thing you must do is ensure that the other machine has the appropriate driver installed. For example, you cannot use a file DSN for an Access database on another computer unless that computer also has the ODBC driver for Microsoft Access installed.

Once you are certain that all the right software and drivers are installed on your target computer, you can copy the file that was created earlier in step 8. It is important that this file be placed in the right directory in order for ODBC to be able to "see it." In many systems, this directory is at "\Program Files\Common

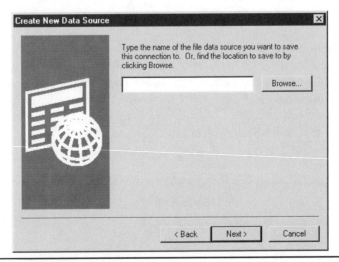

Figure 10.17   Establishing a data source

Files\ODBC\Data Sources." In order to verify the location on your own target system, follow these steps:

1. Choose Settings from the Windows Start menu.
2. Open the Control Panel.
3. Double-click the Data Sources (ODBC) icon.
4. Select the File DSN tab.
5. Click the Set Directory button. A dialog will appear that specifies the correct directory for file DSNs on your target system.

System DSNs

System DSNs are a good "default choice" for Active Server Page developers who don't have any of the "special needs" described earlier. A system DSN is available to all the users on a given system. This doesn't necessarily mean that all users are granted access to the databases pointed to by the DSNs. It merely means that any scripts running on the system where such a DSN is present will be able to "see" that DSN and at least attempt to access it.

Drivers

Earlier in this chapter, you learned about the Microsoft OLE DB provider for SQL Server. This is just one of many drivers available for accessing many different kinds of data. Microsoft Access and Microsoft Oracle are two other extremely popular data sources for use with ASP scripts.

Microsoft Access

The Microsoft Access database uses a native storage format known as the JET engine. This engine can provide extremely fast access to relatively small quantities of data and is, therefore, an ideal choice for use in single-user, desktop applications. It begins to fall short, however, when the amount of data (or number of users wanting access to that data) grows beyond a certain point.

If your ASP application deals with less than 1 gigabyte of data and anticipates fewer than 5–10 simultaneous users at any point in time, a Microsoft Access database can provide a cost-effective alternative to more sophisticated storage like SQL Server or Oracle. To use such a database from your Active Server Pages, add either a system or file DSN for it to your system using the methods outlined earlier.

24x7   Securing an Access Database

One of the most frequent questions asked by Active Server Page developers working with Access databases is, "How can I protect my Access databases from tampering?" It is a fair question. Developers spend a lot of time making sure that their ASP scripts run securely. It would be a shame indeed to lose important data because your database itself was left unprotected.

There are two simple things that you can do to increase the security of your Access databases enormously. First make sure that your database is located in a directory *outside* the boundaries of your Web site. This way, even if the permissions on your directories are set improperly, it will be impossible for hackers to locate and download your database over the network.

The other thing you can do with an Access database, which very few developers seem to realize, is password-protect it. To password-protect an Access database, follow these steps:

1. Open Microsoft Access.
2. Choose Open from the File menu.
3. Select your database.
4. Choose Open Exclusive on the Open button's drop-down list.
5. On the menu bar, choose Tools, Security, Set Database Password.
6. Enter your chosen password in the Set Database Password dialog.
7. Click OK to confirm your changes.

The connect string for your database must now include a password that matches the one you entered in the Password dialog. The username you provide, if any, is irrelevant.

```
cn.open "accessdb", "blahblahblah", "password"
cn.open "accessdb", "nouser", "password"
cn.open "accessdb", "", "password"
```

Oracle

Oracle is one of the oldest and most respected database servers on the market today. It has a well-deserved reputation for almost never crashing and, on the rare occasion that it does crash, losses of data are almost unheard of. Balanced against these strengths is its traditional Achilles heel: cost of ownership. Full-time Oracle

DBAs must administer almost all professional Oracle databases. The cost of the base software is also rather pricey in comparison to some other solutions, such as SQL Server.

If your organization has data stored in Oracle, however, there are excellent ways available to use it directly from your Active Server Pages. Arguably the best way is the Microsoft OLE DB provider for Oracle. In order to use it, you must first ensure that the client software for Oracle, which is provided by Oracle, is installed on the machine where your ASP scripts will execute.

At this point, you may use Oracle data from your scripts just as you would any other data source. Simply use the string "MSDAORA" as the setting for your Connection object's Provider property.

```
<%
    Option Explicit

    Dim cn

    Set cn = Server.CreateObject("ADODB.Connection")
    cn.Provider = "MSDAORA"

    cn.open "oracledb", "user42", "8pass23"

    ' Rest of your code goes here
%>
```

If you get an error on the line of your script that attempts to set the provider to use the Microsoft OLEDB provider for Oracle, it probably means that this driver is not available on your system. To correct this, download the newest version of this driver from http://www.microsoft.com/data.

Connection Pooling

Connection pooling can greatly enhance the performance of your Active Server Page applications. Without connection pooling, every request for a new connection to a database that comes in from your ASP scripts must be serviced from scratch. This means that a brand new connection must be created, given to your application, and then completely destroyed when your application is finished with it (see Figure 10-18).

In contrast, connection pooling maintains a certain number of connections to your database in a constantly ready state. This means that requests made by your Active Server Page applications for new connections can usually be serviced directly from the pool of existing connections. This eliminates the

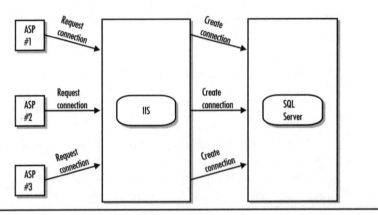

Figure 10.18   ASP performance without connection pooling

performance-intensive task of creating a new connection from scratch (see Figure 10-19).

ODBC Connection Pooling

One of the first kinds of connection pooling made available for use with Active Server Pages was ODBC connection pooling. Under this kind of pooling, the ODBC driver manager maintains a pool of connections for direct use by your applications. The advantage to this is that it is transparent to the code making use of these connections—everything is handled for you by ODBC. The disadvantage is that this pooling will not help any of your scripts that use non-ODBC drivers, such as the Microsoft OLEDB drivers for SQL Server and Oracle.

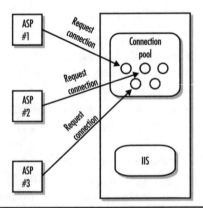

Figure 10.19   ASP performance with connection pooling

To turn on connection pooling, follow these steps:

1. Select Settings from the Windows Start menu.
2. Open the Control Panel.
3. Open Administrative Tools.
4. Open Data Sources (ODBC).
5. Choose the tab Connection Pooling (see Figure 10-20).
6. Select the driver for which you would like to enable connection pooling from the list and double-click it.
7. Make sure that "Pool Connections to This Driver" is enabled (see Figure 10-21).
8. Click OK to confirm your selection.
9. Click OK again to confirm your selection.

Component Services

If you intend to use OLEDB providers to access your data, you should consider encapsulating all your data access code in components running under Microsoft Component Services. Situations where this might arise include working with

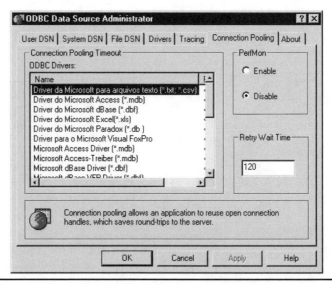

Figure 10.20 The Connection Pooling tab of the ODBC Data Source Administrator

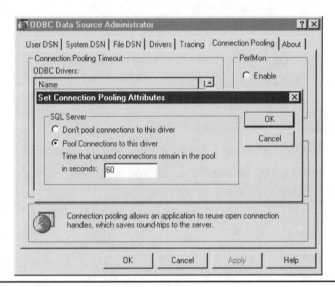

Figure 10.21 Enabling connection pooling to a driver

SQL Server and Oracle databases, which have an excellent OLEDB provider available directly from Microsoft.

Component Services automatically provide pooling for OLEDB connections. In order to use this function, load your components that access OLEDB data sources into Component Services.

```
<%
    Option Explicit

    Dim obj
    Dim strEmployeeName

    ' Instantiate a component to perform our data access
    Set obj = Server.CreateObject("MyData.Customers")

    ' Get the name associated with this employee #
    strEmployeeName =obj.getNameForNumber(4272)

    Set obj = Nothing
%>
```

This sample code is for using a component running under Component Services to access your data source and return some useful information.

The getNameForNumber method is be responsible for making the actual connection to the database. This allows Component Services to serve the connection from its internal pool.

```
Option Explicit

public function getNameForNumber(intEmployeeNumber)
    Dim cn as ADODB.Connection
    Dim rst as ADODB.Recordset

    Set cn = new ADODB.Connection
    Set rst = new ADODB.Recordset

    cn.provider = "MSDAORA"
    cn.open "employees"

    rst.open "select name from employees where number = " & _
        intEmployeeNumber, cn

    getNameForNumber = rst.fields(0)

    cn.close
end function
```

Design Tip   *In order for connection pooling to work most effectively, it is important that your scripts not leave connections open for any longer than is absolutely necessary. Notice that this method opens a connection, retrieves its information, and then closes its connection. This would be a bad design in situations where connections had to be constantly recreated from scratch because of the time required to create connections. In a situation where connections are pooled and ready, however, this is the appropriate way to design your applications.*

Coding Database Connections

The way that you code your attempts to connect to databases from ASP can be a major source of bugs in your applications. Some of these bugs are the result of improper syntax in your connection requests. Others involve the tricky formatting of DSN-less connection strings.

Syntax
Many of the errors surrounding ADO connections from Active Server Pages stem from the switch in naming conventions for the ADO objects. The earliest

versions of ADO used the name ADO.Connection for referring to the Connection object. Later, it was changed to ADODB.Connection. For this reason, the following simple script generates an error if you attempt to run it.

```
<%
   Option Explicit

   Dim cn

   Set cn = Server.CreateObject("ADO.Connection")
%>
```

Getting an error here mystifies many developers, who think that a script this simple should never fail. If you have been using ADO ever since its earliest days, you should always remember to check your scripts for the presence of the string "ADO" and replace every one with "ADODB." This prevents you from getting into any serious problems with name changes.

Connection Strings

The people who run Windows Web servers are often different from those who write the Active Server Pages applications that run on those machines. This can lead to problems where ODBC data source names are concerned. Suppose that you wrote a series of scripts intended to work with the DSN named "alcatraz." You might create this DSN and have your application working fine, but there is nothing to stop an administrator from later removing or renaming this DSN for some reason. In the event of this happening, your entire application would grind to an immediate halt.

One way to prevent these kinds of situations from arising is to make use of so-called DSN-less connection strings. A DSN-less connection contains all the information that ADO needs in order to build a connection to an external data source. This removes the need for a specific DSN containing this information in the ODBC data sources. One example of a DSN-less connection string might be

```
"uid=sa;driver={SQL Server};server=teriyaki;database=sales"
```

This line tells ODBC to connect to the "sales" database on the server named "teriyaki" using the SQL Server driver and a username of "sa." This username is assumed not to need a password. If it had, the string "pwd=<<password>>" could be used to specify it.

You may elect to use this connection string in your code where you would typically place the DSN for your data source.

```
cn.open "uid=sa;driver={SQL
Server};server=teriyaki;database=sales"
```

Alternatively, you might make use of the Connection object's built-in ConnectString property.

```
cn.connectstring = "uid=sa;driver={SQL Server};_
    server=teriyaki;database=sales"
cn.open
```

Design Tip *It is slightly more efficient for ODBC to use connection strings like these shown here than DSNs. For this reason, when performance is a concern, you might want to consider using these strings instead of DSNs.*

Returning Recordsets from Your Data

This is the second in a three-chapter look at debugging data issues under Active Server Pages. In the previous chapter you learned about debugging ASP connections to various and sundry data sources. In this chapter, you will learn how to troubleshoot problems encountered while trying to return recordsets from data sources to your Active Server Pages.

Using Disconnected Recordsets

The preferred method for manipulating data in your ASP scripts is through the use of disconnected recordsets. Disconnected recordsets offer performance benefits (in the areas of memory and connections) and database support. They are also, when returned from COM components, a way that your ASP scripts can collect the data they need to operate.

Performance Benefits

The use of disconnected recordsets in your Active Server Pages offers the opportunity for performance benefits in two keys areas. The first benefit is a reduction in the amount of memory required on the database server's machine. The second benefit is a reduction in the total number of connections that must be maintained between the database server and Internet Information Server.

Memory

When you open an ordinary recordset under Active Data Objects, a good-sized portion of memory is consumed on the database server. This is because all the data in your recordset must be maintained on the server, in isolation from all other recordsets currently being manipulated on the same server.

```
<%
   Option Explicit

   Dim strQry

   Dim cn
   Dim rst

   Set cn = Server.CreateObject("ADODB.Connection")
   Set rst = Server.CreateObject("ADODB.Recordset")

   cn.open "albums", "producer", "43fds77"

   strQry = "SELECT name, artist, year "
```

```
    strQry = strQry & "FROM records "
    strQry = strQry & "WHERE producer = '" & Request("producer") & "'"

    rst.open strQry, cn

    Do until rst.EOF
        rst.MoveNext
    Loop
%>
```

If five Web clients created separate sessions with your ASP application and each executed this script simultaneously, you might imagine the situation as looking like Figure 11-1.

Note that the memory used on the database server is equal to the size of the recordset multiplied by the number of clients currently using server-side copies of it. The main benefit of using disconnected recordsets, from a standpoint of memory, is that it offloads this burden to the client requesting it.

```
<!--#INCLUDE FILE="adoconsts.inc" -->

<%
    Option Explicit

    Dim strQry

    Dim cn
    Dim rst

    Set cn = Server.CreateObject("ADODB.Connection")
    Set rst = Server.CreateObject("ADODB.Recordset")

    rst.RecordsetLocation = adUseClient

    cn.open "albums", "producer", "43fds77"

    strQry = "SELECT name, artist, year "
    strQry = strQry & "FROM records "
    strQry = strQry & "WHERE producer = '" & Request("producer") & _ "'"

    rst.open strQry, cn, adOpenForwardOnly, adLockBatchOptimistic

    Set rst.ActiveConnection = Nothing

    Do until rst.EOF
        rst.MoveNext
    Loop
%>
```

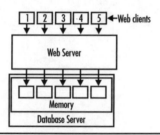

Figure 11.1 Storing recordsets on the database server

Notice first that the RecordsetLocation property of the recordset has been set to the constant adUseClient, which is intended to indicate that a client-side cursor should be used. Next, notice that additional parameters are passed to the recordset's open method to indicate that the recordset should be opened in a way that allows movement only from start to finish through the recordset, with a minimum of record locking. The final new action in this code is the line that sets the recordset's ActiveConnection to Nothing, so that the connection can be reclaimed as soon as possible.

Error Watch *Remember, if you are going to use constants like those shown in the previous example listing, they must be defined somewhere in your ASP script. In this example, we chose to place these constants into a separate file named ADOCONSTS.INC, which we then included in our script using a server-side include directive.*

After modifying the preceding code to use disconnected recordsets, the situation now looks like Figure 11-2.

This example may surprise you. There are five Web clients, and you were told that disconnected recordsets store their data on the client. So why are all the

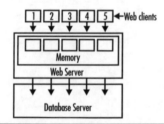

Figure 11.2 Storing disconnected recordsets on the Web server

recordsets here located on the Web server? The reason for this is that, as far as Active Data Objects are concerned, the client of the database server is your Active Server Pages application. The Web clients are clients of your application, not the database server itself.

This means that the memory burden associated with maintaining these recordsets has effectively been moved from your database server to your Web server. This is usually a good trade, because database servers typically require more memory just to operate than do Web servers. The reason for this is that database servers achieve peak performance when the data being requested by clients is already located in memory, rather than having to be read in from disk. The best way for database servers to achieve this is to store as much data in memory at a time as possible. This invariably leads database servers to use every bit of memory available on their system.

Connections

The other benefit to using disconnected recordsets is that they allow you to reduce the number of simultaneously open connections on your database server. If you compare and contrast the structure of the previous two code listings for a moment, you will quickly see why this is the case. The first listing performs the following steps:

1. Open the connection.
2. Open the recordset.
3. Work with the data.
4. Close the recordset (implicit).
5. Close the connection (implicit).

Steps 2 through 4 are all executed while the database connection is still open. Step 3 may be particularly lengthy, also.

In contrast, the second listing performs these steps:

1. Open the connection.
2. Open the recordset.
3. Close the connection.
4. Work with the data.
5. Close the recordset (implicit).

Notice that only step 2 is performed while the database connection is open in this listing, resulting in a vast decrease in the amount of time that the connection must be kept open. The most time-intensive step, working with the data, is delayed until after the connection has already been closed.

The reduction in the length of time that connections are kept open reduces the number of simultaneous connections that the target database server must be able to support. This is because, with less time open per connection, the chance that multiple clients will want to have connections open at the same time is considerably decreased. You might imagine the phenomenon looking like Figure 11-3.

Database Support

Support for recordsets of various kinds varies greatly from one database to another. On one hand, this may mean that some databases support client-side cursors while others do not. On the other hand, most client-side cursor support is dependent on the capability of a database server to maintain bookmarks in a recordset. Support for bookmarks also varies among database servers.

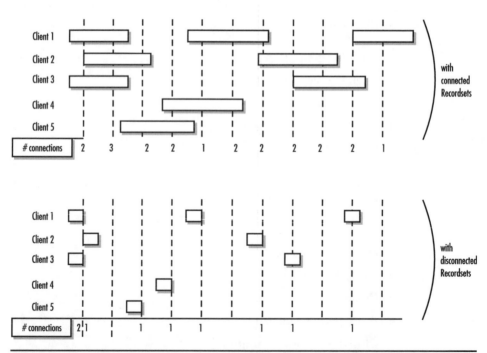

Figure 11.3   The difference in connection times when using disconnected recordsets

Client-side Cursors

A cursor is the bit of a database system that defines how the records in a recordset can be used and accessed. For example, some cursors allow records to be accessed in any order while others require that they be traversed in a forward-only manner. Some cursors support only the reading of data from your recordsets while others allow you to freely write to your data as well.

In order for a database to support disconnected recordsets, it must minimally offer support for the maintenance of recordsets on the client, as opposed to the server. Fortunately, most major database servers now offer such support, including SQL Server and Oracle.

Bookmarks

A lack of support for bookmarks in a database or its driver will typically not prevent the creation of a disconnected recordset. It may, however, prevent changes to such a recordset from being merged back into the database from which the data was originally taken. This will cause your scripts to fail at whatever point you first call the UpdateBatch method on your recordset.

```
<!--#INCLUDE FILE="adoconsts.inc" -->

<%
    Option Explicit

    Dim strQry

    Dim cn
    Dim rst

    Set cn = Server.CreateObject("ADODB.Connection")
    Set rst = Server.CreateObject("ADODB.Recordset")

    rst.RecordsetLocation = adUseClient

    cn.open "albums", "producer", "43fds77"

    strQry = "SELECT name, artist, year "
    strQry = strQry & "FROM records "
    strQry = strQry & "WHERE producer = '" & Request("producer") & "'"

    rst.open strQry, cn, adOpenForwardOnly, adLockBatchOptimistic

    Set rst.ActiveConnection = Nothing
```

```
Do until rst.EOF
    rst.fields(3) = "1967"
    rst.MoveNext
Loop

rst.ActiveConnection = cn
rst.UpdateBatch
%>
```

This code represents a further modification to the examples at the start of this chapter. Here, we have added a line that sets the year in which each album was produced to "1967" by looping through every record in the dataset. After this is done, the recordset is reconnected to the database and the changes are transmitted to the server through the UpdateBatch method.

Design Tip *Modifying data this way is extremely inefficient. Preferably, changes such as those shown earlier would be made either via a single SQL statement or, even better, through a stored procedure. For more information, see the following chapter.*

The problem here is that, unless the database server supports bookmarks, it will be incapable of figuring out which rows in the disconnected recordset correspond with which rows in the server's own storage. This will result in the generation of an error and the termination of your ASP script, along with the loss of all your changes!

To prevent this situation, always verify that your database and database driver support the modification as well as creation of disconnected recordsets. The OLEDB drivers for SQL Server and Oracle both work fine for this purpose.

Returning Recordsets from Components

One of the best ways to use disconnected recordsets is by returning them from COM components. This way, your ASP scripts can instantiate custom objects to collect the data they need to operate. The benefit to this is that it represents a true encapsulation of data access issues from the business logic and user interface of your Web applications. This would make it much easier to change database servers or data schemas in the future, should the need ever arise.

Cloning

To return a disconnected recordset from a COM component, you should first clone it. Your code may then close the original and return the clone. This is the best way to ensure complete separation of your ASP code and your database server. Here is some typical ASP code that might use such a component:

```
<%
    Option Explicit

    Dim obj
    Dim rst

    Set obj = Server.CreateObject("Custom.GrabSomeRecords")

    Set rst = obj.ReturnRecordset("dolphins")

    do until rst.eof
        response.write rst.fields(0) & "<br>"
        rst.movenext
    loop
%>
```

This code relies completely on the Custom.GrabSomeRecords object to establish a connection to the database, select some appropriate records, and return them. If this component failed to generate a recordset and return it, the preceding script would fail completely. For this reason, a more bulletproof way of stating this code is

```
If obj.ReturnRecordset("dolphins", rst) Then
    Do until rst.eof
        response.write rst.fields(0) & "<br>"
        rst.movenext
    Loop
Else
    Response.Write "No recordset returned!"
End If
```

This way, the return value of the COM function can be used to indicate whether the attempt to retrieve a recordset succeeded.

```
Option Explicit

public function ReturnRecordset(species, prst)
    On Error Goto Oops

    Dim cn as ADODB.Connection
    Dim rst as ADODB.Recordset
```

```
Set cn = new ADODB.Connection
Set rst = new ADODB.Recordset

with rst
   .CursorLocation = adUseClient
   .CursorType = adOpenStatic
   .LockType = adLockBatchOptimistic
   .ActiveConnection = cn
   .Open "select * from ocean where species = '" & species & "'"
   .ActiveConnection = Nothing
end with

Set prst = rst.clone
rst.close
cn.close

ReturnRecordset = True

exit function

Oops:

ReturnRecordset = False

end function
```

Here, the code is using an On Error construction to ensure that, if anything breaks, the return value of the function will be explicitly (rather than implicitly) set to False. Using a With…End With construction like that shown in the code listing allows Visual Basic to improve component performance by retaining a reference to the object being worked with between calls. The cloning occurs towards the end of the listing and allows the original recordset to be closed immediately, along with the connection.

SQL

The most common way to interact with data sources under Active Server Pages is via the Structured Query Language, or SQL. The peculiar constructions and rules of this language can create a certain number of issues for ASP programmers in their own right. In this section, you will learn about a number of the most common issues and how to avoid them.

24x7   Passing Recordsets through Process Boundaries

In Chapters 7 and 8, you learned a great deal about the differences between in-process and out-of-process COM components. From the perspective of an ASP developer, a fundamental difference between the two lies in their performance under Internet Information Server. IIS can treat calls to in-process components just like calls to its own internal procedures, because such components execute completely within Internet Information Server's own process space. However, calls to out-of-process components must pass through the process boundaries of both IIS and the component itself.

At the time of this writing, there is a bug that affects the way this works under Active Server Pages and Active Data Objects. If you try to return disconnected recordsets to your scripts from out-of-process components, you might receive either an "Out of Memory" error or an "Unspecified Error" message. Both of these are completely erroneous and are actually caused by the way that disconnected recordsets are passed through process boundaries. You might recall that this is called *marshalling*.

For more information on this bug, consult Microsoft Knowledge Base article Q237536.

Special Characters

There are three kinds of special characters that can lead you into problems when working with Active Server Pages: quotes, wildcards, and spaces.

Quotes

Single quotes are often used to distinguish string constants from the rest of a line of SQL code. For example, in the code segment below, the last name of the customer is enclosed in single quotes to indicate that it is a string value ('Roose').

```
<%
    Option Explicit

    Dim cn
    Set cn = Server.CreateObject("ADODB.Connection")

    cn.open "companyinfo", "sa", ""

    cn.execute "delete from customers where name = 'Roose'"
%>
```

The problem arises with strings that contain single quotes themselves. This is most commonly caused by apostrophes for contractions and last names.

```
cn.execute "delete from customers where name = 'O'Leary'"
```

When the database tries to interpret this SQL command, it will see it in two parts:

1. delete from customers where name = 'O'.

2. Leary'.

Part 1 is perfectly valid, but part 2 is absolute nonsense as far as SQL interpreters are concerned. For this reason, a database engine will throw out the entire SQL command and not execute either portion.

The way to overcome this is to make sure that any single quotes contained within your string constants are replaced by two instances of the single quote. You can do this by leveraging the new *replace* statement available in VB Script.

```
do until rst.eof
    lastname = rst.fields(0)
    lastname = replace(lastname, "'", "''")
    cn.execute "delete from customers where name = '" & lastname & "'"
    rst.movenext
loop
```

This code shows how replace can be used to ensure that there are no single quotes within your string constants without even knowing at compile time what strings are going to be a part of your SQL statements. Using this above, a last name such as Roose would remain completely unchanged, while a last name like O'Leary would become O''Leary.

Error Watch *It is important to note that two single quotes are not the same as a single double quote. Most database engines do not use double quotes within their SQL statements at all. Consult the documentation for your database's SQL implementation for further information.*

Wildcards

Wildcard characters allow you to create SQL that works against data that matches certain prespecified patterns, rather than absolute string literals. Suppose, for instance, that you want to delete all the customers from your database who have a last name starting with the letter "F." You might write a script that looks like this:

```
<%
   Option Explicit

   Dim cn
   Set cn = Server.CreateObject("ADODB.Connection")

   cn.open "companyinfo", "sa", ""

   cn.execute "delete from customers where name like 'F%'"
%>
```

Here, we have replaced the usual equal sign with the keyword *like* and substituted a % sign to represent all of the characters of which we were unsure. This is just one of the wildcard characters available to you under SQL Server. Your exact options vary with your choice of database server.

The potential trouble with this approach would arise if you ever want to actually use any of these wildcard symbols as literals in your search strings. Consider the case of the underscore symbol, which (under SQL Server) stipulates that exactly one character in a given string may be anything. You might have a table in your database where the full names of all your employees are stored as follows:

```
Ada_Michaelson
Ada_Zepherson
Adam_Horowitz
Sarah_Rotterman
Tyler_Peters
```

How could you use SQL to delete all the employees with the first name "Ada" without also grabbing "Adam"? A first approach might be something like

```
cn.execute "delete from employees where name like 'Ada_%'"
```

But SQL Server would interpret the underscore as a wildcard that would match against any single character, followed by the percent sign, which is a wildcard matching any string of characters. This would result in deleting Adam as well as the two Adas.

In order to use any character that is a wildcard as if it were just a literal character inside of a LIKE clause, you should preface it with an *escape*

character. The escape character under SQL Server is the backward slash (\).
Here's how you would use this character in the preceding example:

```
cn.execute "delete from employees where name like "Ada\_%"
```

This lets SQL Server know that you really want to match the underscore in your
string against an underscore in the data.

Spaces

A difference in the number of spaces surrounding string literals in your SQL
and the fields in your databases can also cause many errors in your Active
Server Pages. For a full discussion of this phenomenon, refer to Chapter 12.

Multiple Recordsets

ADO allows Active Server Page developers to work with queries that return
more than a single recordset. In this section, you will learn how to avoid some
of the pitfalls that often accompany this functionality.

Creating Multiple Recordset Queries

Most SQL queries result in the return of a single recordset to the client application.
All the code listings so far in this book have been of this type. It is possible, however,
to create SQL queries that return multiple recordsets of data. Here is an example of
code that would do this:

```
<%
    Option Explicit

    Dim cn, rst
    Dim strQry

    Set cn = Server.CreateObject("ADODB.Connection")
    Set rst = Server.CreateObject("ADODB.Recordset")

    cn.open "corpinfo", "bigboss", "hrfuwhhb"

    strQry = "SELECT name, title, manager "
    strQry = strQry & "FROM employees "
    strQry = strQry & "COMPUTE count(*) BY manager "

    rst.open strQry, cn
%>
```

This code uses a SQL keyword that you may not have encountered before: COMPUTE. This keyword allows you to include aggregate functions, such as SUM and COUNT, in the same SQL query as one that produces detail rows. The only problem with this is that, under Active Data Objects, the aggregate totals created by the COMPUTE keyword are returned in a separate resultset.

If you retrieve only the first recordset, as we have done in previous chapters, you will completely miss the aggregate totals. This is a frequent bug in Active Server Page scripts that use multiple recordset queries.

Using NextRecordset

Fortunately, ADO provides a way for you to access all the recordsets returned by a query like the one shown earlier. The Recordset object includes a method called NextRecordset which either

- Returns the next recordset in the query's results, or
- Returns nothing.

Therefore, by repeatedly calling the NextRecordset method and checking for a return value of *nothing*, it is possible to write code that is guaranteed to access all the recordsets returned by a query.

```
<%
   do until rst is nothing
      do until rst.eof
         ' Do useful stuff here
         rst.MoveNext
      loop
      set rst = rst.NextRecordset
   loop
%>
```

Code like this could be placed at the end of the previous example to navigate however many resultsets were generated by the SQL query shown. Notice that the normal loop through the rows of the recordset is present here, but only within the framework of a larger loop. It is this larger loop that performs the work of iterating through the recordsets themselves and checking for the end of the list of recordsets, as indicated by the return of *nothing*.

Different SQL Dialects

Active Server Page developers are likely to encounter many more SQL dialects than their counterparts who develop only desktop applications. It is important that you understand the relationships between some of the more common dialects.

ANSI SQL

ANSI SQL is the standard for SQL set by the American National Standards Institute. Like most standards, it is almost never encountered in its completely unadulterated form. Most of the major database engines have extended (rather than compromising) this standard, however. This means that if you limit yourself just to using the portions of SQL that are ANSI-compliant, you should find it relatively easy to use your code with just about any serious database platform.

Jet SQL

Microsoft Access uses a flavor of SQL that can be referred to as Jet SQL. *Jet* is the name of the database engine upon which Microsoft Access is based. Jet SQL implements almost all the ANSI standard, except for the following:

- COMMIT
- GRANT
- LOCK
- The use of the DISTINCT keyword inside of aggregation functions
- LIMIT TO xxx ROWS

Transact-SQL

Transact-SQL is the name of Microsoft's SQL dialect for use with their SQL Server product. You will have to use some of the peculiarities of Transact-SQL if you plan on doing any kind of advanced work with the SQL Server database. For example, stored procedures are defined and called largely by rules defined under the Transact-SQL standard.

PL-SQL

Oracle offers an implementation of SQL that is, perhaps, closest to the standard set by the American National Standards Institute. They have also, however, introduced a number of extensions that are intended to support more procedural operations than are normally available. These extensions are referred to as PL-SQL.

Modifying Data

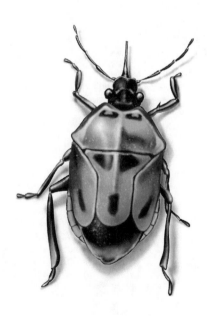

This is the third chapter in a three-chapter look at debugging your Active Server Pages' data. In this chapter, you will learn about the many issues that may arise when you try to modify data from your ASP scripts.

Stored procedures (also known as *static procedures*) are bits of data-tier code that are stored on the database server. Calling these procedures from your Active Server Pages can both decrease the possibility of bugs and improve your scripts' performance. The performance of your Active Server Pages can vary greatly, depending upon whether you choose to use stored procedures in your code.

Parsing Scripts with Stored Procedures

Every time you build and execute a SQL statement "from scratch," the database server must begin by compiling your statement and checking it for errors. If there are no errors, the server must then determine the optimal strategy to use in executing your request. Then, and only then, can the database server proceed to actually carry out your instructions. This entire process must be repeated the very next time you execute your statement.

```
<%
    Option Explicit

    If Request("animals") = "" Then
%>
    <FORM METHOD="POST">
    Which animals shall we delete?
    <INPUT TYPE="checkbox" NAME="animals" VALUE="Pig">Pig
    <INPUT TYPE="checkbox" NAME="animals" VALUE="Cow">Cow
    <INPUT TYPE="checkbox" NAME="animals" VALUE="Chicken">Chicken
    <INPUT TYPE="checkbox" NAME="animals" VALUE="Otter">Otter
    </FORM>
<%
    Else

        Dim cn
        Dim strQry, i

        Set cn = Server.CreateObject("ADODB.Connection")

        cn.open "farmdb", "farmer", "bauer"

        For I = 0 to request("animals").count - 1
            strQry = "delete from animals "
            strQry = strQry & "where name = '" & request("animals")(i) & "'"
            cn.Execute strQry
        next

    End If
```

This code builds a form that accepts a list (in the form of checkboxes) of animals to delete from the farmer's database. It then runs through all of the items in the list, constructing and sending a command string for each item that requests the deletion of the appropriate db row. Because each of these command strings are being rebuilt "from scratch" with every iteration of the loop, the database server will have to go through complete recompilation and optimization *every time the code calls cn.Execute.* As a flowchart, you might imagine it this way:

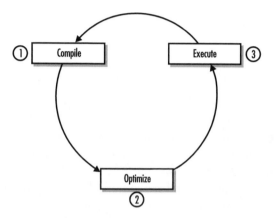

A better way to achieve the same results without recreating the query string over and over again would be to use a stored procedure. Here is what the previous code would look like if it were rewritten to use this technology:

```
<%
    Option Explicit

    If Request("animals") = "" Then
%>
    <FORM METHOD="POST">
    Which animals shall we delete?
    <INPUT TYPE="checkbox" NAME="animals" VALUE="Pig">Pig
    <INPUT TYPE="checkbox" NAME="animals" VALUE="Cow">Cow
    <INPUT TYPE="checkbox" NAME="animals" VALUE="Chicken">Chicken
    <INPUT TYPE="checkbox" NAME="animals" VALUE="Otter">Otter
    </FORM>
<%
    Else

        Dim cn
        Dim cmd
        Dim i

        Set cn = Server.CreateObject("ADODB.Connection")
```

```
        Set cmd = Server.CreateObject("ADODB.Command")

        cn.open "farmdb", "farmer", "bauer"

        cmd.CommandText "killer"
        cmd.CommandType = adCmdStoredProc
        cmd.ActiveConnection = cn

        For I = 0 to request("animals").count - 1
            cmd(0) = request("animals")(i)
            cmd.execute
        next

    End If
```

The main changes introduced into the code involve the removal of the strQry string variable and the addition of the cmd object variable. The CommandType property of the cmd object alerts Active Data Objects to the fact that "killer" is to be interpreted as the name of a stored procedure. Without this disclosure, the database might attempt to process the word "killer" as a SQL instruction, and this attempt would fail for obvious reasons.

The most important thing to notice about the changes to the code is that everything boils down to the swapping of a single variable with multiple values. This occurs within the For-Next loop on the line

```
cmd(0) = request("animals")(i)
```

This line is telling Active Data Objects to replace the first variable during each iteration of the For-Next loop. This variable replacement allows you to change the exact SQL that will be executed by the database without requiring recompilation or re-optimization. The process looks like this:

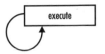

Creating Stored Procedures

Now that you understand what stored procedures are and what they can do for your Active Server Page applications, it would probably help you to know how they can be created. The exact process for this varies from one database server to the next. In the next sections, you will learn how to create procedures for Oracle and SQL Server.

Stored Procedures in Oracle

Under Oracle, the main language for stored procedures is known as PL-SQL. Describing the intricacies of PL-SQL is beyond the scope of this book, but here is an example of how you might declare a procedure such as "killer" from the previous examples:

```
CREATE OR REPLACE PROCEDURE killer (
    p_animal_name VARCHAR2) IS
BEGIN
    DELETE FROM Animals WHERE Name = p_animal_name;
    COMMIT;
EXCEPTION
    WHEN OTHERS THEN
        ROLLBACK;
        RAISE;
END killer;
```

This code is asking Oracle to create a stored procedure named "killer" that takes a single parameter as input. This parameter is the variable that you saw being swapped in the For-Next loop in the ASP examples above. It defines the stored procedure as being virtually the same as the SQL that you saw in the very first ASP example, except that it uses a variable named p_animal_name to determine which row(s) to delete, rather than having it hard-coded. In the event of success, all changes are committed. In the event of failure, everything gets rolled back.

Error Watch *This particular stored procedure has been created in the default package, which requires no special naming. More often, stored procedures under Oracle are grouped into different packages that must be named along with the procedure itself in any code that wishes to call its functionality. So, for example, if the preceding procedure occurred in a package named utils, the line naming the procedure under ASP would have to be*

```
cmd.CommandText "utils.killer"
```

Stored Procedures in SQL Server

The language used to create stored procedures under SQL Server is significantly less verbose. The language is known as Transact-SQL and looks like this:

```
CREATE PROCEDURE killer
    @p_animal_name VARCHAR (30) As
    DELETE FROM Animals WHERE Name = @p_animal_name
```

In the case of SQL Server, the OR REPLACE verbiage is dropped from the creation attempt. If you would like to write over a given stored procedure, you must first erase it with a DELETE PROCEDURE request, such as

```
DELETE PROCEDURE killer
```

Also notice that the variable names in Transact-SQL are preceded by the @ sign. This makes it easy to tell at a glance which portions of a stored procedure under SQL Server are intended to be passed as parameters at runtime.

Data Type Issues

There is at least one benefit to using stored procedures with your Active Server Pages, besides the enormous improvements in performance that they offer. This additional benefit is the ability to easily execute queries containing data that is neither text nor number. For example, suppose that the farmer in our previous code listings now wants to delete rows from the database based on their date of entry. Some code to accomplish this might run as follows:

```
strQry = "DELETE FROM Animals "
strQry = strQry & "WHERE PurchaseDate = #" & Request("dte") & "#"
```

This code uses an approach that is perfectly acceptable to a Microsoft Access database: denoting date information by enclosing it in pound signs. Unfortunately, Oracle and SQL Server have their own, mutually exclusive ways that they like to see date information presented. If you write your Active Server Pages today in a way that specifically caters to the needs of a particular database software, then your pages will all break tomorrow when you decide to use a different database.

So, the key is to find some way of presenting dates and other kinds of "special data" (such a binary pictures, for example) to your database without committing yourself to never changing your server software. Parameters provide an ideal solution to this issue. A parameter exists in the format native to the database currently in use and can usually be replaced with a similar data type on a new database system without requiring any change to your Active Server Page code.

```
cmd(0) = cdate("3/11/2000")
```

If the stored procedure above were altered to accept date information as input, this statement could be used to insert a date, whether the receiving DB server were Oracle, SQL Server, or Access.

24x7 Runtime Type Discovery

Not knowing the data types of a stored procedure's parameters is a common source of errors for Active Server Page developers. Fortunately, ADO provides an eloquent solution to this dilemma. By leveraging the Refresh method of the Command object's Parameters collection, you can ask ADO to discover and return information about a stored procedure's parameters at run time! You can then use this information to ensure that the remainder of your code behaves appropriately.

The following code accepts the name of a stored procedure as input, along with the name of a database, username, and password. It uses these three pieces of data to return the name and data types (as integer constants) for every parameter on the requested stored procedure in the specified database. You can use code like this in your own projects to ensure that you never attempt to pass data of the wrong type to a parameter.

```
<%
    Option Explicit

    If Request("paramname") = "" then
%>
<FORM METHOD="POST">
DB Name:<INPUT NAME="db"><br>
Username:<INPUT NAME="user"><br>
Password:<INPUT NAME="password"><br>
Procedure Name:<INPUT NAME="procname"><br>
</FORM>
<%
    Else

        response.write "<table border>"

        Dim cn
        Dim cmd
        Dim prm

        Set cn = Server.CreateObject("ADODB.Connection")
        Set cmd = Server.CreateObject("ADODB.Command")

        cn.open request("db"), request("user"), request("password")

        cmd.CommandText request("procname")
        cmd.CommandType = adCmdStoredProc
        cmd.ActiveConnection = cn
        cmd.Parameters.Refresh
```

```
    For each prm in cmd.Parameters
        response.write "<tr>"
        response.write "<td>" & prm.name & "</td>"
        response.write "<td>" & prm.type & "</td>"
        response.write "</tr>"
    Next

    response.write "</table>"

End If
%>
```

Referential Integrity

Referential integrity refers to the rules that specify the relationships that must be maintained between the entities in a database schema. One example of a common referential integrity rule is the so-called "one to many" rule. You would use this rule to require that for every one row in a given table, "Fathers" for example, there can be many rows in another table, such as "Daughters." Note in the case of this example, however, that the rule works slightly differently in reverse. A single row in the Daughters table can be related to at most one row in the Fathers table. This makes sense.

Attempts to perform database operations that violate previously existing rules of referential integrity are a common source of bugs in Active Server Page applications.

Deleting Rows

Trying to delete rows from one table that are still related to rows in another table may fail due to referential integrity rules. Consider the following situation:

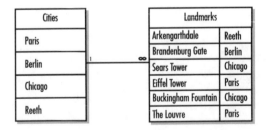

This diagram shows the relationship that exists between cities and their landmarks. Notice that the one-to-many relationship demands that a city may have several landmarks, but any given landmark can only be in a single city. Now, suppose that you tried to execute the following bit of ASP code:

```
<%
    Option Explicit

    Dim cn
    Set cn = Server.CreateObject("ADODB.Connection")

    cn.open "cities", "demolitionman", "boom"

    cn.execute "DELETE FROM Cities WHERE Name = 'Paris'"
%>
```

This code basically tries to remove the entire city of Paris from the database. The only problem is, a couple of the landmarks left in the database would still point to a city that no longer exists. When this situation occurs in a relational database, the records that are left without relations are referred to as *orphans*. Orphaning is typically forbidden once relational integrity has been declared, so this code would not succeed if attempted.

Typically, the way that this situation is solved is to first delete the record on the "many" side of the "one-to-many" relationship. This is because the phrase "many" really means "however many you like." This includes the concept of not having any related records at all. Once you have deleted the "many" rows, the "one" row will not present a problem.

```
<%
    Option Explicit

    Dim cn
    Set cn = Server.CreateObject("ADODB.Connection")

    cn.open "cities", "demolitionman", "boom"

    cn.execute "DELETE FROM Landmarks WHERE City = 'Paris'"
    cn.execute "DELETE FROM Cities WHERE Name = 'Paris'"
%>
```

Unique Identifiers in a Table

A concept that often goes hand-in-hand with referential integrity is that of constraints. A *constraint* is a rule that you add to a database schema to enforce things like referential integrity. Arguably the thing most commonly enforced by constraints is uniqueness within a given table. Because this falls within the realm of a single entity, it is not technically referential integrity. It is, however, a common enough source of errors in ASP scripts to warrant special mention here.

Imagine a table created to hold information about all of a certain company's employees. Many different employees can share the same name, so this doesn't make a very good choice for a unique identifier. Also, many different employees could start on the same day at a company, so this doesn't make a good identifier. In many countries, the government assigns a number to every individual that is guaranteed to be unique (such as the social security number in the United States). This is an excellent choice for placing a uniqueness constraint.

If you should ever run code that attempts to add a record with a nonunique ID number, your Active Server Page will fail to update the database. This is technically an error in your ASP script, but it may be exactly what you want to have happen in this instance. It would make no sense for a company to have two employees with the same Social Security Number in the United States. Readers in other countries can certainly think of similar examples for their own situations.

Modifying Views

The final problem that referential integrity can lead your Active Server Pages into occurs when you attempt to make use of views in your applications. A *view* is a term applied to any artificial creation in your database that facilitates the examination of data from one or more tables. For example, you might create a view called SafeCustomers for use by your low-level employees. This view might be based on the same Customers table that your senior staff are allowed to access directly. The only difference might be that you could choose to leave more sensitive information (such as credit card numbers) off the SafeCustomers view, even if it formed a part of the original Customers table.

In Microsoft Access, you might use queries for this purpose. Under Oracle, you would use objects that happen to actually be called Views.

Creating a View object under Oracle is very straightforward and can help to illustrate the difference between what is possible with views and what is not. An Oracle user simply prefaces a standard SQL query with the phrase "create view <viewname> as." This text

```
create view moneyowed as
select account_no, sum(due)
from account_t a, item_t b
where b.ar_account_obj_id0 = a.poid_id0
group by account_no
```

will create a View object named moneyowed that links data in the account_t and item_t tables to produce a report showing the total amount owed by each customer.

This kind of view works perfectly with Active Server Pages and can be treated just like any other table under ADO. However, *you must never try to update the data in a view!* Views like this are strictly read-only creations, and any attempt to alter their contents will fail miserably.

Storing Data with AppendChunk

The AppendChunk method is provided by Active Data Objects to facilitate the storage of binary data from your Active Server Pages. It can be useful for occasions when you would like to put something such as a picture or a piece of software into a relational database.

The problem that many ASP programmers encounter when they first begin using this method, however, is that all of the data they store winds up being double its original size. A picture that is received as 4K winds up being 8K when it is stored in the database. A program that is just a little larger than 1MB is over 2MB when stored. What is wrong here?

The issue turns out to be in Active Server Pages' lack of support for anything but the Variant data type. With Variant data, all calls to AppendChunk will default to the Unicode encoding scheme—which typically requires two bytes for every one byte used under Western encoding schemes.

The way to get around this issue is, fortunately, quite simple. You just need to create a COM component to do the database access for you. You can pass your data to a method on the component as a Variant and let the method convert your Variant to a specific data type before saving it to the database.

```
Option Explicit

public function saveToDB(vData) as boolean
    Dim cn as ADODB.Connection
    Dim rst as ADODB.Recordset
    Dim bt as Bytes()

    Set cn = new ADODB.Connection
    Set rst = new ADODB.Recordset

    cn.open "pictures", "artist", "d432k"
    rst.cursortype = adOpenKeyset
    rst.locktype = adLockOptimistic
    rst.open "landscapes", cn, , , adCmdTable
```

```
    Redim bt(len(vData))
    bt = vData

    rst.addNew
    rst.AppendChunk bt
    rst.Update

end function
```

Spotting Errors in Character Fields

Character fields present the most diabolical and difficult-to-spot of all errors in Active Server Page development! There is nothing special about character fields, so you wouldn't expect this. But try to find the bug in the following code:

```
<%
    Option Explicit

    Dim cn
    Dim rst

    Set cn = Server.CreateObject("ADODB.Connection")
    Set rst = Server.CreateObject("ADODB.Recordset")

    cn.open "wtf", "programmer", "iketitk"

    cn.execute "insert into data values ('hey ')"

    rst.open "select count(*) from data where token = 'hey'", cn

    if rst.fields(0) < 1 then
        response.write "ERROR - no matching records!"
    else
        response.write "Look at the listing a little closer..."
    end if
%>
```

If you read the listing *very* carefully, you will eventually find the source of the error. Finding this sort of error is, as pointed out earlier, one of the hardest things to catch in your code. The reason why no matching records are returned by the query at the end of the script is that the number of spaces surrounding the text "hey" varies by one character. This kind of thing is almost impossible to spot by visual inspection.

This case is actually one of the more trivial manifestations of this problem. In this listing, the number of padding spaces has been determined by the code itself.

In other cases, moving data from one database to another can cause the data to be padded with spaces sufficient to fill the size of the text field serving as the destination. For example, on many database servers, if you create a text field of size 15 and try putting the word *Hello* into it, the string that will actually be stored is

```
"Hello          "
```

(Note the extra blank spaces.) For this reason, you should use variable-length text fields as much as possible when storing text data.

The other thing that you can do to reduce the number of this kind of error in your Active Server Pages is to use the keyword LIKE whenever possible when comparing text strings in your database. The LIKE keyword allows for the use of wildcards in your text strings so that matches that differ only by the number of surrounding spaces will still be counted as hits. If this idea were put into practice in the preceding example, it might look like this:

```
<%
    Option Explicit

    Dim cn
    Dim rst

    Set cn = Server.CreateObject("ADODB.Connection")
    Set rst = Server.CreateObject("ADODB.Recordset")

    cn.open "wtf", "programmer", "iketitk"

    cn.execute "insert into data values ('hey ')"

    rst.open "select count(*) from data where token LIKE 'hey%'", cn

    if rst.fields(0) < 1 then
        response.write "Did you use LIKE this time?"
    else
        response.write "See, wildcards help!"
    end if
%>
```

CHAPTER 13

Style Guide

A t this point in the book, you have learned about all of the major pitfalls and gotchas that are part of developing with Active Server Pages. In this chapter, you will learn about some general points of ASP style. By consciously applying the principals outlined in this chapter, you can greatly reduce the number of bugs in your Active Server Page applications—often before they even arise!

Source Control

The use of source control is essential on any large development project. Under source control, the changes made by multiple developers working on multiple pieces of a project can all be easily tracked and recorded. In the event that any of the changes turn out later to have been ill advised, it is possible to undo those changes through a process known as *source rollback*.

The specific kind of source control that is offered by Internet Information Server is known as *version control*. When you enable version control for an Active Server Page application, IIS will begin requiring that any development tool wanting to work with any file in that application must first "check it out." Visual Interdev is just one example of a development tool that follows the check-out procedure when used in Master mode under version control.

Once a file is checked out, no other user can come along and check out the same file until that file is checked back into the system. This way, version control helps prevent multiple users from making changes that might be incompatible to the same file at the same time. For example, suppose this sort of script exists on your Web server:

```
<%
    Response.Write "Yo, dude!"
%>
```

Now, suppose that one developer would like to change it to read

```
<%
    Response.Write "Well met fellow, hail!"
%>
```

And another developer would like to change it to read

```
<%
    Response.Write "Yo, dude!"
    Response.Write "Can you hear me?"
%>
```

Under a sophisticated conflict resolution system, both of these changes would be permissible, because they don't really conflict with each other. If both of these changes were allowed (or *merged,* to use the proper term) the code would wind up looking like this:

```
<%
    Response.Write "Well met fellow, hail!"
    Response.Write "Can you hear me?"
%>
```

Unfortunately, this functionality is not offered by either IIS's built-in version control system or the Microsoft Source Safe system that comes as a part of Microsoft Visual Studio.

Fortunately, IIS offers the capability for any version control system to plug in to its interface, provided it meets certain guidelines. In order to turn on version control in an ASP application, follow these steps:

1. Choose Programs from the Windows Start menu.
2. Open the Administrative Tools program group.
3. Click Internet Services Manager.
4. Expand the tree view in the left panel until you see the icon for your ASP application.
5. Right-click the application's icon and choose Properties from the pop-up context menu.
6. Choose the Server Extensions tab.
7. Select the version control software of your choice from the drop-down list labeled Version Control.

General Coding

The use of source control is one way to prevent errors that can arise when multiple developers try working on the same pages at the same time. There are many guidelines you can follow as you write your code that will limit errors created by single developers working in isolation, too. In this section, you will learn about many of these guidelines.

Reducing the Number of Pages

One of the surest ways to reduce bugs in your Active Server Pages is to reduce the total number of scripts in your applications. Every script is an additional piece of code that needs to be checked for errors. By limiting the total number of scripts, you limit the number of places that need to be inspected for bugs so that you can spend more time on each possible weak point.

Testing for Field Blankness

The most common way that Active Server Page developers limit the number of pages in their applications is by using a single script both to present a form and then to process that same form. This is achieved by checking a particular field on the form for blankness when the script first executes. If the field is blank, then the user must not have had the opportunity to fill it in yet. In this case, the form is displayed to take the user's response, and the script terminates.

On the other hand, if the field is seen to be nonblank, then the rest of the script executes and processes whatever was placed on the form in the previous step. Once this processing is finished, some kind of response is sent, and the script terminates again. The flow is shown in Figure 13-1.

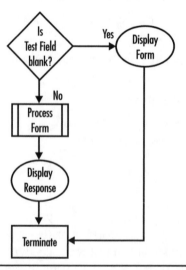

Figure 13.1   A simple logic flow

You can see numerous examples of this coding style throughout the earlier portion of this book. Here is just one short, trivial sample:

```
<%
   If Request("Planet") = "" Then
%>
<FORM METHOD="Post">
Target planet? <INPUT NAME="Planet">
</FORM>
<%
   Else
      Response.Write "This is the processing portion of the script!"
   End If
%>
```

Using Server.Transfer for Actions

This approach will reduce the number of scripts in your applications. If nothing else, it will cut in half the number of special scripts that you need either to create forms or respond to them. But what about situations where you need more flexibility than a single script seems capable of providing?

Consider the logic flow shown in Figure 13-2.

In the figure, the trivial code sample from earlier has been expanded to suggest a few possible ways in which the Planet data might be used. It might be the destination for a rocket launch, the subject of an attack, or the recipient of terra-forming efforts. One way of approaching this problem might be to hyperlink multiple pages from this one, each intended to handle a different one of these three actions.

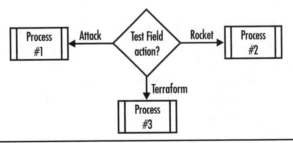

Figure 13.2   A complicated logic flow

A more sophisticated way, however, would be to retain the single-page design. You can differentiate the action that must be taken on the information in the form and then redirect to different pages using Server.Transfer. This doesn't reduce the number of pages, but it does centralize the decision-making logic in the same place as the form that drives it—which is a very good thing.

```
<%
   If Request("Planet") = "" Then
%>
<FORM METHOD="POST">
Target planet? <INPUT NAME="Planet"><br>
Target action: <SELECT NAME="action">
<OPTION>Rocket
<OPTION>Attack
<OPTION>Terraform
</SELECT>


</FORM>
<%
   Else
      If Response("action") = "Rocket" then
         Server.Transfer "rocket.asp"
      ElseIf Response("action") = "Attack" then
         Server.Transfer "attack.asp"
      Else
         Server.Transfer "terraform.asp"
      End If
   End If
%>
```

Using Variables

The way that you use variables in your ASP applications can have a dramatic effect on the number of errors in your scripts. Whether you enable Option Explicit, how you incorporate constants, and the way that you name your variables are just a few of the issues that you will learn about in this section. When you are done reading this section, you should understand many things that you can do with the variables in your scripts to reduce bugs and decrease ASP errors.

Option Explicit

Putting the phrase *Option Explicit* at the top of your scripts may initially make things harder on you as a developer. The reason for this is that, by including this line in your code, you are asking the Active Server Pages interpreter to require that all variables in your script be declared prior to their use. This means that code like the following would not work at all:

```
<%
    Option Explicit

    alpha = 2
    beta = 2

    kappa = alpha + beta
%>
```

If you tried to run this code, it would bomb out immediately with this error:

So, why make things harder on yourself by requiring that all of your variables be declared prior to their use? By putting Option Explicit in your scripts, you prevent a potentially much worse kind of error than that shown above. If you allow variables to be used without prior declaration, it becomes impossible for Active Server Pages to distinguish a misspelling of an existing variable from a declaration of a new one. In this case, the script will proceed without raising an error—but with completely different results than you were probably desiring.

```
<%
    alpha = 2
    beta = 2

    kappa = alfa + beta
%>
```

In this case, the variable kappa would be left containing the value 2 instead of 4. This is because the variable alpha has been misspelled as *alfa*, which had no previous existence in the script. Alfa is, therefore, created on the spot and initialized to a value of 0. This is completely not what was intended. Had the code been written to use Option Explicit, the misspelling would have been caught during an early test run and the potential for an ongoing and difficult-to-find bug like the one shown earlier would have been averted.

```
<%
   Option Explicit

   Dim alpha, beta

   alpha = 2
   beta = 2

   ' The following line will now generate a visible and easy-to-solve
   ' error, rather than possibly sneaking along undetected

   kappa = alfa + beta
%>
```

Constants

You should endeavor to do three things with constants in your Active Server Pages:

- Use constants wherever the alternative would be a numeric value whose significance would be impossible to understand without additional explanation.
- Segregate all the constants for your application in a single file that you then incorporate into your script using the server-side include directive.
- Name your constants using all capital letters, such as PI or DISTANCETOTHEMOON.

The first point appears to be a bit of a mouthful, but most Active Server Page developers understand it the moment they see an example of code written by someone who completely *doesn't* understand it.

```
<%
   Option Explicit

   Dim obj, result
   Set obj = Server.CreateObject("Lawn.Tractor")

   obj.WheelAlignment = 412
   obj.Gear = 3

   result = obj.Drive(32, 333, 67)
```

```
   if result = 4912 then
      response.write "What the hell was this developer
thinking??!!"
   else
      response.write "Is the fact that this isn't 4912 good or
bad?"
   end if
%>
```

Okay, there's a bug in this code—can you find it? Of course you can't. It is completely unclear to anyone (other than the insane developer who created it) exactly what any of this code is trying to do. You might guess that the constant value 3 is a request to put the tractor into third gear, but can we really be sure?

```
<!-- #Include FILE="tractors.inc" -->
<%
   Option Explicit

   Dim obj, result
   Set obj = Server.CreateObject("Lawn.Tractor")

   obj.WheelAlignment = jdtStraightAhead
   obj.Gear = jdtExplodeOnContactWithRoots

   result = obj.Drive(jdtSlow, jdtTurningRight, jdtInReverse)

   if result = jdtExplosion then
      response.write "Oh oh - that's going to be a liability lawsuit"
   else
      response.write "You survived mowing the lawn - congratulations!"
   end if
%>
```

Suddenly, everything becomes so much clearer. We can see that the wheels are supposed to be set straight and that we would like to execute a slow turn to the right in reverse. Suddenly, we are also able to see that the source of our error was that the 3 wasn't a request for third gear but was, in fact, a special setting that asks the tractor to explode upon any contact with roots. Oops.

Now that you've gotten to the bottom of this mystery, you can turn your attention to the second point. All the constants used in the preceding code are actually defined in a separate file that is included by a directive at the top of the script. You could, of course, decide to define all these constants in the same script where you use them. This would be much more cluttered, however, and would prevent you from reusing the same constants in multiple scripts!

Naming Scheme

The names that you choose for the variables in your ASP scripts can help to reduce bugs in your applications. This is possible through the use of a predetermined naming scheme that allows developers to deduce information about the scope and data type of variables simply by looking at them.

The naming scheme most commonly encountered when working with Microsoft technologies is known as *Hungarian naming*. There are two reasons for this (slightly odd) moniker.

- Naming your variables using this scheme will make them look a little bit more like Hungarian, or any other language that has a predilection for long strings of consonants devoid of vowels.

- The person who devised this naming scheme, Dr. Charles Simonyi, was originally from Hungary.

The basic concept is that you take a variable's name and preface it with characters that indicate its data type and scope. The characters are typically short abbreviations for the data type or scope to which the variable belongs. In the case of COM components built into Visual Basic for use with your ASP scripts, you might use a scheme like the following:

Prefix	Meaning	Example
boo	Boolean	booIsAnObnoxiousHabit
bte	Byte	bteNextCharacterInStream
cur	Currency	curCustomerBalance
dte	Date	dteBillingDay
dbl	Double	dblNationalDebt
int	Integer	intNumberOfChildren
lng	Long	lngGrainsOfSandOnTheBeach
obj	Object	objUnknownCOMComponent
sng	Single	sngSatisfiedCustomersCount
str	String	strCustomerName
vrt	Variant	vrtTemporyHolderForEverything

It is interesting to note that Option Explicit does *not* require the use of a particular data type, which is why Variant appears on this list. Under Active Server Pages themselves, in fact, only the Variant option from this list is available. In this case, however, it is more or less customary to use Hungarian notation to indicate the type of data that *should* be stored in a variable.

A character may also be used to indicate the scope of a variable in your Active Server Pages. This character is placed before all other characters in the variable's name. There are three variable scopes supported by ASP: local, session, and application. Here is how you might use Hungarian notation to convey variables in each of these categories:

```
<%
    Option Explicit

    Dim lstrTargetCity ' A local, string variable
    Dim sintErrorCount ' A session-level, integer variable
    Dim acurDailyPurchases ' An application-level, currency variable

    lstrTargetCity = Request("TargetCity")
    sintErrorCount = Session("ErrorCount")
    acurDailyPurchases = Session("DailyPurchases")
%>
```

Design Tip *The previous listing coincidentally illustrates another important point of variable usage. You should always store values taken from intrinsic objects in temporary variables if you plan to make repeated references to them. The reason for this is that it is much more performance-intensive to repeatedly reference an object's property than to reference a simple variable. When you are done using whatever value is being referenced, you may store it back in the intrinsic object if it is an object property that supports writing as well as reading, such as on the Session and Application objects.*

Variable Scope

Decisions about variable scope can have an enormous impact on the quality of your Active Server Page code.

Best Practices

There are two ways in which you can guarantee that your ASP scripts will be in line with the best practices of ASP variable scooping. The first of these is to avoid using script-level variables with procedures. The second is to avoid multipage lifespans.

Avoiding Script-Level Variables with Procedures

A script-level variable is any variable that is declared outside of a specific procedure in your VBScript code. They are not problematic in and of themselves, and they are an excellent way to hold information under most circumstances. The problem arises when you start using variables dimensioned at this scope to pass information into your procedures.

```
<%
    Option Explicit

    Dim status
    Dim count

    count = 20

    waitForAWhile

    if status = 1 then
        response.write "That worked fine!"
    else
        response.write "That broke!"
    end if

    sub waitForAWhile
        dim I
        for I = 1 to count
            ' Do some stuff here
        next
        status = 1
    end sub
%>
```

In this example, the first mistake is in using the count variable to dictate to the waitForAWhile routine how many times it should iterate through the loop. Any information that you want to pass into a procedure under Active Server Pages should come through a parameter on that procedure.

The second mistake is the use of the status variable to return either success or failure to the calling script. Any information that you want to return from a procedure under Active Server Pages should be a part of that procedure's return value. This will require the use of a function rather than a subroutine.

```
<%
    Option Explicit

    if waitforAWhile(20) = 1 then
        response.write "That worked fine!"
```

```
      else
         response.write "That broke!"
      end if

      function waitForAWhile(count)
         dim I
         for I = 1 to count
            ' Do some stuff here
         next
         waitForAWhile = 1
      end function
%>
```

This code has improved enormously on the previous example. The number of times that the For-Next loop inside the waitForAWhile procedure iterates is now determined on the basis of the count parameter, rather than a script-level variable. This limits the amount of code that needs to be checked in the event that the loop is seen to iterate incorrectly.

Furthermore, the success or failure of the procedure is now conveyed back to the calling code using the function's return value. This limits the amount of code that would need to be checked in the event that the value returned is soon to be incorrect.

Avoiding Multipage Lifespans

It is generally not the best idea to keep object references in Session- or Application-level storage. The reason for this is that it is extremely hard on the performance of Internet Information Server. One reason for this performance hit is the additional memory required to store objects across multiple page invocations. Another reason is the limited threading model used by IIS Sessions and Applications.

24x7   Memory and Threading

Storing objects in Session- or Application-level storage requires more memory than simply invoking them on a page-by-page basis. The reason for this is that, in a Session or Application context, an object must be retained in memory even between page requests. Given enough users and enough objects, this could easily grow to overburden many Web servers.

The limited thread model supported by the Session and Application objects is another reason that you shouldn't keep objects around between page requests. An apartment-threaded object stored in the Application object will only be serviceable by the thread that created that Application. There is only one such thread in any given ASP application. However, only the thread that created a given Session may service the objects stored at a Session level. There is only one such thread for every user of your application.

For more information on this topic, refer the section on object storage in Chapter 7.

Objects

For all the admonitions about not storing objects at the Session or Application level, there are rare occasions in which such a decision may be justifiable. The most common example would be the use of the Application object to store a database connection.

Database Connections

Active Server Pages provides the intrinsic Application object specifically for data that will be shared in common by all the scripts in an ASP application. Most developers make very infrequent use of this capability. In general, the stateless nature of the World Wide Web does not lend itself very well to the cross-Session communication possibilities of the Application object.

The one case in which many developers make use of the Application object's storage abilities is when database connections are required. Most enterprise-level databases are licensed on a per-connection basis, so limiting the number of connections between an ASP application and a database may lead to enormous dollar savings. In the case of more modestly priced "desktop" databases, support for multiple connections may not even be available.

In both of these cases, ASP developers often store their database connections in the Application object. If you choose to follow this path, make your code a part of the GLOBAL.ASA file's Application_OnStart event.

```
Sub Application_OnStart
   cn = Server.CreateObject("ADODB.Connection")
   cn.open "dbname", "user", "password"
   Set Application("cn") = cn
End Sub
```

You should unpackage the connection into a local variable at the start of every page that will be using it. This way you can avoid the high performance overhead associated with repeated calls to the Application object's methods and properties.

```
<%
    Option Explicit

    Dim cn

    Set cn = Application("cn")

    ' REST OF CODE GOES HERE
%>
```

Threading Models

If you plan to store your own COM components in the intrinsic Session or Application objects, you should make sure that they are apartment threaded. This threading model provides the best blend of concurrency and consistency for your components under Active Server Pages.

Concurrency   Apartment threading provides concurrency for your COM components by allowing multiple processes to access the same component simultaneously. This is particularly important for Application-level objects because one object must be shared between all the clients currently using the application. If you try to use single-threaded components in this situation, you will notice long hangs when multiple scripts try to access your component simultaneously.

Consistency   Apartment threading prevents different threads from accessing the same portions of your components' code simultaneously. The advantage to this is that you don't need to be as worried about different threads interacting in ways that cause each other to fail. The usual level at which multiple threads are prevented from coexisting is that of a single procedure. This affords particular protection to values stored in local variables within your COM components.

To enable apartment threading in your Visual Basic ActiveX DLL projects:

1. Open your project in the Visual Basic IDE.
2. Select Properties from the Project menu.

3. Select the General tab on the Project Properties dialog, if it has not already been displayed.

4. Make sure that Apartment Threaded is selected in the drop-down list box labeled Threading Model.

Architecture

Architecture refers to the way in which the various pieces of your ASP applications fit together. Some of these pieces are the intrinsic objects provided by Active Server Pages. Others are the COM components that you create yourself or purchase from third-party developers. Still others are the bits of data provided to your scripts by data sources such as database servers and Internet connections.

In order to create the most bug-free Active Server Page applications, you must be willing to analyze the architecture of your systems. The choices you make in fitting together the pieces of your applications can exert a vast influence over the potential for errors in your scripts.

Intrinsic ASP Objects

Intrinsic ASP objects include

- Application
- ASPError
- ObjectContext
- Request
- Response
- Server
- Session

In this section, you will learn about the best practices for integrating these objects with the rest of your application's code.

Referencing from COM Components

It is technically possible to reference ASP's intrinsic objects directly from the internals of your COM components.

Error Watch *The conduit for such communications is typically Microsoft's Component Services. Once you ensure that your components will be running under Component Services, you can obtain handles to all the intrinsic ASP objects through the ObjectContext object's Item collection. If you attempt to call the GetObjectContext procedure from a component that is not running under Microsoft's Component Services, you will get an error!*

```
Option Explicit

public sub interactDirectlyWithTheClient()
    Dim oc as ObjectContext
    Dim rqst as Object
    Dim rspns as Object

    Set oc = GetObjectContext
    Set rqst = oc.Item("Request")
    Set rspns = oc.Item("Response")

    if rqst.Form("Name") <> "" Then
        rspns.write "Hello there, " & rqst.Form("Name")
    else
        rspns.write "Why didn't you give your name?"
    end if
end sub
```

This code is perfectly legitimate insofar as it contains bug-free, usable VBScript code. The only problem is that it is a complete violation of the principals of encapsulation. The best practices for ASP development dictate that your scripts—and your scripts alone—should be responsible for all direct interaction with your users. In this case, a COM component is completely bypassing your ASP code to talk directly to the users. This would make it impossible for a developer casually reading your ASP code to easily see all of the information that is passed to and from the user.

Getting Input

The best way to process user input from your COM components is by passing it as parameters on your method calls.

```
<%
    Option Explicit

    Dim obj
    Set obj = Server.CreateObject("Interactions.Greeting")

    Call obj.respondDirectlyToTheClient(Request.Form("Name"))
%>
```

The preceding ASP code invokes a modified version of the COM component discussed in the previous section. It passes the Name field from the user's input form so that the component doesn't have to access it directly. The code for the method in the component would now look like this:

```
public sub respondDirectlyToTheClient(strName as Variant)
    Dim oc as ObjectContext
    Dim rspns as Object

    Set oc = GetObjectContext
    Set rspns = oc.Item("Response")

    if strName <> "" Then
        rspns.write "Hello there, " & strName
    else
        rspns.write "Why didn't you give your name?"
    end if
end sub
```

Sending Output

The revisions introduced earlier get you about halfway toward total encapsulation. Your component is now receiving input via parameters rather than direct access to the intrinsic ASP Request object. However, it is still sending output directly to the Web client via direct access to the intrinsic ASP Response object.

```
<%
    Option Explicit

    Dim obj
    Set obj = Server.CreateObject("Interactions.Greeting")

    Response.Write obj.handResponseToASP(Request.Form("Name"))
%>
```

This is the 100 percent encapsulated version of the ASP script. The component returns its output to the ASP script. The ASP script is then responsible for writing to the Web client. A developer reading just this script would immediately recognize that some kind of output is being controlled by the COM component. This would prevent any number of possible misunderstandings that could lead to the introduction of countless bugs.

```
public function handResponseToASP(strName as Variant) as Variant

    if strName <> "" Then
        handResponseToASP = "Hello there, " & strName
```

```
      else
         handResponseToASP = "Why didn't you give your name?"
      end if
end sub
```

Working with Data

Active Server Pages provide developers with a number of ways to access databases. Not all of the options available are equally ideal from the standpoint of performance improvement and bug reduction. As a general rule, iterating through the recordset is the worst possible approach to data access. The direct execution of SQL code is somewhat better, and the direct invocation of stored procedures is even better yet. The absolute best way to access data from Active Server Pages, though, is through data objects.

Iterating Through Recordsets

The absolute worst approach to working with data under Active Server Pages is to waste time iterating through complete recordsets. This situation typically arises in cases where a modification needs to be made to several rows in a table but perhaps not all of them.

```
<%
   Option Explicit

   Dim cn, rst
   Set cn = Server.CreateObject("ADODB.Connection")
   Set rst = Server.CreateObject("ADODB.Recordset")

   cn.open "pencils", "sharpener", "igsowotb"
   rst.cursortype = adOpenKeyset
   rst.locktype = adLockOptimistic
   rst.open "pencils", cn, , , adCmdTable

   do until rst.eof
      if rst("darkness") = 2 then
         rst("color") = "black"
         rst.update
      end if
      rst.movenext
   loop
%>
```

This code shows one possible way to set the color of every pencil in a table with a darkness of 2 to "black." The reason that this is a poor way to write ASP code is that it requires the retrieval of *every single row in the table* in order to operate on just some subset of those records. It would be much better just to ask the database server to specifically target records meeting the desired criteria.

Command Executions

You can ask the database server to specifically target records meeting your desired criteria through the use of SQL. By passing SQL requests directly to your data source, you can avoid the need to convey entire recordsets beyond your database server and IIS. Here is an example of how you might rewrite the preceding example using direct SQL:

```
<%
   Option Explicit

   Dim cn
   Set cn = Server.CreateObject("ADODB.Connection")

   cn.open "pencils", "sharpener", "igsowotb"
   cn.execute "update pencils set color = 'black' where darkness = 2"
%>
```

Stored Procedures

Stored procedures offer you a way to encapsulate your data-access logic and keep it separate from the rest of your ASP code. The benefits of this are thoroughly described in Chapter 12, and you should refer to it for more information. Suffice it to say here that the use of stored procedures wherever possible should be considered the next-to-best practice for data access under Active Server Pages.

Data Objects

The most elegant solution to accessing data from your Active Server Pages is to encapsulate all such access in data objects. A *data object* is a custom component that you create to automate the performance of various operations on your data that you feel are likely to be repeated more than once. One great benefit to this is that, once you get it debugged right, you can reuse the same code with multiple scripts and multiple applications. Another benefit is that you can share your objects with others and be reasonably sure that your data will remain safe—even in the hands of an inexperienced ASP developer!

The code for your data objects should subscribe to the same set of style guidelines that you have learned about earlier in this chapter. Probably the ideal data object serves as a wrapper for a stored procedure. This way, you can accomplish two levels of encapsulation in the pursuit of guaranteed data integrity.

```
<%
    Option Explicit

    Dim obj
    Set obj = Server.CreateObject("ASPExample.DataObject")

    Call obj.setPencilColor("black", 2)
%>
```

This code instantiates a data object and then calls a method on it named setPencilColor. This method is listed here. Examining the next listing, you can see that it is essentially just a wrapper for a stored procedure. The parameters passed to this method are passed to the stored procedure exactly as received.

```
Option Explicit

public sub setPencilColor(strColor, intDarkness)
    Dim cn as ADODB.Connection
    Dim cmd as ADODB.Command

    Set cn = new ADODB.Connection
    Set cmd = new ADODB.Command

    cn.open "pencils", "sharpener", "igsowotb"

    cmd.CommandText "setPencilColors"
    cmd.CommandType = adCmdStoredProc
    cmd.ActiveConnection = cn

    cmd(0) = strColor
    cmd(1) = intDarkness

    cmd.execute
end sub
```

CHAPTER 14

Performance Issues

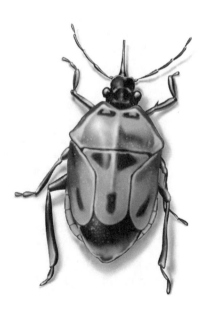

Welcome to the final chapter in *Debugging Active Server Pages*! At this point, you have learned more about debugging ASP scripts than you probably ever thought there was to learn.

In the previous chapter, you added an additional layer of sophistication to your skills by learning the points of style that can help prevent bugs before they occur. In this chapter, you turn your attention to the performance issues that should form the focus of all development efforts—once you have assured yourself that the bugs have been removed.

General Coding

The code that you use to create your ASP scripts exerts a fundamental influence over the performance of your Active Server Page applications. Making the wrong decisions as you create your code can cause an otherwise excellent application to draw far too many system resources to be useful. Conversely, planning all your code in advance with performance in mind ensures that any application you develop will fall well within the limits of any hardware on which you choose to run it.

Buffering

When it comes to performance, there is only one correct choice that you can make about buffering: Use it. You may recall from previous chapters that buffering allows Internet Information Server to hold onto all of the output generated by your ASP scripts until they have run to their conclusion. Then, if a script has completed successfully, all that stored-up output is sent to the Web client in a single burst of connections. On the other hand, if the script encounters an error somewhere along the way, all of the output up to the time of error is thrown out, and only the error is sent along to the Web client.

From a performance standpoint, the benefit of buffering is that it reduces the total number of times that connections need to be opened and closed with the Web client. Without buffering, you might think of a single script as working as shown in Figure 14-1.

Notice in the figure that the connection between the Web server and the client is opened and closed several times as the script generates delays in producing its output. If buffering were turned on in this same situation, the process would look more like what is shown in Figure 14-2.

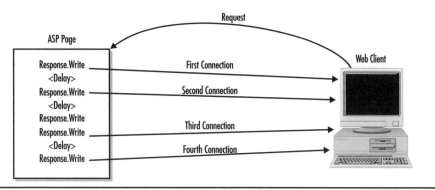

Figure 14.1   How a script works without buffering

The benefit to reducing the number of times that connections must be opened and closed lies in the overhead associated with establishing connections over the Internet. In order to establish a single connection, the target computer must be located using DNS, contacted, and then a protocol must be negotiated; then and only then may data transfer be attempted. If you turn on buffering, this process need be undergone only once for each page visit, greatly reducing the load on your server.

To turn buffering on for your Active Server Pages, you may either add the line

```
Response.Buffer = True
```

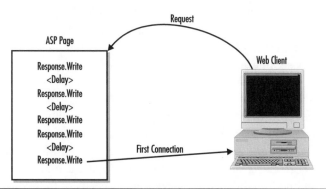

Figure 14.2   How a script works with buffering turned on

to the start of every script for which you would like output to be buffered. Or you can follow these steps to enable buffering for your entire Active Server Page application:

1. Select Programs from the Windows Start menu.
2. Open the Administrative Tools group.
3. Select the Internet Services Manager.
4. Expand the tree control on the left to reveal the application that you suspect might have its buffer capability turned off.
5. Right-click this application.
6. Choose Properties from the pop-up context menu.
7. Click Configuration in the Application Settings section of the dialog.
8. Select the App Options tab.
9. Verify that the Enable Buffering" box has been checked.
10. Click OK or Apply to verify your changes.

Connections

Most Active Server Page applications need to establish connections to external systems in order to perform useful work for their clients. For example, a Web site used to track the current value of major league baseball trading cards might require at least one connection to a database of recent trading card sales. A more ubiquitous example is the fact that every Web application ever designed has required at least one connection in order to be used at all: the connection between the client (usually a Web browser, such as Internet Explorer) and the server (in this case, Internet Information Server).

ConnectionTimeout

Every time that Internet Information Server establishes a connection with a Web client somewhere out on the Internet, at least one of its threads becomes a prisoner to the performance of that connection. This is because, whenever a Web client requests such a connection, IIS "spawns off" a thread that is charged with doing nothing other than servicing the needs of that connection. This thread lasts as long as the connection remains open; it is then recycled for use with other connections.

As you might imagine, the total number of threads available represents a limited resource on your server. Even on a machine with enormous amounts of memory and processor speed, there has to be some finite limit on the total number of threads that can be coordinated by IIS at the same time. This represents one of the key factors limiting the number of simultaneous connections to your ASP applications.

Now, imagine the case of a connection to your application that is established from a very remote part of the world. For the sake of argument, let's pretend that your ASP scripts are being used by a race of intelligent reptiles with very slow modems operating out of secret bases located hundreds of miles beneath the Earth's crust. (This scenario may seem farfetched, but this chapter is the final one in the book and you deserve at least a little bit of amusement for having studied so hard to get here.)

The problem with your applications being used by people with very poor Internet connections is that it can take a very, very long time for data to travel back and forth between your server and their clients. During this whole time, the threads charged with maintaining their connections are essentially held hostage—unable to tend to the business of helping other users until their current transactions are finished.

If your resources are limitless, you might consider increasing your memory size and processor speed indefinitely until all users can be served, regardless of bandwidth. If you are like most businesses, however, you will be more interested in getting the greatest possible return on your investment. The best way to do this from the standpoint of ASP performance is to put a limit on the time that you will allow a single connection to remain inactive.

By lowering the amount of time that you are willing to allow a connection to remain inactive, you are directly limiting the amount of time that you are willing to allow a single thread to remain hostage by a single user's slow Internet connection. This will help the performance of your ASP application by reducing the total number of threads that must share the CPU during periods of high simultaneous usage. It may, on the other hand, frustrate your users with slow Internet connections (such as the reptiles under the earth's crust) when they receive continual timeout errors. You must determine your comfort level with this as a trade-off.

To set the ConnectionTimeout of your application, you must run a script like this:

```
<%
   Option Explicit

   Dim iisobj
   Set iisobj = getObject("IIS://localhost/w3svc/1/root")

   iisobj.ConnectionTimeout = 10

   iisobj.setInfo
%>
```

In this case, we are assuming that the application to be limited is the first node in the ADSL tree for this Windows server's Web tree. If you are not sure about this value for your own application, consult your system administrator. The relevant value in the preceding script is 10, which is asking for a 10-second limit on an inactive connection. If you wanted a longer or shorter limit, you would adjust this value accordingly.

Storing Connections

You have now seen how to limit the connections between your application and its users out on the Internet. Now what about the connections between your application and the server applications that provide it with data? Under Active Data Objects, these applications might be database servers such as Oracle or SQL Server, or they might be something as unconventional as an e-mail server. Whatever the case, you always use the same object to establish a connection: ADODB.Connection.

```
<%
   Option Explicit

   Dim cn
   Set cn = Server.CreateObject("ADODB.Connection")

   cn.open "tradingcards", "defaultuser", "defaultpass"

   Set Application("cn") = cn
%>
```

This script establishes a connection to some unknown data source and then saves it in the intrinsic Application object. As discussed in Chapter 13, this decision can sometimes be justified when the total number of connections supported by a data source is low and every script within a given application must make use of that same source. In situations where ample connections are available, however, this method of storing the database connection can become a real bottleneck to performance in your ASP applications.

The reason for this is that an object stored within the intrinsic Application object can be serviced only by the single thread that first created the ASP application. This means that all data access attempts from all the sessions currently open on your application must be queued up for time with this single thread (see Figure 14-3).

As noted earlier, if you are only allowed a limited number of connections (per-connection licensing, for example), this strategy may be your best alternative. However, if you have enough connections to go around, you should consider either

- Storing connections in the Session object rather than the Application object, or

- Instantiating a new connection at the start of any page that needs it

The benefit to the first approach is that you are saved the considerable time and CPU burdens associated with creating and recreating connections to your data source on an as-needed basis. The downside is that it requires that one database connection be maintained and left open for every one session currently open on your ASP application. This might be a resource burden that your data source can tolerate, depending on its design and licensing situation.

The benefit to the second approach is that it doesn't leave connections open on your data source. This can be much easier on the resources of your data source

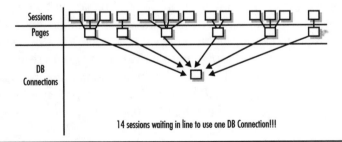

Figure 14.3   Queuing up data access attempts

and potentially much cheaper if your data source is licensed on a per-connection basis. On the other hand, the time that it takes to open a new database connection can be considerable and will slow down every page in your application that requires the use of such a connection. The additional burden that this continual creation and recreation of data source connections will place on your Web server's CPU is also something to take into consideration.

Sessions

In the previous section, you learned about the connections that your ASP application must establish in order to conduct its business. A series of connections between Internet Information Server and a *single* client can be logically grouped together in the form of an ASP session. A session begins with the first visit to your application by a given client and ends with the last visit to your application by that same client, or when it is abandoned by your code.

This raises the question: How can Internet Information Server possibly know when a given client has accessed my application for the final time?

This question is relevant because, as long as IIS believes that a session with a given client is still open, it will continue dedicating resources to its preservation. This may mean additional memory for the storage of variables placed into the intrinsic Session object. It might also mean CPU cycles for the constant monitoring of activity on that session. Clearly, the less time your applications keep each session open, the better for the overall performance of your Web server.

There are two ways to define the ending of sessions to IIS:

- Through the use of the Session.Timeout property, or
- By explicitly requesting the termination of a session with Session.Abandon

The Session.Timeout property tells IIS how long you would like it to wait between requests from a single client. If the amount of time that elapses between requests from a single client ever exceeds this threshold, that client's session is considered expired and is removed. The benefit to this, from the perspective of ASP performance, is that this removal allows IIS to reclaim all the memory and CPU resources that had been tied up in maintaining the session. However, if you set the timeout threshold too low, you may experience loss-of-state bugs. These bugs are discussed at length in Chapter 4.

To set Session.Timeout to a length that you feel is reasonable, use code such as the following:

```
<%
    Session.Timeout = 15
%>
```

In this case, the limit is set to 15 minutes. If a client waits more than 15 minutes between requests to your ASP application, it will experience a complete loss of its session. The shorter you set this value, the quicker IIS can reclaim the resources associated with dead sessions. The risk of sessions being killed "before their time" also increases proportionately.

In some applications, it might be possible to know immediately when a particular session is finished. For example, in an online-shopping application, it might make sense to destroy a client's session as soon as that user has checked out and paid for all their purchases. As another example, in an online game, you might decide to get rid of a user's session as soon as the player's character "dies." If your application fits either of these models, you can greatly improve the performance of your Active Server Pages by using the Session.Abandon method.

```
<%
    If EverythingIsOverForThisUser Then
        Session.Abandon
    End If
%>
```

Using code like this, you can specifically instruct IIS to destroy a session and reclaim its resources. You would do this as soon as you were certain that the client associated with the session was completely finished with their business at your site. This allows for the most immediate reclamation of memory and CPU resources.

Components

Your choice of ASP components can either increase or decrease the performance of your Active Server Page applications.

Out-of-Process Components

The cross-process messaging that is required to communicate with out-of-process components makes them less than ideal as an alternative for performance-sensitive ASP applications. This topic is discussed at some length in Chapter 7.

There is another aspect to out-of-process components that can make them even more of a performance burden on your Active Server Pages. Out-of-process components can be set to create their own process whenever your scripts instantiate a new instance of them. This means that there will be one new process on your server for each instantiation of such a component. Insofar as processes represent considerably more of a resource burden on your server than threads, this makes these kinds of out-of-process components true resource hogs.

To avoid this phenomenon in your applications, make sure that the Instancing property for your out-of-process components is never set to SingleUse.

In-Process Components

In-process components are typically the best performance value in terms of COM components. Even so, there are two ways in which you can adversely impact the performance of ASP scripts with COM components. The first is by leaving them outside of Microsoft Component Services. The second is by choosing an inappropriate threading model for their design.

Microsoft Component Services provides a wide variety of support for improving the performance of your COM (and COM+) components. One example of this is the tendency for components running under Microsoft Component Services to instantiate much quicker than components outside the scope of this technology. In fact, it is more common to think of components under Component Services as being activated and deactivated rather than created and destroyed. The enormous time savings during the activation of new COM component instances can greatly improve the performance of your ASP scripts.

If you are creating your in-process components under Visual Basic, there can only be one appropriate choice of threading model: apartment threading. Apartment threading allows multiple threads to service your components simultaneously without fear of collisions between them. For more information on this, refer to the previous chapter.

Performance Monitor

The Microsoft Performance Monitor allows you to precisely quantify the responsiveness of your Active Server Pages. Even better, it allows you to visually

track changes in this responsiveness over time. The main interface for the
Performance Monitor is through the Microsoft Management Console. To start
the Performance Monitor, follow these steps:

1. Choose Programs from the Windows Start menu.
2. Open the Administrative Tools program group.
3. Click Performance.

At this point, you will be presented with a window that looks like Figure 14-4.

In order for Performance Monitor to begin providing you with useful
information, you must choose the specific pieces of real-time data that you would
like to track in the graphing area of the window. For measuring Active Server
Page performance, we are particularly interested in two data parameters.

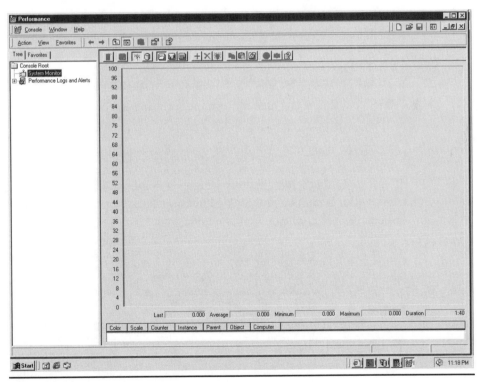

Figure 14.4   Performance Monitor without any data

Requests Queued   This represents the total number of requests from Web clients that are waiting to be processed by Active Server Pages. Too high a number here would indicate insufficient performance from your ASP applications.

%Processor Time   This option allows you to see how much idle time the processor(s) on your system are experiencing. A lot of idle time is a sign that your scripts are, at least, not overloading the processing capabilities of your server machine. On the other hand, too little activity here might suggest that a lot of I/O blocking is occurring.

To add these data items to the Performance Monitor, follow these steps:

1. Right-click the graphing portion of the Performance Monitor window.
2. Choose Add Counters from the pop-up context menu to open the dialog shown in Figure 14-5.
3. Make sure "Select Counters from List" is enabled.
4. Select Processor from the Performance Object drop-down menu.
5. Select % Professor Time from the scrolling list box.
6. Click Add.
7. Select Active Server Pages from the Performance Object drop-down menu.
8. Select Requests Queued from the scrolling list box.
9. Click Add.
10. Click Close.

(If you study this screen intently whenever someone important enters the room, such as your boss, you will look professional and important.) This table will help you derive useful information from this screen.

	Requests Queued	**% Processor Utilization**
Good	A horizontal line, meaning that the number is remaining constant.	A line that is mostly low, meaning a good amount of idle time.
Troubled	A line with significant peaks and valleys, indicating that some users are waiting longer than others for the server to respond.	Less than 50%, meaning that there is more processing power available, but something is preventing its use.
Critical	A diagonal line that grows from left to right, meaning that client requests are taking too long to finish and are stacking up.	A diagonal line that grows from left to right, meaning that jobs are taking too long to process and are stacking up.

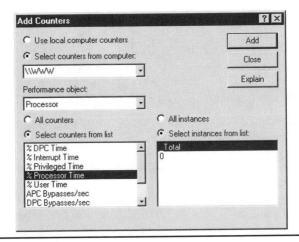

Figure 14.5   The Add Counters dialog

You can avoid developing a troubled ASP application by correctly setting the ASPProcessorThreadMax parameter for your Internet Information Server. Increasing this parameter allows IIS to bring additional threads into existence to service additional client requests. This has the effect of squeezing additional performance out of your existing processors. For more information, see the section on the Metabase at the end of this chapter.

Components   The first things you should check are any custom COM components that may form a part of your ASP solution. For example, calling the method shown from any Active Server Page would be guaranteed to put your system into a critical state. Infinite loops can normally be terminated when they occur in script at the page level. When they occur in COM components, however, you will usually have to reboot your server to regain control!

```
public function loopEndlessly()
   do until false
   loop
   loopEndlessly = "You'll never get to this line!"
end function
```

24x7 **When ASP Becomes Critical**

When you find your performance to have entered the critical situation described in the table, it means that something serious has broken. Usually, some portion of your application has become hung and is sucking away vital resources from the rest of your system. Identifying and releasing the hung portion of your system is the first step in getting out of the critical situation.

Data   The data sources on which your ASP scripts operate can lead you into a critical state, both directly and indirectly. In the direct case, it is possible for a data source to crash in such a way that ASP cannot detect that it is broken—but it still won't respond. In the indirect case, your code may attempt an operation against the data that requires too much time for completion. In both of these cases, you will at a minimum have to restart your data source. At worst, you might have to restart your entire server.

Network   If your Active Server Page application requires network connectivity to locations other than Internet clients making requests, then this is another possible point of breakage that can lead you into a critical state. For example, if your site uses maps from a third-party geography Web site to show users where your stores are located, any failure of this third-party Web site might also cause a critical condition for your own site. Well-designed ASP scripts should always take into account the possibility that resources not under the direct control of developers and system administrators may become unavailable. Your scripts should aim to degrade gracefully under such conditions, rather than become critical cases.

Administration

Professional Web sites running Internet Information Server typically assign responsibility for maintaining and upgrading the Web server software to a single person or group of persons. These individuals are often referred to as system administrators or, to use the Microsoft Certified Professional terminology, system engineers. Their work with IIS is referred to as "administration."

Administrators are usually very concerned about ensuring the best possible performance for IIS. A good part of this is determined by the performance of the Active Server Page applications running under IIS. For this reason, there is a great deal that can be done by administrators to affect ASP performance.

Registry

The registry is the low-level database of system settings that dictates the precise configuration for a vast number of tools and applications under the Windows operating system. You have already seen a couple of registry settings earlier in this book. Generally, if it is possible to configure a tool in the desired way through a standard GUI interface, this is how the configuration should be performed. Direct modification of the Windows registry is recommended only in cases where the tools available through the Windows GUI are inadequate.

Turning on ODBC connection pooling is a case in point. At the time of this writing, there is no good way to request that IIS pool ODBC connections via the Microsoft Management Console interface. It is entirely possible to do so by directly editing the registry, however. To enable ODBC pooling via regedt32, follow these steps:

1. Select Run from the Windows Start menu.
2. Type **regedt32** in the Open text field.
3. Click OK.
4. Bring to the forefront the window labeled HKEY_LOCAL_MACHINE.
5. Expand the tree nodes in this window in the following order:
   - System
   - CurrentControlSet
   - Services
   - W3SVC
   - ASP
   - Parameters
6. Double-click the entry for StartConnectionPool.
7. Enter **1** in the Data text field.
8. Click OK.
9. Close the application.

With ODBC Connection Pooling turned on, IIS will first check for the existence of an open, unused connection on a data source before creating a new one. If such a connection exists, it will reuse it. This is a benefit to performance because it saves the time and memory associated with the constant creation of new database connections.

On the other hand, ODBC Connection Pooling tends to leave connections open for longer than they are actually in use by a given application. This results in a greater number of open connections on a given data source than would ordinarily be the case. If your database software has a limited number of connections, you might want to think twice about using this performance optimization with your Active Server Page applications.

IIS Console

Once upon a time, the IIS console was the only way in which to make administrative changes to the Internet Information Server's configuration and settings. Today, it shares this role with the IIS Administration objects and the ADSI interface. Like working directly with the registry, it is best to attempt administrative changes first through the IIS console, resorting to ADSI only for settings not otherwise available.

Debugging

Where performance is concerned, there is only one right choice for debugging: Turn it off. When Active Server Pages debugging is enabled, Internet Information Server has to work much harder to execute each script in your application. The reason for this is that, besides simply doing the work requested by the code in your scripts, IIS must also keep assiduous records about every step of the work that it is performing. This way, if an error occurs, it can communicate immediately to the debugger everything it might want to know about the current state of the application: where it stopped, what values were currently in the variables, the call-stack list, and so on.

By turning off debugging, you tell IIS that it doesn't have to worry about keeping such detailed records. This allows the server to concentrate completely on executing your ASP scripts in the quickest, most resource-efficient manner possible. Of course, if an error occurs and debugging is turned off, you will not be able to use the Microsoft Script Debugger to get to the root of the problem.

For this reason, you should only turn debugging off to improve performance in applications that have already been thoroughly tested.

To turn off debugging for an Active Server Pages application, follow these steps:

1. Choose Programs from the Windows Start menu.
2. Open the Administrative Tools program group.
3. Click Internet Services Manager.
4. Locate your ASP site in the tree control on the left and right-click it.
5. Choose Properties from the pop-up context menu.
6. Select the Home Directory tab.
7. Click the Configuration button.
8. Select the App Debugging tab.
9. Make sure Enable ASP Server-side Script Debugging is *not* enabled.
10. Make sure Enable ASP Client-side Script Debugging is *not* enabled.
11. Click Apply or OK to confirm your changes.

Caching

To maximize the performance of your Active Server Pages, enable caching. The reason that it helps is that caching drastically reduces the number of times that Internet Information Server has to interpret the code in your scripts. Consider this simple script:

```
<%
    Response.Write "Well, this is pretty simple, isn't it?"
%>
```

Does it really make sense for IIS to reinterpret this script every single time that it is executed? After all, you could run it constantly until the end of time and it should never produce any results other than printing out the simple message shown. So, the ideal situation is for IIS to interpret it once, realize that it will produce the same output every time it is run in the future, and therefore cache its results. All future requests for that page, assuming that the script remains unchanged, should simply receive a copy of the cached results.

This will greatly enhance the performance of your Active Server Pages because transmitting cached results is much less resource intensive than actually interpreting an ASP script. To enable caching in your ASP applications, follow these steps:

1. Choose Programs from the Windows Start menu.
2. Open the Administrative Tools program group.
3. Click Internet Services Manager.
4. Locate your ASP site in the tree control on the left and right-click it.
5. Choose Properties from the pop-up context menu.
6. Select the Home Directory tab.
7. Click the Configuration button.
8. Select the App Mappings tab.
9. Make sure Cache ISAPI Applications is enabled.
10. Select the Process Options tab.
11. Make sure Do Not Cache ASP Files is *not* enabled.
12. Click Apply or OK to confirm your changes.

Metabase

The metabase is a kind of database that IIS maintains for all its configurations and settings. Changing the metabase via the IIS Admin objects represents the main alternative to administration via the Microsoft Management Console. You can make changes to the IIS metabase directly from ASP scripts using the ADSI interface.

ASPProcessorThreadMax

In the section on the Performance Monitor you learned that the ASPProcessorThreadMax parameter controls the number of threads that IIS can create to service requests for your Active Server Pages. It was suggested that you might consider increasing this value if you find that the number of ASP requests queued is fluctuating wildly while your CPU load remains constant. You might have wondered what relevance this setting has to that situation.

Fluctuations in the number of ASP requests queued up suggests that some requests are taking a particularly long time to complete, while others are proceeding at a fairly "normal" rate. When the number of requests in the queue goes up, this means that all the available threads have gotten stuck on whatever is causing the performance bottleneck in your application. When the number of queued requests goes down, this means that, although some threads may be stuck in the bottlenecks, there are at least some threads free to service other requests.

By increasing the number of threads in general, you reduce the risk that all your threads will get caught in the same bottleneck at the same time. If you notice that kind of troubled behavior described in the section on the Performance Monitor, then 100 is usually considered a good value to which you may raise this parameter. Otherwise, you should probably leave this parameter set to its default of 25.

To set ASPProcessorThreadMax to 100, you can run the following script:

```
<%
   Option Explicit

   Dim iisobj
   Set iisobj = getObject("IIS://localhost/w3svc/1/root")

   iisobj.ASPProcessorThreadMax = 100

   iisobj.setInfo
%>
```

Error Watch   *Whenever you run a script, such as the one shown here, that works with the ADSI interface, you must restart the Web server in order for it to take effect. If you do not restart IIS after running the script shown earlier, the number of threads processing your requests will remain unaltered until a restart is performed.*

ASPScriptEngineCacheMax

This parameter tells IIS the maximum number of script engines that it should keep on tap and ready to interpret your pages as they are requested. There are a couple of principals governing the value that you should choose for this parameter. One of them is the total amount of memory available on your Web server machine. The other is how many pages comprise your ASP application, the nature of your scripts, and whether you have enabled caching of your scripts' output.

If your Web server's machine has a limited amount of memory, it would probably be counterproductive to raise the ASPScriptEngineCacheMax above its default value of 50 because each new instance of the ASP script engine requires additional memory in order to stay alive and ready. If this additional resource burden takes memory away from the rest of IIS while it is attempting to service your scripts, the results will be a decrease in performance rather than an improvement!

You should also consider how many unique pages are in your application and whether their output is likely to be cached. If you have just a few simple pages in your application, and they are all likely to have their output cached the first time that they run, there is no need to have additional script engines cached. This is true because a script engine will be used only when interpretation of the code in your pages is required. If IIS is simply retransmitting output from your scripts that it has previously cached, there is no script engine involvement.

If you have a server with plenty of memory and numerous, complicated scripts that are unlikely to ever be cached by IIS, you may use the following script to change the value of the ASPScriptEngineCacheMax parameter. In this case, we have elected to double it to 100. The best setting for your server will vary depending upon the amount of memory and nature of your scripts. You should discover this through trial and error and by keeping an eye on Performance Monitor.

```
<%
   Option Explicit

   Dim iisobj
   Set iisobj = getObject("IIS://localhost/w3svc/1/root")

   iisobj.ASPScriptEngineCacheMax = 100

   iisobj.setInfo
%>
```

External Issues

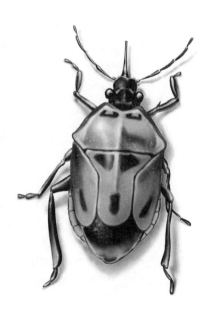

No matter how well you debug your Active Server Pages, there will always be some things that you can't control. In this appendix, you will learn about some of the most common external issues that can cause your ASP applications to break.

Browsers

Browsers can cause your ASP scripts to fail in two primary ways. First, they can cause problems through the ways that they are configured and used by their owners. Second, eccentricities and bugs in the browsers themselves can cause incorrect HTTP procedures that your ASP programs can't quite understand.

Common Problems

Cached pages and chopped URLs are the most common problems stemming from browser issues.

Caching Pages

Having a page cached in your browser may prevent you from seeing it as it currently exists on the server. Under Internet Explorer, you can clear your browser's cache by following these steps:

1. Open Internet Explorer.
2. Choose Internet Options from the Tools menu. You will see the dialog shown in Figure A-1.
3. In the frame marked Temporary Internet Files, click Delete Files.
4. In the frame marked History, click Clear History, and then click OK.

At this point, if you refresh the page you should get the most current version of the server.

Chopping URLs

If you use the GET method to post information to HTML forms under Active Server Pages, you should keep a careful eye on the length of your URLs. Many browsers limit the length of the URLs that they are willing to submit. If you ever get an error that indicates an unrecognized URL from your Active Server Pages, you should make sure that you actually received the whole thing.

```
<%
  Option Explicit

  Dim strURL
```

```
   strURL = Request.QueryString

   Response.Write strURL
%>
```

This script will echo to your browser interface the exact URL requested by your script. If you compare this to the URL you wanted to use and find that it has been truncated at a certain length, you might consider rewriting your scripts to use the POST method instead.

Losing Cookies

Cookies are often used directly by Active Server Page developers to expand the kinds of information that they can store on their Web browser clients. In addition to this explicit usage, however, there is the implicit usage that serves as the basis for much of ASP. Without operational cookies, neither the Session nor the Application objects are available for use by your scripts!

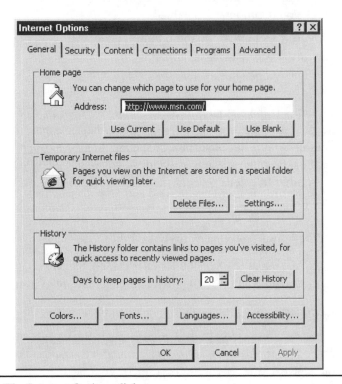

Figure A.1   The Internet Options dialog

Disabled Cookies

Because of the (mostly groundless) security fears that have been hyped by the media in virtually every corner of the globe, many Web users have disabled cookies on their browsers. The fallout from doing this when trying to use Active Server Page applications depends largely on how much your applications use the Session and Application objects. If they use them extensively, then users without cookies may not be able to access your applications at all!

In order to re-enable cookies under Internet Explorer, you can ask your users to follow these steps:

1. Open Internet Explorer.

2. Choose Internet Options from the Tools menu.

3. Select the Security tab in the dialog.

4. Click Custom Level.

5. Find the node labeled Cookies in the drop-down list.

6. Make sure that the radio button under Allow Cookies That Are Stored on Your Computer is enabled.

7. Make sure that the radio button under Allow Per-session Cookies (Not Stored) is enabled.

8. Click OK to confirm your changes.

Step 7 is the absolute most essential. Without it, your ASP applications will never function properly. Step 6 is somewhat optional; if you don't perform it, your cookies will not survive past a single visit to your Web site. This might not be a problem for you, depending on the nature of your site.

In order to re-enable cookies under Netscape, follow these steps:

1. Open Netscape.

2. Choose Preferences from the Edit menu.

3. Select Advanced on the left-hand tree control.

4. Make sure that Accept All Cookies is enabled in the Cookies frame.

Clearing the Cache

Clearing a browser's cache can also cause the loss of stored cookies. The procedure for clearing a browser's cache was outlined in the previous section on page caching. If you think some of your users are doing this, you can either advise them to avoid it or you can redesign your application to store their information on your server and restore it every time they return to your site.

Security Problems

The use of Web browsers as the main client tools for accessing your applications carries with it a certain lack of security. Unlike custom applications, you do not have total control to specify how you would like to prevent unauthorized access to your primary client. You must instead try to make do with the minimal security features provided by the browser manufacturers.

Sharing Computers

As long as companies and families require people to share computers, one of the greatest security risks will remain. The usual physical barriers to accessing another person's computer all disappear as soon as financial necessity dictates that such a computer be shared.

The best way to safeguard your users' security under Windows is to make sure that they always log out when they are finished using the computer. Ideally, everyone using the same computer should log in under a different user account. Such accounts can be created by anyone with administrative privileges on the computer and/or the Windows domain of which it is a member.

Expiration Times

One thing that you can do to make your applications a little more secure is to set your pages' expiration times such that they will never be cached locally on your clients' computers. The benefit to this is that anyone obtaining improper access to your clients' computers will never be able to look at copies of the pages the appropriate users previously visited. This could be extremely important in applications that send confidential information across the Internet, such as credit card numbers.

To make sure that the output of a given Active Server Page can never be stored in the cache of a client browser, add the following code to the top of the page:

```
<%
    Response.CacheControl = "no-cache"
    Response.AddHeader "Pragma", "no-cache"
    Response.Expires = -1
%>
```

This code instructs both HTTP 1.0– and HTTP 1.1–compliant browsers not to cache the content that will follow.

Using Passwords

The simplest way to ensure the security of your Active Server Pages is to always use password protection on your applications. The temptation can be great to use persistent cookies alone for the recognition of your users. An example of this would be an e-commerce site that always says, "Welcome back, So-and-so" whenever you visit it and never asks you to verify your identity before using your credit card information that is stored on their server.

The problem with this approach is that it could be quite easy for a different person to be using the same Web browser on the same machine. This is particularly true in the case of the computer sharing described earlier. Making sure that your users always log off after visiting your site is not nearly as easy for you as a developer as simply adding password verification to the sensitive areas of your sites!

Firewalls and Proxies

Many users and corporations that are concerned about Internet security take the time and trouble of setting up firewall and proxy machines for their Internet access. A firewall is a machine that sits between users and the Internet and prevents anyone or anything undesirable from coming in through the connection. Restricting the ports and kinds of protocols that can be sent through the firewall is the most common approach to this. Prohibiting access by all but a predetermined list of IPs is an even more restrictive way of limiting access.

Proxy servers function in a similar method, except that they work by echoing the requests that they receive from their clients. The only machine that ever truly communicates with the Internet is the proxy server. If the content received by the proxy server is deemed acceptable and safe, it is relayed to the client. Proxy servers are a very common way to restrict content at businesses to work-related topics.

Redirection Problems

The most common problem that Active Server Page developers encounter when working with clients behind a firewall or proxy server is the inability to accept page redirections. For example, a script that executed the following code

```
<%
    Response.Redirect "http://www.interaccess.com"
%>
```

might result in the production of an Object Moved error in the Web browser. This is a sure sign of a problem with proxies and firewalls.

Fortunately, there is a work-around for this problem. If your users report that they are experiencing such errors, simply modify your code as follows:

```
<%
    Response.Clear
    Response.Redirect "http://www.interaccess.com"
%>
```

Adding Response.Clear will typically resolve this peculiar issue with proxies and firewalls under Active Server Pages.

DCOM Problems

Unfortunately, trying to use DCOM through a firewall is a much thornier issue to resolve. DCOM is a technology for using COM components over a network; the components are located on computers other than the one running the client code (see Figure A-2). A client accessing a COM component via DCOM has no idea that the object is on a remote computer—it simply goes about using it as if it were local. All the networking is taken care of by the DCOM extensions to the Windows operating system.

Unfortunately, firewalls like to restrict access between computers based on certain predefined ports (see Figure A-3). For example, port 80 might be allowed between any two computers across the firewall because this is the standard port

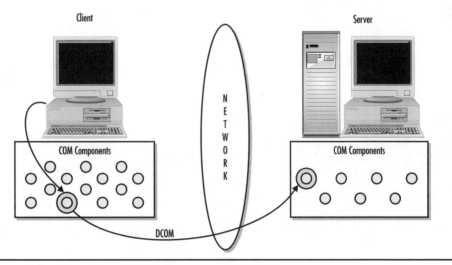

Figure A.2   Accessing a COM component via DCOM

for traffic on the World Wide Web, which is usually seen as harmless. Other ports may be opened on a one-at-a-time basis as client users make requests to the firewall administrator(s) and additional ports are guaranteed to be safe for use.

The problem with this is that DCOM doesn't operate on a single port. Ports for DCOM are chosen and negotiated as required, so that many connections can be made between client and server components. This means that the person administering a firewall must do one of two things if they want to allow DCOM traffic through it:

- Open all the ports on the firewall, which is extremely unsafe and largely negates the value of even having a firewall.

- Configure the firewall to recognize DCOM traffic and allow it—and *only* it—through on any port.

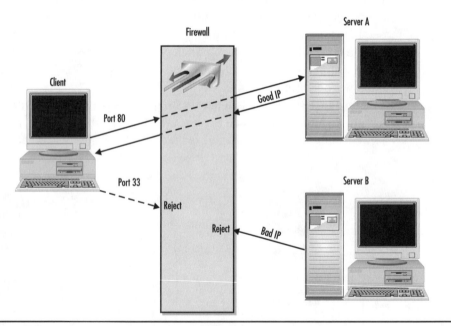

Figure A.3 A firewall limits access between computers.

Microsoft SMTP Server

Many Active Server Page developers are asked at some point in their careers to write an application that sends out e-mails of some sort. In the early days of ASP, this usually required the purchase of a third-party component that handled all the intricacies of Internet protocols such as SMTP and POP. Nowadays, it is much more likely that an ASP programmer will leverage the features of the Microsoft SMTP Server as exposed through the CDONTS object library.

Administrative Problems

Possible administrative problems stem from the workings of the Microsoft SMTP Server itself. The server runs as a service that can be administered via the Microsoft Management Console.

Is It Turned On?

The most basic reason for failure by ASP scripts to send out e-mails when required is that the SMTP service has been turned off. In order to verify that your SMTP server is operational, follow these steps:

1. Choose Programs from the Windows Start menu.
2. Open the Administrative Tools program group.
3. Click Internet Services Manager.
4. Expand the node representing the computer running SMTP.
5. Right-click Default SMTPVirtual Server.
6. Choose Start from the pop-up context menu.

Is the Smart Host Correct?

Microsoft SMTP Server allows an administrator to request that all outbound mail be routed to another server for processing (a *smart host*). This can be useful if your computer is connected to an Internet service provider that offers high-end mail servers for your use. There is no point in putting the load on your own computers when you can offload it to theirs!

To make sure that the smart host for your SMTP server is set correctly, follow these steps:

1. Choose Programs from the Windows Start menu.
2. Open the Administrative Tools program group.
3. Click Internet Services Manager.
4. Expand the node representing the computer running SMTP.
5. Right-click Default SMTPVirtual Server.
6. Choose Properties.
7. Go to the Delivery tab of the Properties dialog.
8. Click Advanced.
9. Verify that the server named in the Smart Host text field is the appropriate machine to receive all your site's outbound mail.

Code Problems

The other group of reasons why your attempts at sending mail might fail originate from actual errors in your scripts. This is fairly common when using the CDONTS object library, as some of the rules concerning its use are unusual and not well documented.

NewMail Object

The NewMail object is good for one use only. Once you have called its Send method, you will need to create another NewMail object before you can use it to send another piece of mail. For example, this code would fail miserably:

```
<%
    Option Explicit

    Dim nm

    Set nm = Server.CreateObject("CDONTS.NewMail")

    nm.From = "dferguson@interaccess.com"
    nm.To = "derek@eviloscar.com"
    nm.Subject = "This won't work!"
    nm.Body = "Don't try reusing this object, or you'll regret it!"
    nm.Send
```

```
      'And this is where it all breaks!
    nm.To = "oscar@eviloscar.com"
    nm.Send
%>
```

This code would have been fine without the attempt to reuse the same NewMail object. It would run and send the first message perfectly, but it would bomb out on the second mail attempt. The only way to rectify this would be to create another NewMail object, set all its properties separately, and send it.

Nontext Materials

Another error that is extremely common when ASP programmers use CDONTS is the inappropriate formatting on nontext content, such as HTML. If you try to send HTML in your e-mails, you must make sure to set the *BodyFormat* and *MailFormat* properties of the NewMail object to 0. If you don't, it will be treated as text.

```
<%
    Option Explicit

    Dim nm

    Set nm = Server.CreateObject("CDONTS.NewMail")

    nm.From = "dferguson@interaccess.com"
    nm.To = "derek@eviloscar.com"
    nm.Subject = "This won't work!"
    nm.BodyFormat = 0
    nm.MailFormat = 0
    nm.Body = "<html><body>Now this <b>really</b>is_cool!</body></html>"
    nm.Send
%>
```

Preventing Bad Input

Inappropriate input is one of the leading cause of Active Server Page failure. Ideally, your pages should be able to withstand anything that your clients may throw at them. In reality, this is often a daunting task, to say the least. Using client-side scripting to "prequalify" some of the data received by your scripts is one way to reduce the number of bugs in your Active Server Pages.

Client-side Scripting

Client-side scripts execute within the framework of your users' browsers, rather than on your Web server. For this reason, Internet Information Server has little or no control over these programs as they run. The exact interpretation of any client-side coding you do is always left up to the implementation of the various browsers.

VBScript

VBScript is the language that you have seen throughout the vast majority of this book. It is a subset of the Visual Basic programming language, which you have already seen. Visual Basic is by far the most popular programming language in the world. For this reason, the VBScript language is often the natural choice when working with any browser that supports it.

The problem is that VBScript is currently directly supported only by Internet Explorer. If you encounter users that complain about your VBScript code not working, chances are good that they are using Netscape or another browser other than IE.

LiveScript, JavaScript, Jscript, ECMAScript

The client-side scripting language supported by the widest variety of Web browsers is commonly known as JavaScript. Netscape originally created JavaScript under the name LiveScript. It was soon renamed JavaScript to cash in on some of the popularity of Java, but they are only casually related.

The benefit of using JavaScript for your client-side scripting is that it is available on both Netscape and Internet Explorer. Its only drawback is that many programmers who are skilled in VB and VBScript are not familiar with it.

Checking Common Data

There are many kinds of data that might cause errors in your ASP applications. A relatively small set of these pieces of data account for a surprisingly large percentage of all data sent across the World Wide Web, however. Three of these, in particular, warrant special attention. They are credit card numbers, location information, and e-mail addresses.

Credit Card Numbers

The rules governing legitimate credit card numbers are very precise and well published. The formula is known as the Luhn check. You can find exact information on how this formula can be used to validate credit card numbers at http://users.knoware.nl/users/eprebel/Numbers/Luhn.html.

Locations

The multitude of places on Earth that can be entered into a simple request for an address boggles the imagination. Street numbers, apartment numbers, buildings, floors, etc., all add to the confusion surrounding what is, for humans, usually fairly simple information to understand.

Because it is difficult to get computers to understand the many varieties of addresses used by people throughout the world, it is usually a good idea to limit yourself to a few basics. If you are in the United States, you might simply verify that a state is, indeed, one of the 50 recognized states and that a ZIP code is actually five or nine digits. In other countries, you might maintain a short list of provinces or counties that you could also verify against.

E-mail Addresses

The exact rules that let you know whether a given e-mail address is formatted correctly are stated in a series of Internet RFCs (Request for Comments). RFCs are the papers in which most of the major protocols used in the Internet are first described and subjected to discussion. The best repository of Internet RFCs can be found at http://www.nexor.com/info/rfc/index/rfc.htm?index/rfc.html.

HTTP Status Codes

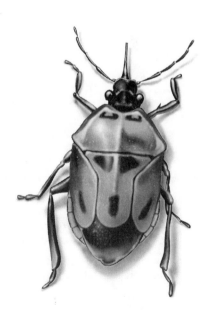

In this appendix, you will find a complete listing of the status codes returned by all HTTP-compliant Web servers. Servers such as IIS use these codes to communicate the success or failure of client requests. Web browser clients, such as Internet Explorer, then use these codes to determine what action to take next. For example, a 200 would tell a Web browser that a page has been successfully returned. However, a 404 would cause most Web browsers to display an error message for their users telling them that the requested page was not found.

Numeric Constant	Symbolic Name	Meaning
100	HTTP_STATUS_CONTINUE	A "keep-alive" message to let the browser know that it may continue making its request.
101	HTTP_STATUS_SWITCH_PROTOCOLS	A message to let the client know that the server has switched protocols.
200	HTTP_STATUS_OK	The Web server has accepted the client's request without error.
201	HTTP_STATUS_CREATED	The Web server has created a new resource in response to the client request.
202	HTTP_STATUS_ACCEPTED	The client's request has been accepted, but the server has not yet finished processing it.
203	HTTP_STATUS_PARTIAL	The metadata being returned by the server is not to be interpreted as complete.
204	HTTP_STATUS_NO_CONTENT	The client's request has been processed, but the server has nothing to say in response.
205	HTTP_STATUS_RESET_CONTENT	The server is requesting that the client (browser) refresh whatever page it is currently displaying.
206	HTTP_STATUS_PARTIAL_CONTENT	Used with the GET method, this indicates that the server is partially finished processing.
300	HTTP_STATUS_AMBIGUOUS	This message indicates that the Web server is confused about what kind of response to send.
301	HTTP_STATUS_MOVED	The requested resource has been permanently relocated.
302	HTTP_STATUS_REDIRECT	The requested resource has been temporarily relocated.

Numeric Constant	Symbolic Name	Meaning
303	HTTP_STATUS_REDIRECT_METHOD	The requested resource has been temporarily relocated; please go there using a GET method.
304	HTTP_STATUS_NOT_MODIFIED	The requested resource as stored on the server is no different from that in the client's cache.
305	HTTP_STATUS_USE_PROXY	Please access the requested resource using the specified proxy server.
307	HTTP_STATUS_REDIRECT_KEEP_VERB	The requested resource has been temporarily relocated; please go there using the same method you just used.
400	HTTP_STATUS_BAD_REQUEST	The server doesn't recognize your request as being legitimate HTTP syntax.
401	HTTP_STATUS_DENIED	The resource requested by the client requires authentication.
402	HTTP_STATUS_PAYMENT_REQUIRED	The resource requested by the client requires payment.
403	HTTP_STATUS_FORBIDDEN	The client's request has been rejected for security reasons.
404	HTTP_STATUS_NOT_FOUND	There is no such resource on the server as the one requested by the client.
405	HTTP_STATUS_BAD_METHOD	The server doesn't recognize your request method as being a legitimate HTTP verb.
406	HTTP_STATUS_NONE_ACCEPTABLE	The client won't accept any of the response types possible.
407	HTTP_STATUS_PROXY_AUTH_REQUIRED	The proxy server making the request must authenticate itself to the Web server.
408	HTTP_STATUS_REQUEST_TIMEOUT	The server got sick of waiting for the client to finish its request and has stopped waiting.
409	HTTP_STATUS_CONFLICT	Another user or process has an exclusive lock on the requested resource.
410	HTTP_STATUS_GONE	The requested resource is no longer on the server.
411	HTTP_STATUS_LENGTH_REQUIRED	The client must specify the length of its request.

Numeric Constant	Symbolic Name	Meaning
412	HTTP_STATUS_PRECOND_FAILED	The server has tested all the preconditions stipulated by the client and at least one has failed.
413	HTTP_STATUS_REQUEST_TOO_LARGE	The length of the client's request is too long.
414	HTTP_STATUS_URI_TOO_LONG	The length of the URI used by the client to reference the resource on the server is too long.
415	HTTP_STATUS_UNSUPPORTED_MEDIA	The data type of the resource can not be handled by the Web server.
449	HTTP_STATUS_RETRY_WITH	The Web server needs the client to perform a certain action before retrying the request.
500	HTTP_STATUS_SERVER_ERROR	Something unexpected and bad has happened to the Web server.
501	HTTP_STATUS_NOT_SUPPORTED	The action requested by the client is legitimate, but it is beyond the capabilities of this Web server.
502	HTTP_STATUS_BAD_GATEWAY	The Web server has been acting as a proxy for another resource and has just received an error.
503	HTTP_STATUS_SERVICE_UNAVAILABLE	The Web server is temporarily incapable of servicing the client's request because of resource limitations.
504	HTTP_STATUS_GATEWAY_TIMEOUT	The Web server has gotten sick of waiting for the specified gateway to respond and has rejected the request.
505	HTTP_STATUS_VERSION_NOT_SUPPORTED	The Web server is incapable of working at the level of HTTP protocol desired by the client.

Active Server Pages Plus

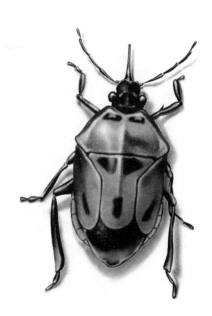

By many estimates, ASP is the single most popular platform in the world for Web application development. With a customer base of well over 1,000,000 developers, it is not surprising that Microsoft has been eager to follow up on the success of this product. ASP+ adds tremendous value to the Active Server platform by incorporating a number of elements from new Internet technologies and Microsoft initiatives.

Foundation Technologies

Many of the new features found in ASP+ can trace their roots to the development of three other "foundational" technologies: Microsoft.Net Frameworks, Visual Studio.Net, and XML.

Microsoft.Net Frameworks

Microsoft.Net Frameworks adds a host of new features and tools to the Windows development environment and might best be described as a "Web services platform."

Common Language Runtime (CLR)

The Common Language Runtime, CLR, provides the underlying support structure for all Microsoft.Net Frameworks other innovations. If you are familiar with Java, you can think of it as Windows' new Virtual Machine.

Microsoft.Net Frameworks introduces the concept of *managed languages*. These languages never compile completely into binary machine language. Instead, they create something known as *IM*, which is a kind of byte code that is interpreted at runtime by the CLR. All managed languages create exactly the same IM, so you may therefore freely mix and match bits of code written in completely different languages.

Because all IM (also known as *managed code*) must pass through the CLR before being executed, far greater opportunities now exist to control the flow of this code as it runs. A few of its benefits include

- **Fine-grained security**   It is possible to allow different users access to different methods on the same object.

- **Reflection**   Components written in a managed language can be thoroughly inspected at runtime by the CLR.

- **SOAP**   Objects can be accessed remotely using XML over a standard Internet protocol, such as HTTP.

- **Memory management**   The CLR will not allow executing IM to corrupt its own memory. It also features a garbage collector, so memory leaks are virtually impossible.

- **Easier deployment**   The CLR uses *assemblies* to store code. See the next section for the benefits of assemblies.

Assemblies

Assemblies are repositories of code described by XML manifests. The level of detailed information supported by XML is what enables the CLR's excellent reflection mechanisms. But there is a much more important benefit to most Active Server Page developers: Components stored in assemblies can be swapped in and out of a running application. You never even need to run regsvr32 on these components!

This means that you should never again have to restart your Web server just to make a change in one of your components! Simply copy your new assembly over the old assembly, and the change should be made. You will not get a "file lock" error like you would now with .DLL files.

Base Class Libraries

To support development under Microsoft.Net Frameworks, Microsoft has created an enormous set of utility classes known as the Base Class Library. These classes are documented exceptionally well in the file COM20SDK\Docs\cpref.htm. A few examples of some of the more compelling ones are

- **System.Net**, which is a network-access library *much* improved over Microsoft's previous offerings (WinInet and the Internet Transfer Control).

- **System.Text**, which provides a host of pattern-matching and text-manipulation routines—almost as good as PERL.

- **System.Web.Util**, which covers every odd task you've always needed to do from a Web site, like access other sites and send e-mails.

24x7   ADO+

The System.Data library implements Microsoft's new data access technology: ADO+. ADO+ throws out a lot of the previous ideas from ADO and starts fresh. Oh joy… not! To begin with, whereas ADO strove to make all data types look as much alike as possible, ADO+ has decided to "play to the unique strengths" of differing data sources by accessing each differently. If you are working with a relational database, for example, the object model that you see will be very different from the object model you would see if you were dealing with a mail system.

The way that ADO+ accomplishes this is through the concept of *managed providers* ("managed" is the big word in dealing with Microsoft.Net Frameworks). A managed provider is a group of classes that exists just below the System.Data name space and is responsible for interacting with a single kind of data source. For example, the classes in System.Data.SQL are those used for talking with SQL Server databases.

For a good example of ADO+ in action, refer to the section on HTML extenders later in this appendix. It is largely incidental to the discussion at that point, but the example in that section uses the managed provider for SQL Server.

Visual Studio.Net

The latest release of Visual Studio incorporates strong support for the Microsoft.Net Frameworks environment.

Availability under ASP+

The single most shocking innovation introduced by Visual Studio.Net is that Visual Basic and a new language called C# both produce IM now, rather than machine language. This change is significant because ASP+ is capable of running any language that can produce IM. For this reason, you can now use the full Visual Basic and C# languages under ASP+ (in addition to JavaScript, which has always been there)!

As just one example of the significance of this step, you can now declare a variable as being a specific type under ASP+. By extension, this means that you can also early-bind to objects, rather than using the Server.Execute method to late-bind.

```
<%
    Dim x as Integer
    Dim y as New Truck.Engine
%>
```

The ASP+ engine completely compiles a page the first time it runs it and retains this compiled version in memory until the page is changed or the server is restarted. By the time this technology is released to the public, it is likely (though not guaranteed) that a tool will exist to precompile all ASP+ pages before they are ever accessed. This will greatly improve performance and allow for the distribution of ASP+ pages in compiled form without source code. This will be useful to those of you (particularly consultants) who want to protect your intellectual property.

Languages

Some languages have been changed radically for Microsoft.Net Frameworks. One language is completely new. One development tool is dead in the water.

Visual Basic 7   Since the bulk of this book has been written in VBScript, there is a section devoted to the differences in the newest version of this language; see later in the appendix.

C++   Visual Studio now offers two versions of C++. One of these is a "managed" version that creates IM and has the limitations on its behaviors that you would imagine: no direct access to memory, and so on. The other is the standard version of Visual C++ that you can continue to use for non-COM+ 2.0 applications.

C#   C# (pronounced "C sharp," which is the key immediately above C in Western musical notation) is Microsoft's new, extremely Java-like language creation. You may have heard about it previously when it was still known as COOL. It is now an official part of Visual Studio 7.0 and may be used to create ASP+ scripts.

Visual Interdev   Stick a fork in it; it's done. If you have any plans to become certified in this tool, I would drop them. There will not be a version 7 of Visual Interdev. It is as dead as dead can possibly be. ASP+ creation has been so tightly woven into the fabric of the other Visual Studio tools that an independent tool is no longer regarded as needed.

XML

The Extensible Markup Language (XML) has received a lot of press lately. Originally, it was proposed to facilitate the transfer of data. For example, an IBM mainframe is built completely differently from a PC, but they can both be made to use TCP/IP and "speak" the HTTP protocol to one another. XML defines a way to package data for transmission over a standard protocol, such as HTTP, so that wildly different systems—like IBM mainframes and PCs—can exchange data.

Recently, XML has begun showing up as the indigenous data storage format for several applications. For example, the configuration files for many Java applications are formatted using XML. The next version of Internet Information Server will also store all of its configurations (the *metabase*) in XML.

With the release of ASP+, XML is poised to begin facilitating the interoperation of software components across system and network boundaries. The SOAP protocol can be used to package requests and their parameters into XML messages that are sent by the client. Then, on the server, SOAP bundles the data returned by the requested object method into XML messages for the return trip back to the client.

This most advanced use of XML is contained with ASP+ in what are known as Web Services. They are discussed in greater detail at the end of this appendix.

Installation

At the time of this writing, ASP+ is not yet available to the general public. For this reason, some of the specific information contained in this section may change by the time that the product is officially released. Consult the product documentation for specific details.

Software

ASP+ is currently available as part of Microsoft's COM+ 2.0 Software Development Kit (SDK). In order to fully utilize all of the advanced functionality that ASP+ makes available, however, you must also install Internet Explorer 5.5.

System Requirements
In order to install and use Internet Explorer 5.5 and COM+ 2.0, you should have

- Windows 2000
- 133MHz or higher Pentium-compatible CPU
- 128MB of RAM
- 2GB hard disk with a minimum of 1.0GB free space
- A monitor with 800x600 resolution @ 256 colors
- CD-ROM

Internet Explorer 5.5

In order to install Internet Explorer 5.5, follow these steps:

1. Gather all the files included with your distribution into a single directory.
2. Run the program "ie5setup."

ie5setup

3. Accept the licensing agreement and click Next.
4. Click Next again.
5. Wait while the Setup program installs Internet Explorer 5.5 on your system (see Figure C-1).
6. After the files are installed, click Finish to restart Windows.

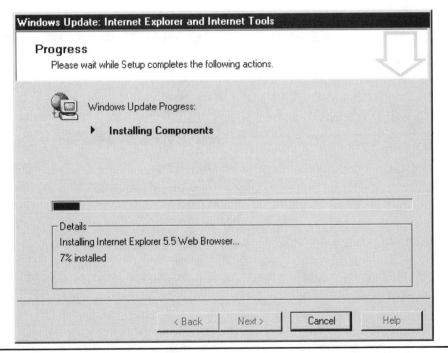

Figure C.1   Installing Internet Explorer 5.5

Once your computer has restarted, you should log in and start Internet Explorer. Select "About Internet Explorer" from the Help menu and verify that you are now using version 5.5 (see Figure C-2).

COM+ 2.0 SDK

In order to install the COM+ 2.0 SDK, follow these steps:

1. Run the Setup program.

2. Click Yes.

3. Wait while Setup extracts the files needed to install COM+ 2.0 on your system.

4. Click Next.

5. Accept the licensing agreement and click Next.

6. On the Install Options screen (see Figure C-3), select "Software Development Kit" and "Documentation," and then click Next.

7. Choose a location to install COM+ 2.0 and make sure that you will be registering the environment variables (see Figure C-4), and then click Next.

8. Wait while Setup installs COM+ 2.0 on your system.

Figure C.2   Verifying the version number of IE

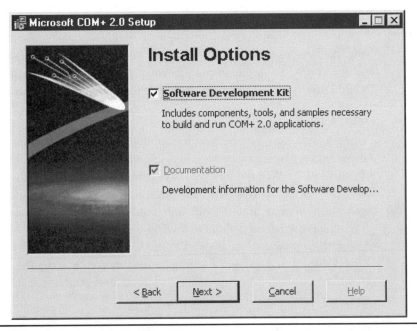

Figure C.3   Choosing installation options

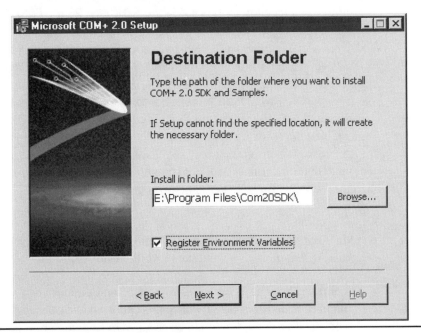

Figure C.4   Selecting the files' destination

Applications

Now that you have installed COM+ 2.0, you are ready to begin using it to run and develop ASP+ applications. However, there are a few basic things that you should know before you begin exploring this new development environment.

Existing ASPs

To begin with, you may be wondering to yourself: "What about my existing Active Server Page applications? Is ASP+ backward compatible, so that they will all still work?" Well, the answer may seem a little strange to those of you familiar with the traditional way of installing Windows software. Your ASP applications should all still work fine, but ASP+ is *not* backward compatible!

What has happened is that the COM+ 2.0 setup program has left ASP unaltered on your system. Instead, it installed ASP+ *in addition* to regular Active Server Pages. It is capable of telling the difference between the two primarily by the differences in their extensions: .asp or .asa for Active Server Pages and .aspx, .asax, .aspc, or .asmx for ASP+.

Samples and Tutorials

One of the best ways to begin learning about ASP+ is by consulting the samples and tutorials included with the COM+ 2.0 SDK (see Figure C-5). They are not fully installed by the COM+ 2.0 Setup program, however, so you will have to do a little additional work in order to get them completely operational on your system.

To begin with, find the icon for the COM+ 2.0 SDK Start Page that should have been placed on your desktop by the Setup program. If you open this, you should see a Web page with links to Samples and Tutorials toward the bottom.

If you click on these links, you should be taken to pages with complete instructions for installing the software appropriately. Printing out these instructions is probably the easiest way to ensure that they remain visible to you as you follow them. From the standpoint of learning ASP+, it is much more important to install the Tutorials than the Samples. Budget your time accordingly.

ASP+ Applications

An ASP+ application typically exists within a single directory (like most standard ASP applications) and contains the following files:

- **config.web**   This is an XML-formatted configuration file that specifies a number of details about how this application should operate. It allows an ASP+ application's configuration to be changed by copying or uploading a new configuration file. This is useful in cases where access to the server's desktop is not possible (as in the case of a commercial Web hosting service).

- **global.asax**   This replaces the traditional global.asa file. Like the global.asa file, it is optional.

- **.aspx pages**   These are known as Web forms under ASP+. They are probably the most like traditional .asp files and are where you will do the vast majority of your ASP+ programming that is not Web Service–related.

- **.asmx pages**   These are where Web Services are implemented.

- **/bin directory**   All the components used by an ASP+ application should be placed in assemblies in this directory. It has the advantage of preventing conflicts between components with the same name in different applications. It also allows components to be added to ASP+ applications by copying or uploading them into this directory, which is useful when access to the server's desktop is not possible.

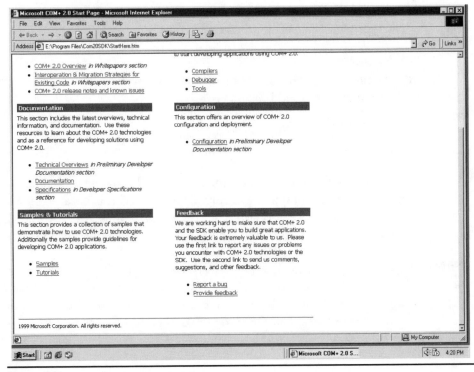

Figure C.5   The COM+ 2.0 SDK Start page

Web Forms

Web Forms are the ASP+ equivalent of traditional Active Server Pages. Microsoft has added value beyond the traditional ASP scripts, however, by adding a multitude of new server-side controls. These controls make performing common tasks that were once very difficult and time-consuming under Active Server Pages much quicker and less tedious. Perhaps most importantly, these new features result in the generation of pure, truly platform-independent HTML!

HTML Controls

The easiest way to get started with ASP+ is to see a quick example. Consider the following, amazingly primitive, Active Server Page.

```
<FORM METHOD="Post">
    <INPUT NAME="simple" ID="simple">
</FORM>
```

If you run this script, you will get a blank text field. Type something and press Enter to submit the form. You will get exactly the same form again—whatever you typed will disappear.

ASP+ Enabling

To begin reaping the benefits of ASP+, all we have to do is add a "RUNAT" clause to the Form and Input tags.

```
<FORM METHOD="Post" RUNAT="server">
    <INPUT NAME="simple" ID="simple" RUNAT="server">
</FORM>
```

Now, try running this script again. This time, if you type something and hit Enter, whatever you typed will stay in the field. This is because by adding the "RUNAT" clause to an HTML control, you are telling ASP+ to actually think about the control as if it were running on the server rather than the client.

Error Watch *It is easy to forget to add the RUNAT parameter to the FORM tag. If you add RUNAT to every control within your form, but leave it off the FORM tag, things will not work. This bug can be difficult to track down, so always remember to check the FORM tag in addition to whatever controls seem to be experiencing difficulties.*

State Maintenance

To see how running a control on the server differs from running it on the client, examine the source HTML in Internet Explorer as shown in Figure C-6.

The first thing you might notice is that ASP+ has automatically generated a unique ID for our form, "ctrl0." This is what ASP+ will do with any form element for which you neglect to specify your own ID. IDs are what the server uses to refer to your form elements, so it is essential that every element have such an ID.

The other thing that you might notice about this HTML is that a completely new field, "__VIEWSTATE," has been created. This is where ASP+ now maintains all session state information, such as that stored in the Session object. This is very important to understand, and quite wonderful once you grasp its significance. *All session-level data maintained by your ASP+ scripts will be stored in the hidden "__VIEWSTATE" field that is returned to the client with each page request.*

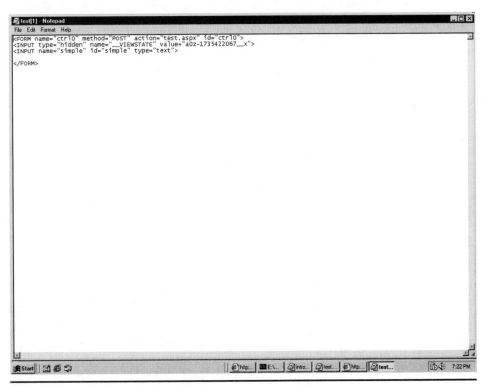

Figure C.6　HTML source for forms run on the server

Why is this so much better than storing this information on the server, like ASP? To begin with, it offloads some of the resource burden from your Web servers, which can help their performance and lower hardware costs. More importantly, it sidesteps the issues with maintaining session state that have always made using Web farms with ASP applications very difficult. Recall the discussion in Chapter 4 about how to jump through these hoops? Well, if you're going to use code like this, you can just forget all about it and let ASP+ do the work for you!

You might be concerned that round-tripping session data between the client and the server at every page request is going to substantially increase the wait times for your pages. Don't worry: The __VIEWSTATE data is compressed and will almost never grow noticeably in size. You might be concerned that a hacker will alter the contents of __VIEWSTATE while it is on their client and resubmit it with bogus data. Don't worry: The value is "signed" cryptographically, so any alteration will be immediately spotted by ASP+ and thrown out. Is this nice, or what?

Leveling

It is important to realize that nothing but standard, platform-neutral HTML is being used to accomplish any of this. If you would like to be a little more aggressive on this point, however, ASP+ provides a mechanism to support your efforts. It is called the *ClientTarget* page directive.

Simply put, ClientTarget allows you to specify whether you want the HTML generated by ASP+ to be the absolute most advanced that it knows about, the absolute most platform-independent that it knows about, or the best that it thinks a given client can tolerate.

<%@ Page ClientTarget = "Uplevel" %>	ASP+ generates the best-looking, most responsive HTML/DHTML of which it is capable. No regard is given to the nature of the client making the connection. If it can't deal with it, too bad!
<%@ Page ClientTarget = "Downlevel" %>	ASP+ generates the most widely usable, standards-abiding HTML of which it is capable. If it looks horrible, too bad!
<%@ Page ClientTarget = "Auto" %>	ASP+ tries to figure out what client you are using and give you the best HTML/DHTML that it thinks you can handle. Of course, the closer your browser is to Internet Explorer, the better!

Page directives like these must always occur at the top of your ASP+ script, before all other content.

Web Controls

Adding the RUNAT clause to your form elements will go a long way toward solving the session maintenance problems just described. But there is much, much more to Web forms under ASP+ than that! In order to move to the next level, you must start using Web controls.

HTML Proxies

The first group of Web controls that we will look at can be thought of as HTML proxies. These are controls that "live on" the server but have exact analogs in HTML. For this reason, every HTML proxy that you put in your ASP+ scripts will result in the creation of exactly one "pure-HTML" control on the client at runtime.

To see them in action, continue the example from the previous section. Pressing Enter is a rather primitive way to submit a form, so add a button—better yet, add two.

```
<INPUT ID="a" VALUE="1" TYPE="submit">
<INPUT ID="b" VALUE="2" TYPE="submit">
```

Now, imagine some ASP code that will change the text field on this page to contain "ONE" if you click the first button, or "TWO" if you click the second. Give up? It is a very nontrivial task to write ASP code that does this, because HTML buttons were never designed to drive events on the server. They were intended only to give the user some way to request that his client submit the form.

```
<SCRIPT RUNAT="Server">
   private sub a(obj as Object, e as EventArgs)
      If obj.text = "1" Then
         simple.value = "ONE"
      ElseIf obj.text = "2" Then
         simple.value = "TWO"
      End If
   end sub
</SCRIPT>

<FORM METHOD="POST" RUNAT="SERVER">
   <INPUT ID="simple" RUNAT="SERVER">
   <asp:button id="a" text="1" type="submit" onclick="a" runat="server"/>
   <asp:button id="b" text="2" type="submit" onclick="a" runat="server"/>
</FORM>
```

Starting at the bottom, probably the first thing you notice is that the HTML buttons have been replaced by this new "asp:button" monstrosity. This is your first example of an HTML proxy control. Don't worry: It only looks like this on the server. On the client, it creates the same old, pure, platform-neutral HTML buttons—but *these* buttons can drive events!

Error Watch   *If you put an OnClick parameter on a standard HTML button, you will get bizarre errors in your Web browser. The reason for this is that, under standard HTML, the OnClick keyword will be used to run a client-side script, rather than a server-side script.*

At the top of the script you can see the code for the event that these buttons fire. This is written in Visual Basic.Net, which is why it takes an Object and EventArgs parameter. Additional differences between Visual Basic.Net and previous versions of this language are discussed later in this appendix.

Notice that the script block at the top of the previous listing manipulates the Value property of the text field name "simple". One reason for using the HTML proxy objects rather than their regular HTML analogs is that the proxies feature a much more consistent naming scheme for their properties. For example, if you created the simple control this way

```
<asp:textbox id="simple" runat="server"/>
```

you could change the code in the SCRIPT block to refer to the control's text property instead. This is the same as the property used, for instance, to get at the caption on the buttons in this form. The naming scheme used within the HTML proxies seems much more natural to most people familiar with Microsoft technologies.

Other HTML proxies include dropdownlist, listbox, radiobuttonlist, and checkboxlist. Space prevents going into detail about them here, so consult the documentation for further information. (Note: Microsoft lumps them in with some of the extenders described next and refers to them as *Intrinsics.*)

HTML Extenders

Another kind of ASP+ control creates standard HTML, but not just a single control. You can think of these as HTML extenders, because they extend the capabilities of ordinary HTML. The two HTML extenders that are probably the most fun to work (and impress your boss and coworkers) with are the DataGrid and Calendar. Imagine that you are given the following development project:

> "Build a Web page that allows users to see information available about employees with a given date of birth. The data will all be stored in a table called EMPLOYEES on a SQL Server database named HR.

Your code should be able to automatically adapt to frequent changes in the design of this table (different columns, data types, and so on). For usability purposes, users should be able to pick dates using a graphical calendar, but it must be rendered in pure HTML for cross-platform compatibility."

Trying to meet these design goals using standard Active Server Pages would present several points of frustration. To begin with, you'd need to write your own code to generate an HTML table from the employee data given to you. You wouldn't be able to make any assumptions about the number or types of data columns, so you'd have to code for many conceivable possibilities.

Furthermore, creating an HTML calendar is no small feat. Just drawing it on the screen requires quite a bit of effort. Adding a way to flip forward and backward in months adds another layer of complexity. Finally, coding the calendar in such a way that it can be used to submit the form would require quite a bit of JavaScript magic because hyperlinks are normally quite different from Submit buttons.

Fortunately, ASP+ has you covered:

```
<script runat="server>
   private sub page_load(x as object, y as eventargs)
       Dim strDate as String
       Dim strQry as String

       Dim cn as System.Data.SQL.SQLConnection
       Dim cmd as System.Data.SQL.SQLDataSetCommand
       Dim ds as System.Data.DataSet

       strDate = cal.SelectedDate.Format("d",null)
       strQry = "select * from employees where birthdate = '" & _
           strDate & "'"

       cn = new System.Data.SQL.SQLConnection("hr")
       cmd = new System.Data.SQL.SQLDataSetCommand(strQry, cn)
       ds = new System.Data.DataSet()

       cmd.FillDataSet(ds, "employees")

       TheGrid.DataSource = new System.Data.DataView(ds.Tables(0))
       TheGrid.DataBind()
   end sub
</script>

<FORM METHOD="POST" runat="server">
   <asp:calendar id="cal" runat="server"/>
   <asp:datagrid id="TheGrid" runat="server"/>
</FORM>
```

There is a lot of information to absorb in this example, so let's start with the form at the bottom. There are two controls, both of which are the kind of HTML extenders that were alluded to earlier. The first of these is a calendar control and the second is the datagrid control. Both of these look funny on the server, but result in pure HTML on the client (see Figure C-7).

The code in the page_load event at the top of the script is probably of next most concern. The very existence of this event and its close relative, page_unload, are new to ASP+. The code used to access the database within this event is making use of ADO+. The System.Data classes are all of the "general purposes" classes provided for working with any kind of data. The System.Data.SQL classes are specific to SQL Server. Once the data is retrieved, it is fed to the datagrid control and bound with just a couple lines of code. The beauty of this is that no matter how the design of the Employees table is changed, your code will continue to function as required!

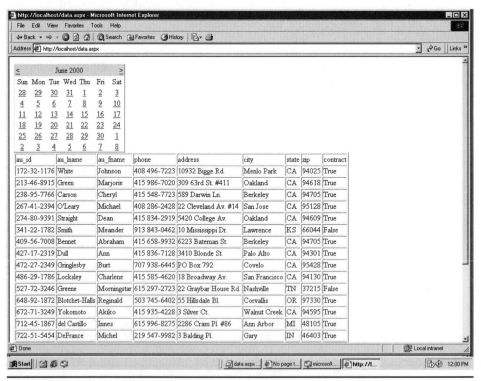

Figure C.7   How the datagrid and calendar controls appear on the client

Other HTML extenders include linkbutton, repeater, and datalist. Space prevents going into detail about them here, so consult the documentation for further information.

Validators

How many times have you been asked to write an ASP application that collects some kind of data and makes one or more fields "required"? For example, "Make sure that the customer puts in their telephone number so that we can call them if there is a problem with their order." The Validator controls included with ASP+ make it much easier to perform this kind of validation.

```
<%@ PAGE ClientTarget="Downlevel" %>

<SCRIPT RUNAT="server">
   private sub page_load(o as Object, e as EventArgs)
      if Page.IsValid then
         summary.text = "The Page is Good!"
      else
         summary.text = "There is a Problem!"
      end if
   end sub
</SCRIPT>

<FORM METHOD="POST" RUNAT="SERVER">
   <asp:label ID="summary" runat="server"/>
   <asp:textbox ID="phone" runat="server"/>
   <asp:RequiredFieldValidator
      ControlToValidate="phone"
      ValidatorDisplay="VisibleStaticLayout"
      InitialValue="" Width="100%" runat="server">
      * </asp:RequiredFieldValidator>
</FORM>
```

Start, as usual, by studying the form at the bottom of this page. You haven't seen the "label" control before, but it is pretty basic; it is just a nice way to reserve some space on the page so that you can programmatically insert text into it at a later point in time (as indeed the script does). The other new bit is the RequiredFieldValidator. Notice that it specifies that it wants to validate the "phone" field. It then gives some formatting parameters and ultimately seems to be enclosing an asterisk. The asterisk is the mark that will appear in this location whenever validation fails.

In the SCRIPT block at the top of the page, the code uses the page_load event to check the IsValid property of the Page object. If any of the validators on a given page ever fail, this property will return False; otherwise it will always return True. This way, you can take some action that may differ for validated versus nonvalidated pages. In the case of this script, it places a different message in the Label field, as shown in Figure C-8.

There are many other Validators available under ASP+:

- **RangeValidator**   Verifies that the value of a given field falls within a certain range. For example, that an employee's salary is greater than $50K but less than $100K.

- **CompareValidator**   Compares multiple fields to make sure that they "make sense." For example, that the years of experience claimed by a job candidate is less than their age.

- **RegularExpressionValidator**   Makes sure that the data entered for a given field matches the format used by data of that sort. For example, that a telephone number looks like "(XXX) XXX-XXXX."

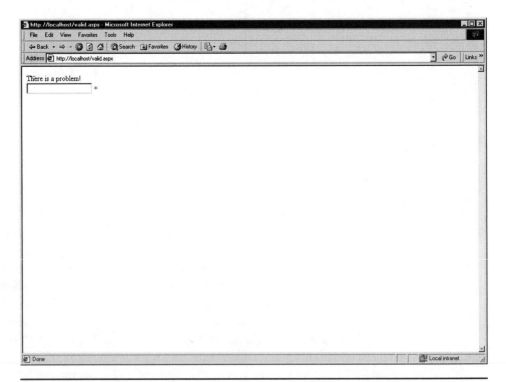

Figure C.8   A validator in action

- **CustomValidator**   Validates complicated multifield situations. For example, a customer must enter a date of birth for their spouse if they say they are married but may leave it blank if they are single.

- **ValidationSummary**   Provides a single message for a multitude of failures. It is a more sophisticated way of performing the Page.IsValid check shown before.

Pagelets

Pagelets are a clever way that ASP+ allows you to create your own controls. These controls generate pure HTML, just like all of the built-in ASP+ controls, and best of all, they are written in regular ASP+.

Consider the common case of checking out your purchases at an online store. Usually, at some point, a page presents itself that asks for your billing, shipping, and (occasionally) contact addresses. These three addresses may all consist of exactly the same fields: name, street, city, state, and ZIP. Using standard Active Server Pages, you would need to create 15 fields in order to encompass all the address information (3 addresses * 5 fields each = 15).

Under ASP+, you could create a pagelet called "Address" and place three instances of it on your form. Here is what such a pagelet might look like:

```
Name: <asp:textbox id="name" runat="server"/><br>
Street: <asp:textbox id="street" runat="server"/><br>
City: <asp:textbox id="city" runat="server"/><br>
State: <asp:textbox id="st" runat="server"/><br>
Zip: <asp:textbox id="zip" runat="server"/><br>
```

Error Watch   *Notice that the ID for State is "st" rather than "state." This is because "State" happens to be the name of a procedure that is defined on the Control base class on which all ASP+ controls are based. Fortunately, if you make this mistake, the compiler will alert you to the fact and abort execution of the page.*

As you can see, the code for the pagelet is pretty straightforward. It is just a bunch of ASP+ textbox controls. Now, here is an ASP Web form that uses three instances of this pagelet to create three addresses:

```
<%@ Register TagPrefix="nifty" TagName="address"
Src="address.aspc" %>

<FORM METHOD="POST">
   Billing Address<br>
   <nifty:address id="billing" runat="server"/><hr>
   Shipping Address<br>
```

```
    <nifty:address id="shipping" runat="server"/><hr>
    Contact Address<br>
    <nifty:address id="contact" runat="server"/><hr>
</FORM>
```

By using the Register page directive at the top of the script, you define your own ASP+ control and tell the compiler where to locate the source for it. Note that pagelets are stored in files with an extension of .aspc. The remainder of the script uses this newly defined control just as it would use any of the controls that are included with ASP+ "out of the box." The output produced by this script is shown in Figure C-9.

If you pull up the HTML source for this under Internet Explorer (or any other browser you choose to use), you will see that ASP+ creates IDs for the controls on your pagelets via concatenation.

```
<input name="billing:name" type="text" id="billing_name">
```

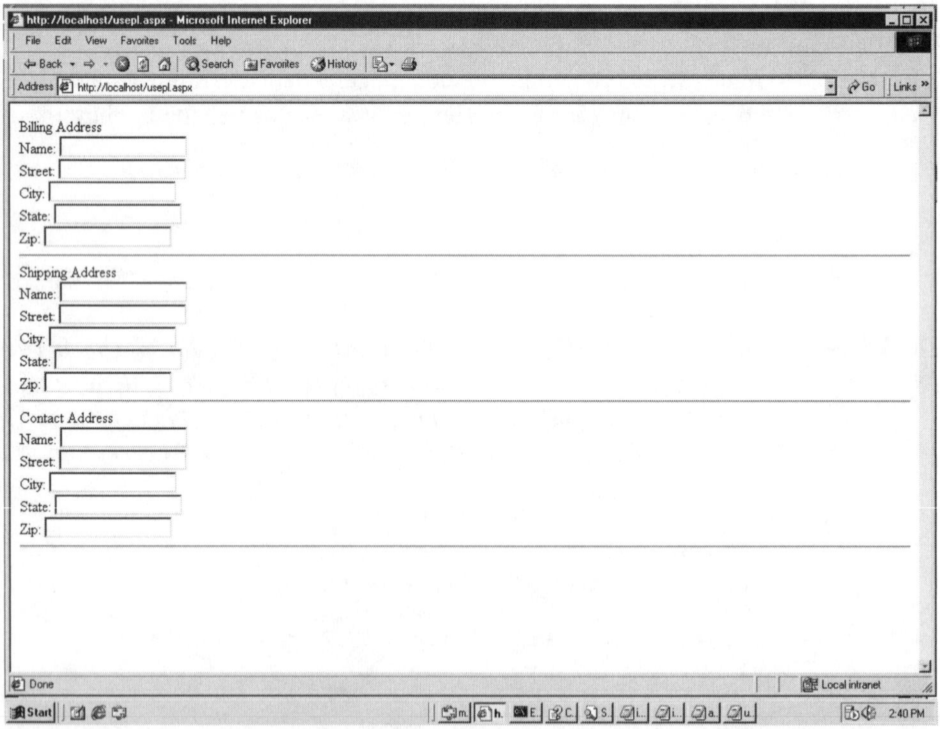

Figure C.9   Using the Address pagelet

This is the HTML created for the Name field on the Billing pagelet. If you want to manipulate it using ASP+ code, you would refer to it as billing_name.

Design Tip *You are no longer allowed to freely mix-and-match languages within the same script under ASP+. The workaround for this is to put any code that uses a different language into a separate pagelet and include it in your main ASPX file. Using this technique, you can once again have as many languages within the same script as you like.*

Visual Basic.Net

All the examples in this book prior to this appendix used VBScript. In this appendix, we have switched to Visual Basic.Net. The reason for this change, as mentioned at the start of this appendix, is that ASP+ uses the complete Visual Basic programming language, rather than its VBScript subset. Visual Basic.Net is vastly different from previous versions of this language, however, and you need to know about some of the more peculiar aspects of the new version in order to use ASP+ properly.

Data Types

Some of the most significant changes to Visual Basic involve the data types available within this language.

Variant and Object

The Variant data type is no longer available under Visual Basic.Net. The Object data type has replaced it. This is not really the same Object data type that you had under previous versions of Visual Basic. Previously, the only kinds of data that could be stored in Object variables were true objects—so "simple" data type, like integers and strings, would be rejected. Under Visual Basic.Net, *everything* is an object, so the following code works fine:

```
<%
   Dim z as Object
   z = 42
%>
```

Namespaces

To support the base class libraries made available by the Microsoft.Net Frameworks, Visual Basic now has the concept of *namespaces*. If you've ever worked with Java, you will recognize them instantly. If you've ever worked with the previous full versions of Visual Basic, you can think of them as being rather like references.

To understand the benefit of namespaces, consider our earlier example with the calendar and datagrid. Some of the class names for ADO+ got to be exceedingly long because we were forced to give their complete names every time we referred to them. If we had imported their namespaces into our code instead, we could have made the rest of our code much easier to read and maintain.

```
<%@ IMPORT NameSpace="System.Data" %>
<%@ IMPORT NameSpace="System.Data.SQL" %>

<SCRIPT RUNAT="SERVER">
   private sub page_load(o as Object, e as EventArgs)
      Dim cn as SQLConnection
      Dim cmd as SQLDataSetCommand
      Dim ds as DataSet
   end sub
</SCRIPT>
```

By asking ASP+ to include the System.Data and System.Data.SQL namespaces in your code, you can refer to classes within those name spaces using their "short names." This is similar to adding a reference to Active Data Objects to a Visual Basic 6 project, so that you can instantiate a Connection object, rather than an ADODB.Connection object.

Syntax

The syntax for many of the more common operations under Visual Basic has also changed significantly. You have already seen many examples of this previously in this appendix.

Declarations, Initializations, and Instantiations
There are a number of changes to the way that variables are declared and set equal to various values.

No "Set" or "Let" Keywords You may already have noticed the absence of the "Set" keyword in our previous examples. To set a variable equal to an instance of an object now, use this format:

```
varname = new WhateverObject
```

Initialization Can be Combined with Declaration   Under previous versions of Visual Basic you often had to create new variables in two steps. The first step was to declare the variable, and the second step was to set it equal to an initial value. You may now combine these steps:

```
Dim cn as SQLConnection = new SQLConnection("blahblah")
```

The "New" Keyword Always Creates Immediately   Under previous versions of Visual Basic statements of the following form used to delay the actual creation of the object until it was first used in code:

```
Dim z as new Testing.Object ' "z" is in some strange "limbo" now
z.doSomething ' This is where Testing.Object is created!
```

Under Visual Basic.Net an instance of Testing.Object would be created immediately on the first line of code.

Declarations Can be Combined with Commas   Under previous versions of Visual Basic the following line of code would declare x as being a Variant and y as being a String:

```
Dim x, y as String
```

The appropriate way to have declared two strings would have been

```
Dim x as String, y as String
```

This is very different from languages such as C and Java, so it has been changed in Visual Basic.Net to conform with the standards used by other languages. In VB.Net, the following statement, for example, declares three variables of type Integer:

```
Dim x,y,z as Integer
```

Arrays   The following method of declaring arrays is no longer supported:

```
Dim x(3 to 7) as Integer
```

Any use of the "to" keyword in this sense will generate an error. All arrays must also start at 0. Therefore, the only appropriate way to declare a single-dimension array is to use this form:

```
Dim x(5) as Integer
```

Procedure Calls

There have been a number of changes in the way that procedures are called under Visual Basic.

Parenthesis Are Required for Any Procedure with Parameters   You are no longer able to call a procedure like this:

```
Response.Write "Hello, World!"
```

Instead, you must enclose your parameters in parentheses at all times.

```
Response.Write ("Hello, World!")
```

Parameters Default to ByVal   Under previous versions of Visual Basic, parameters were passed by reference, unless otherwise stated. This meant that procedures were, by default, free to alter the values of variables passed to them. Visual Basic now passes all parameters by value, unless otherwise stated. This means that in order to modify the values passed to your procedures, you must specifically request that their parameters be passed ByRef:

```
private sub add_two(ByRef nmbr as Integer)
   nmbr = nmbr + 2
end sub
```

Parameter-less Default Properties Are Gone   It was common in very early versions of Visual Basic to specify that one property on an object was to be that object's default property. For example, on a Customer object, the customer's social security number might be set as the object's default property. Developers working with this object, then, could access the social security number by naming the instance of the object without even specifying the property.

```
ssno = objCurrentCustomer ' YOU CANNOT DO THIS
```

This format is no longer allowed. The actual name of the property must always be given, even if it is a default.

```
ssno = objCurrentCustomer.ssNumber ' YOU MUST DO THIS
```

This restriction does not apply, however, if the default property requires any parameters.

```
Ssno = objCurrentCustomer("jeff") ' THIS STILL WORKS
```

Classes

Classes have been greatly expanded and brought up to full compliance with object-oriented standards for Visual Basic.Net. Consult the documentation for full details.

File Format   It is now possible to put multiple classes in the same file. Classes are distinguished primarily through the use of the keyword "class" rather than the files in which they are contained.

Method Overloading   Multiple methods can share the same name and be distinguished solely on the basis of different parameter sets. For example, within the same class, you can define a method

```
public sub wait()
```

that pauses for 30 seconds, and a method

```
public sub wait(n as Integer)
```

that pauses for the number of seconds indicated by *n*.

Inheritance   Classes now support the concept of *implementation inheritance*, which allows them to receive much of their behavior from other classes defined as their "base." Visual Basic supports only single-class inheritance. Methods in a class default to nonoverridable but may also be tagged as "override permitted" or "override required."

Shared Variables   Visual Basic.Net supports the concept of static class members. A *static class member* is a variable that is shared across all instances of a given class. It can be useful for sharing data between objects of the same type.

Constructors and Finalizers   Visual Basic.Net now has full-fledged constructors that can be used to initialize new instances of a class. It also features *finalizers* that run when dereferenced objects are reclaimed by the garbage collector.

Web Services

One of the most exciting new features of ASP+ is the capability to create Web Services. Using Web Services, Active Server Page developers can free themselves completely from the constraints of plain HTML and begin leveraging the full power of the extensible markup language, XML.

Purpose

The earliest Web pages communicated data solely in one direction: from the server to the client. Users requested static HTML and had little or no opportunity to interact with the software operating "behind the scenes." Eventually, CGI allowed for the submission of data in the shape of HTML forms. Scripts running on the server were then able to generate HTML on the fly and return it to the requesting client.

The weakest link in this chain has often been HTML. As a language, it deals almost entirely with describing how data should *look* rather than on what it *means*. This is usually okay when a human is available to interpret the output of a given script or page. It becomes completely inadequate in cases where automated processes must interact with one another.

For example, consider the case of a Web site that offers free delivery to your doorstep of its goods. In order to make this a profitable venture, the Web site is capable of offering their services only within a three-mile radius of their physical headquarters. To prevent people outside this radius from placing orders, they have decided to look up the latitude and longitude for every shipping address that is entered into their system and verify that it is no further than three miles away. Rather than purchasing their own geographical database and building their own system, they have decided to use the services of a popular "free maps" site out on the Internet. The high-level diagram for their system looks like Figure C-10.

The e-commerce site requests latitude and longitude information from the free maps site using standard HTTP "POST" requests and receives HTML in response. This HTML contains a great deal of extraneous data about how the page should look if it were to be presented in a Web browser, so the e-commerce site must first parse through all this to find the relevant data. It then passes this data through its own business rules to determine whether the customer is in range before making a response to the customer one way or the other.

The problem arises the first time that the free maps site decides to change the way in which they present their latitude and longitude data. This may be as

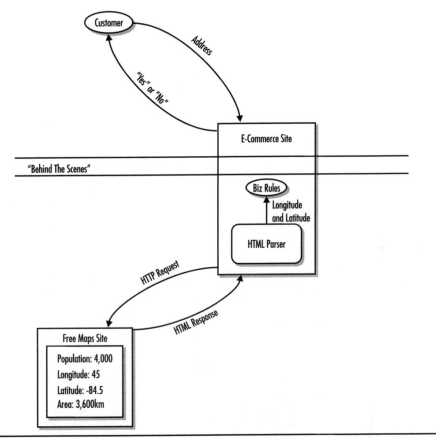

Figure C.10   When one Web site relies upon another for data

simple as adding a few spaces in the wrong place. This changes the HTML in a
way that the parser is not expecting, so malfunctions begin occurring, resulting in
errors, or bogus responses to customers (see Figure C-11).

   ASP+ Web Services provide a way for sites such as the free maps site to
provide data for external consumption without locking themselves into any
particular presentation format. The way it accomplishes this is through the use of
XML. Microsoft.Net Frameworks objects are exposed to external consumers
using the SOAP protocol discussed at the start of this appendix. Results are then
returned in XML using this same protocol. Because XML describes data rather

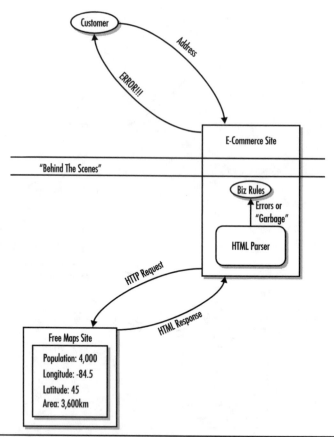

Figure C.11   When a needed Web site changes its HTML

than presentation, it becomes much less likely that client tools will be broken by changes on the server. Figure C-12 outlines what this would look like for our example scenario.

Creation

ASP+ makes it easy to create objects that interact with virtually any platform: Solaris, Mac OS, Linux, and so on. The glue that holds these differing systems together is XML, HTTP, and the SOAP protocol definition. The tool that enables this cohesion under ASP+ is the Web Service.

   To learn how easy it can be to create a simple Web Service, examine the next listing. This code implements the "free maps" Web site described in the

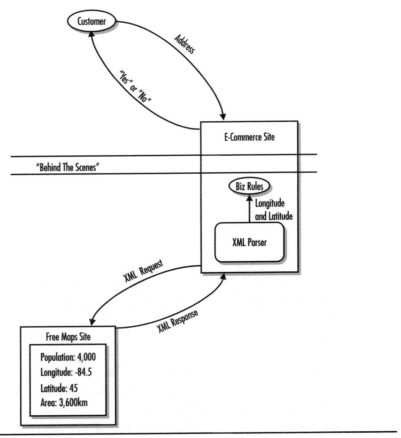

Figure C.12   E-commerce and maps using Web Services

examples from the previous section. It also gives you a brief glimpse of
Microsoft's newest development language, C#.

```
<%@ WebService Language="C#" Class="Geocoding.Example" %>

namespace Geocoding
{
   using System.Web.Services;

   public class Location
   {
      public int Longitude = 45;
      public int Latitude = -87;
```

```
    public Location()
    {
    }
}
public class Example : WebService
{
    public Example()
    {
    }

    [WebMethod]
    public Location Demonstration(string nowhere)
    {
        return new Location();
    }
}
}
```

The listing begins with a page directive telling ASP+ which language to use and which class to register as the "focal point" for this Web Service. The remaining code defines two classes. Both classes define empty constructors. The first class, Location, exists solely to give the second class, Example, a structure in which to return its data.

Example defines a method, Demonstration, which takes a string and returns a Location object. Notice that this method is decorated with "[WebMethod]," which alerts the ASP+ compiler to make this method available for access over the Internet via XML/SOAP/HTTP.

In order to begin experimenting with this Web Service, place the listing in a file with an .asmx extension and load it into a Web browser. You should see a screen like the one in Figure C-13.

Without any additional effort on your part, ASP+ generates a test page for all your Web Services, like the one shown in Figure C-13. You will get a page like this one whenever you access a URL of the following form:

```
http://server/filename.asmx
```

Every method in your Web Service tagged with the "[WebMethod]" phrase should have its own black-and-yellow box on these pages with a description of the parameters and return values for that method. If you scroll down to the box for your Demonstration method, you will see that it also has a text box and a button labeled "Invoke." By filling in this text box and clicking the button, you can execute the Demonstration method with the value in the text box passed to

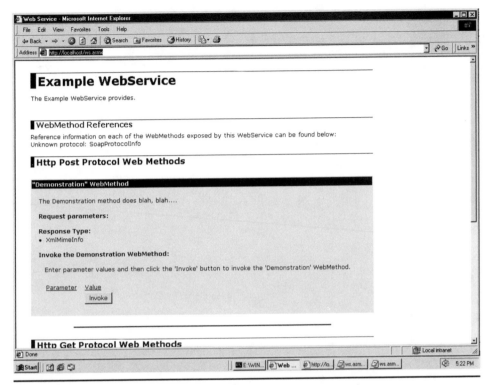

Figure C.13 Web Service experimenting page

the named parameter. If you try this from Internet Explorer, you will get a page like the one shown in Figure C-14.

Internet Explorer is an XML-enabled Web browser, so it is capable of displaying the raw data returned by your Web Method. Notice that it is a complete XML description of the Location object returned by your procedure. Now, examine this URL:

```
http://server/filename.asmx/MethodName?parametername=value
```

The real beauty of Web Services is that *any tool on any platform* that understands XML and HTTP can make a request across the Internet to URLs of this format and

- Invoke a Microsoft.Net Frameworks object running on a Windows machine
- Understand the results returned by simply parsing XML

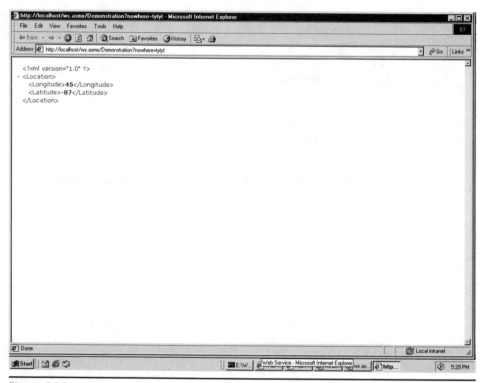

Figure C.14   XML returned by a Web Method

You may envision this as a truly multiplatform, Internet standards–based replacement for DCOM and CORBA.

Letting the World Know

Once you've created your Web Services, ASP+ provides a couple of excellent tools for sharing them with others.

SDL

SDL stands for *Service Definition Language*. This is an XML schema that allows a SOAP service (such as an ASP+ Web Service) to describe its features, functionalities, and usage to any client tool that understands SDL. The newest release of Visual Studio is a good example of a client tool that will understand SDL. It allows Visual Studio.Net to connect to a new site running unfamiliar Web Services and find out all about how they should be invoked and used, thereby assisting the developer in adding them to his or her project.

A sample SDL is shown in Figure C-15. You can have ASP+ generate one of these automatically for any of your Web Services by requesting a URL of the format

```
http://server/filename.asmx?sdl
```

DISCO

In order for a client tool, such as Visual Studio, to request SDLs for Web Services with the intention of understanding how they work, it must first know of their existence. DISCO is a Microsoft technology aimed at helping client tools discover available Web Services on new servers. Using DISCO, for example, you might connect to a large bookseller's Web site with Visual Studio.Net and find out that it offers three new Web Services: author biographies, price comparisons, and live chats.

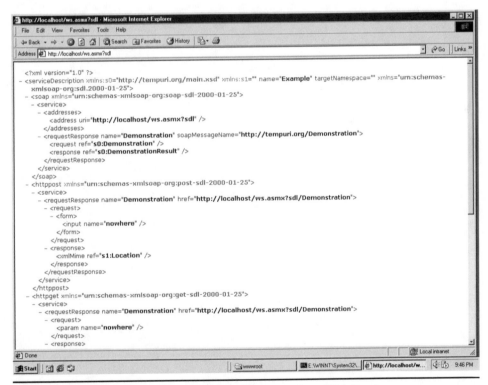

Figure C.15   ASP+ automatically generating an SDL for a Web Service

Index